Penguin Critical Studies

Milton: The English Poem

Dr Moseley was educated at Queens ~~~~~~~~~~~ ~~. He has taught Medieval and Renaissance literature i~~ ~~~~~~~~~~ge for many years and still sees reading books as a serious activity.

For Penguin he has edited two of Chaucer's *Canterbury Tales*, the Knight's and the Pardoner's, and a monograph on Shakespeare's *Richard III*. Penguin also publishes his *Shakespeare's History Plays*: *'Richard II' to 'Henry V': The Making of a King*, and his edition of *The Travels of Sir John Mandeville*, an author still too little known and enjoyed, for whom he retains his early enthusiasm. Dr Moseley is also the author of the first introductory anthology on the fascinating Renaissance form of the emblem, *A Century of Emblems*, published by Scolar Press.

in piam memoriam
F. E. M.

Penguin Critical Studies
Advisory Editor: Bryan Loughrey

John Milton

The English Poems of 1645

C. W. R. D. Moseley

Penguin Books

PENGUIN BOOKS

Published by the Penguin Group
Penguin Books Ltd, 27 Wrights Lane, London W8 5TZ, England
Penguin Books USA Inc., 375 Hudson Street, New York, New York 10014, USA
Penguin Books Australia Ltd, Ringwood, Victoria, Australia
Penguin Books Canada Ltd, 10 Alcorn Avenue, Toronto, Ontario, Canada M4V 3B2
Penguin Books (NZ) Ltd, 182–190 Wairau Road, Auckland 10, New Zealand

Penguin Books Ltd, Registered Offices: Harmondsworth, Middlesex, England

First published by Scolar Press 1991
Published in Penguin Books 1992
10 9 8 7 6 5 4 3 2 1

Printed in England by Clays Ltd, St Ives plc

Contents

Preface

In 1915, my mother, just 14, left school to work in an aircraft factory. The education she had even while at school was in many ways sadly deficient in the things we consider important; the study of English poetry and other literature, for example, was largely reduced to learning large gobbets of it by rote. This should have put her right off it, yet at the end of her long life, when her eyes no longer allowed her to read much, she drew much strength and joy from those long passages of verse she had memorized as a girl: and particularly from Milton. To hear her recite *L'Allegro* or parts of *Samson Agonistes* with feeling and intelligence made one wonder whether literature could be simply pigeonholed as a subject, as too many of us tend to do; whether all the clever analytical assaults on Milton had not in fact missed something utterly basic: that his poetry was hugely enjoyable even by those without the benefit of a university education. The 'dislodgement of Milton', the attacks made by F. R. Leavis and others, passed her by, for she never even knew he was lodged, so to speak. She just loved his poetry with a discriminating intelligence and commitment that put many critics to shame. The fact that an old lady of limited education could feel such acute pleasure in Milton's verse should give pause to those who, for one reason or another, ignore or dismiss him.

I share her belief that, whatever else it is, Milton's poetry can be greatly enjoyable. It is in the hope that I can persuade those who see him from afar merely as a forbidding eminence to share this view that I have written this book. I do not pretend that Milton is an easy poet, for that he is certainly not; nor that he makes no demands on us save that we capitulate to the almost narcotic richness of some of his verse. I am not belittling the problems that there are for us moderns in attempting to read, with something approaching understanding, poetry written by a man of unusually wide learning for an audience that lived in a world utterly different from our own; that lived on different assumptions and with a different understanding of man and his place in the universe. (Those difficulties are there in reading any old books, after all.) A man – as Milton was – of the later Renaissance in the peculiar form it took in England, a man living through and responding to the most politically and philosophically turbulent period in Britain's entire history up to the present, will not be understood if we approach him on our terms. We have to learn his language and that of his age if we want to hear what he has to say rather than make him parrot our own preconceptions. But, in the end, what we are after is an understanding that will enable us to enjoy him, to see, however dimly, through his eyes, and evaluate what we see. It is that intelligent pleasure in art and poetry and music which, as Milton himself said, can 'bring all Heav'n before [our] eyes' that we seek.

Quotations from Milton's *Poems both English and Latin* (1645), in this book are, unless otherwise indicated, from that edition as represented by a copy in the British Library, Ashley 1179. For quotations from and references to his other works I have used *John Milton: Complete Poetry and Major Prose*, ed. Merritt Y. Hughes (Odyssey Press, New York, 1957); *Milton: Complete Shorter Poems*, ed. John Carey (Longman, London, 1971); and *Milton: Paradise Lost*, ed. Alastair Fowler (Longman, London, 1971). I am greatly indebted to these three books. Translations from Latin are my own unless otherwise stated.

It would be grossly ungrateful not to acknowledge the help and encouragement I received during the preparation of this book from Dr Brian Last, Dr Stephen Coote, and Mr Jonathan Riley. Mrs K. W. Drysdale was, as usual, an incisive critic; and my wife's patience, once again, was exemplary.

Reach, Cambridgeshire   C.W.R.D.M.

Part One
'POETIC BIRTH': AN APPROACH TO MILTON'S EARLY POETRY

1 A Brief Apology

Milton was never an easy poet, even when the assumptions on which he wrote his poetry were in large measure still shared by those people who came to read him. But in the last 20 years or so we have lived through a social and intellectual revolution the full consequences of which have not yet fully been digested, and most if not all of those assumptions have gone for the majority of new readers. Our society is much more pluralist; it has quite different notions about the individual, his psyche, and his relationship to his fellows than those held in the seventeenth century – even though it could be argued that the roots of this new growth lie back in that period and before. Moreover, our understanding (if it can be called that) of education and its purpose has changed radically, so that a generation has grown up to whom the knowledge and values that men for centuries took for granted as important and valuable have not been passed: and it needs only one span of a bridge to collapse for people on opposite banks to be cut off from each other.

Western civilization has been built on two pillars: the Bible and the inheritance from Greece and Rome. For the first time since the paganism of early Anglo-Saxon England, there is a generation of young people growing up and attending university the majority of whom have only the sketchiest knowledge – or none whatsoever – of the Bible. This is a serious matter, for whatever one's religious beliefs it is a matter of sheer historical fact that the response to the Bible in past times affected the politics, law, commerce and morality of Europe. Some of the values of our civilization which we say we most value today, like the dignity of the individual, have grown out of and fed on the morality and understanding of the universe offered by the Bible. We shall not only get nowhere in trying to understand what men wrote and how they acted in the past if we ignore this: we shall also get nowhere in

3

understanding how we are as we are, for we are our fathers' children. Further, for the first time since the Renaissance most educated men and women no longer think it necessary to know anything about the philosophy, law, history and literature of the ancient world, whose direct heirs we are. Again, they are the poorer; but when such knowledge is assumed by artists and writers from the Middle Ages to the Second World War, we moderns who lack it cannot begin to understand what they have to say.

Not only is it no longer possible for highly intelligent newcomers to him to read Milton without substantial help – they always did need it – but also a lot of the books that were so valuable as introductions are themselves no longer easily accessible because they assume a knowledge and a set of values which most of their readers no longer have. Hence my attempt in this book to provide a guide that will go some way to smoothing the path of those whom, with the enthusiasm of the missionary, I would like to persuade that not only is reading Milton enormously pleasurable, but it is also a valuable and challenging, even disturbing experience. In this first chapter I sketch what I see as some of the main areas of difficulty and interest, and, so that readers may start the business of reading the texts as soon as possible, outline ways in which Renaissance poetry and the conventions it employs differ from those of our day. The next chapters briefly describe the background to Milton's life and work, and then, in Part II, I concentrate first on the presentation as a whole of *Poems of Mr John Milton, both English and Latin*, published in 1645, and then devote separate chapters to suggesting ways of reading individual poems and some groups of poems.[1] Those last chapters are designed to have considerable overlap with each other and with the material in Part I of the book, so that they can be freestanding, and, if so desired, be read as introductions to individual poems or groups of poems.

I have to admit, however, that the book would not need to have been written if its readers would get themselves copies of the Bible, Plato, Vergil and Ovid and read them. (That would also be a considerably more enjoyable way of spending money and time.) For the awkward and unpopular fact is that Milton was a Christian poet, and a learned one: he assumed his readers to be Christian also and expected them to attempt to be learned.[2] To be fair in reading him – we do not necessarily have to agree with him – we should try to know what he believed and what he knew; and also to know how he understood the craft of poetry. Otherwise we are merely making noises in an echo-chamber, not hearing what he has to say to us. That we do not think as they did about these matters does not necessarily mean our ancestors were wrong and we are right – or, indeed, vice versa; it is possible that we might learn a great deal of profit from them, and it is good for us to be forced to justify, even modify, what we take for granted. The virtual abandonment of the roots of Western culture since the disastrous decades of the 1960s and '70s, when barbarism, not needing to invade, was welcomed by those who should have known better, has cut us off from many things, many ideas, many values of which the world has increasing need as it careers towards the disaster that seems so imminent. Our age of perplexity and plain fear can learn much from the way people came to terms with the perplexity and fear of another age in general crisis, the seventeenth century. It might even be that the morality and values Milton and his contemporaries thought about so keenly and passionately could show us a way forward; or, at least, give us fortitude to meet our fate.

Poets and Poetry: Some Attitudes and Conventions

The profession of poet, which Milton consistently saw as his major job, would hardly find a place today in any conventional list of employment opportunities for graduates. Such people, and of course others, undoubtedly write poetry, but the activity is regarded even by the majority of those who suffer from it as something marginal to the professional and economic core of their lives. Few people now turn naturally to the poet for a diagnosis of our moral and social condition; and even poets themselves would be wary of claiming the sort of high moral authority, as the public conscience of the age, that was natural to Milton, Dryden, or Pope. Wordsworth had no doubts about Milton's authority and public importance, as one of the most Miltonic of his sonnets, written in the middle of another period of convulsive change, indicates:

> Milton! thou shouldst be living at this hour:
> England hath need of thee: she is a fen
> Of stagnant waters: altar, sword and pen,
> Fireside, the heroic wealth of hall and bower,
> Have forfeited their ancient English dower
> Of inward happiness. We are selfish men;
> Oh! raise us up, return to us again;
> And give us manners, virtue, freedom, power.
> Thy soul was like a Star, and dwelt apart;
> Thou hadst a voice whose sound was like the sea:
> Pure as the naked heavens, majestic, free,
> So didst thou travel on life's common way,
> In cheerful godliness; and yet thy heart
> The lowliest duties on herself did lay.

6 'Poetic birth'

There has been a fundamental shift, which probably began with the Romantics, in our view of the nature and function of poetry. Over the last two centuries it has become more private, more intimate, more concerned with the individual and his concerns and nature, and the big poem that addresses itself to the general condition of humanity – like Eliot's *The Waste Land* or David Jones's *In Parenthesis* – is exceptional. The diagnostic, public moral function became part of the job of the novel as it developed through the nineteenth century and into the twentieth. It seems that societies need to contemplate their reflection in art in order to understand and judge themselves, but the art in which they do it does not remain constant. They might do it through painting and the visual arts, as the Dutch seem to have done in the seventeenth century, or through the sub-world of the grand nineteenth-century novel – like *War and Peace* or *Middlemarch*, or Balzac's *Comédie Humaine*. And today we may be witnessing another of those massive shifts in modes of expression and communication that make the reading and understanding of what preceded them so difficult. For, while serious novelists can – just – make a living nowadays by their art, it is noticeable how much creative talent is attracted into the ubiquitous chattering medium of television, and how the version of reality it presents is the *only* artistic input that the vast majority of our contemporaries receive. Television has come to offer linguistic, behavioural and moral models for most of our contemporaries; our politicians have to master the medium if they are to survive – though there is no obvious connection between looking and sounding good on the box and ruling justly; and television fills the secret worlds of our minds, for good or ill, with images, an ephemeral common mythology, that affect our responses to the world we live in. Against this the poet counts for little.

Poetry like that of Milton and his contemporaries was directed at a small minority of educated people – exactly the people to whom the publisher, Humphrey Moseley, addressed the preface to *Poems* (1645) – who had an importance and influence quite disproportionate to their numbers. Poetry was, in the exact sense of the word, an aristocratic medium. Those who did read it took it very seriously. What seems so odd, and forbidding, to us – Milton's perfectly serious and consistent dedication of his life to the practice of poetry as a public duty – is only explicable on contemporary terms, which express and refine an understanding of poetry that goes back directly to Dante and Petrarch, and beyond them to Horace, Cicero and Vergil, and to the poets (whom we call prophets) of ancient Israel. That view of poetry is an important part of a comprehensive attempt to understand the phenomenon of Man – as a mind, as an individual, as a political animal – and his place in the universe.

Furthermore, the emphasis of Renaissance philosophical, scientific and religious enquiry were very different from ours. Yet when we moderns come to read the art of that period, in nine cases out of ten we read it as if it had been written yesterday: John Donne's attitude to sexual love, for example, and the poetry that arose from it, is assumed to be the same as ours, when it patently was not. All too often we assume he was 'sincere' – as if that mattered in a good poem! – when there is no guarantee that any lady at all was the object of some of the verse that makes freshmen swoon.

One major legacy of *The Lyrical Ballads* (1798) was the redefinition of a poem as an impulse growing directly out of the emotional stresses of the poet. The poem's centre is now the thinking and *feeling* poet, and it becomes, in Wordsworth's phrase, 'a spontaneous overflow of powerful feelings', refined and modified by the poet's intellect: the poem derives from later contemplation of the emotion experienced as a result of an unplanned stimulus. Its value can easily be taken to lie in how 'true', 'honest' or 'sincere' the poem is – though it is very doubtful whether Wordsworth would have gone all the way with this view. And if the poem comes thus to be seen as an emotional or moral process of discovery, of self-knowledge and of change, it follows that its structure ought to mirror that process – the notion that the form of the poem is organic to its impulse, that the individuality of the emotional impetus will, like water finding its own level, seek out naturally its most appropriate shape. In theory, the poet does not know where the poem is going when he begins to write. The irregularity of form or structure in many post-Romantic poems is anticipated in, for example, Coleridge's *Dejection: An Ode*: the first version of the poem is an intensely personal process of self-discovery and emotional exploration which begins in a moment of perceived and painful disequilibrium and records Coleridge's gradual achieving of a new understanding of himself and a new emotional balance. The poem stops because the emotional drive has exhausted itself, not because the form demands it do so.

Pre-Romantic poetry does not work like this at all. There is no doubt that many poems are, for want of a better word, 'sincere' in the modern sense, but that sincerity is not an important validating element. A good poem to an imaginary lady – perhaps like Marvell's *To his Coy Mistress* – is more to be admired than a bad, deeply felt poem to a real one. The poem is as much an artefact, shaped and polished to do a particular job, as a kettle or carving knife. It follows that the concept of form as organic will not apply, while on the other hand a concept of form as an appropriate frame for, and signal to the audience about, the total meaning of the poem will be normal – like the total design of a picture. For it was a universally held cliché in the Renaissance that poetry and painting are closely related arts, working in similar ways through the same sort of convention.[3]

So, choosing the rigid sonnet form, for example, for a love poem or a devotional poem will qualify and perhaps throw into ironic relief the ideas discussed in the words, because the form already has associations and values for the audience – just as the design of the picture qualifies its subject. The sonnet, moreover, cuts right out certain subjects and certain levels of expression, for it is as difficult to write a hilarious sonnet as it is to write a sublime limerick.

The choice of form, obviously, has to be decorous – 'fitting' – to the subject: *Lycidas* in the metrical form Peter Quince liked in *A Midsummer Night's Dream* (III. i. 20), in lines of 'eight and six' syllables, would sound merely silly. In reading Renaissance poetry, therefore, we ought to be prepared to give detailed attention to form as an important signal about the sort of expectations we should have of the poem's level and meaning. Form can indeed be remarkably specific in defining or supporting the subject of the poem. George Puttenham, for example, in Book II of his *Arte of English Poesie* (1589) talks (pp. 75 ff.) about the use of visual shape in poems, and says that 'round' or 'circle' poems – that is, poems that return to their beginning in some formal or structural way – are 'the most excellent of all the figures' . . . bear[ing] a similitude with God and eternitie.' (This is not without importance for the *Nativity Ode*.) The form of a poem is always some sort of signal; it can also be a symbol of something in or beyond its ostensible subject, and we shall have to return to this issue below (p. 12f).

Similarly, the level and register of language conveys a good deal. Nowadays the study of rhetoric has been virtually forgotten, and the word itself has become a term mainly of abuse – thrown at the speeches of those politicians, for example with whom we do not agree, and virtually a synonym for lying. Yet in the Middle Ages and Renaissance, rhetoric was an important part of education: not only the art of using words, written or spoken, to best advantage, but also, philosophically, one of the keys to the understanding of how men behave in society. (It is significant that the only place Aristotle discusses psychology is in his *Rhetoric.*) For the range of language that can be used and understood is a good measure of what can be thought and how healthy a society is (a fact which, looking at the tabloid press today, gives one cause for alarm about modern society). Renaissance men in surprising numbers had a specialist knowledge of rhetoric: they knew not only how to use it themselves but also how to judge its use by others, and knew what to expect from certain rhetorical structures and devices. This made them not only capable of incisive reading and understanding of a text, but also self-conscious about their own immediate reading at that moment.

Comus's language and style, for example, are meant to do two things: in showing him trying to persuade, its rhetorical structure and semantic content at the same time show how little chance he has of so doing (see p. 196).

What we are up against (in both pre- and post-Romantic art) is best summed up in the word 'convention': that is, an area of unstated agreement between author and audience where the terms do not need spelling out. A Renaissance audience would glean important clues about how to read a work by recognizing its genre, its form, its level of language and style, and the ways in which characters, for example, relate to norms to which a set of values is already attached: all these can be confirmed or denied. It follows that works of art relate dynamically to what their predecessors have established as normative in an audience's mind, and that the vast amount of allusion to Classical and contemporary art and literature with which the reader of Milton has to cope and which his introducer has to explain is in no sense merely decorative. Renaissance and medieval poems derive a great deal of their force from being bounced off other poems that the audience could be expected to know: they are not mere sparkles in the dark, but relate to everything else like the elements of reflection in a kaleidoscope. Thus, a new poem really is new, but at the same time could not exist without the old ones that formed its creator's and its audience's minds: all, old and new, are an ordering of thought and experience and everything that concerns us as human beings into words, which, obviously, are *not* the same as the things they represent. Part of the discussion of any poem, therefore, must be the validity of its own discourse, and its relation to the examples of its genre that have preceded it. Recognizing the *whole* story of Orpheus as handled in Vergil and Boethius, and the issues the myth symbolized, behind passing allusions in *L'Allegro, Il Penseroso* or *Lycidas* for example, is crucial to understanding what Milton is saying in his new poem (see pp. 67ff, 138f). The tension between memory and the present poem makes the point. Similarly, recognizing who Thyrsis, Damoetas and Lycidas were, or the context of the quotation on the title page of Poems (1645) (see p. 82), adjusts our focus as we read *Comus* or *Lycida*s – or, indeed, the whole 1645 volume.

Properly used, convention can be a liberating thing for audience and artist, a great force for subtlety and economy. Recognition of genre brings with it expectations of what that genre might discuss; recognition that a poem is an 'imitation' – we might say a 'free reworking' or 'updating' – of an earlier (often Classical) poem means that the new audience gets three areas for the price of one – their memory of the old poem, their experience of the new, and the interesting and provocative tension set up between, say, the original version and context of Psalm 114 and the context of Milton's versions (see p. 115). Convention also includes symbols of agreed meaning, or frames of reference, and how it works in general may perhaps be made clearer by looking at one very important convention, that of pastoral. When at the beginning of *Lycidas* Milton signals it, he economically alerts his readers to an area of discourse and a mode of expression which prepares them for what he will do in the poem; conversely, when Wordsworth subtitled *Michael* 'A Pastoral Poem', he *ironically* elicited this same response in order to emphasize how different his poem is from what is expected: its force is immeasurably increased when it is set against literary pastoral in language, story, character and theme.

The Pastoral Convention

It might seem the height of silliness to set plays, poems or indeed pictures in a world populated only by shepherds who seem to have nothing to do but make love and sing songs. It is used so much in the Renaissance precisely because, since everybody recognized its arti-ficiality and its tenuous links to the real life of shepherds, no one was likely to mistake what it said on the surface for a transcription of reality. It was a sort of test tube in which important and often topical ideas could be isolated for examination and discussion. (It could also be used unseriously, or badly, on a much lower level, to signal a set of emotional expectations and clichés as empty as the vapid banality of some modern love songs.) Milton used it extensively in the Latin and English poems of *Poems* (1645), and a glance at its development helps us to grasp why he did so.

Pastoral's origins lie, especially, in the *Idylls* of Theocritus, where fictionalized shepherds sit around singing in a Sicily of exemplary climate and undemanding sheep, and in the *Eclogues* of Vergil, where the actual jobs of shepherds and farmers hardly appear at all. Already there is that linking, destined to be very long-lived, between the imagined world of pastoral and the lost Golden Age of Saturn that Ovid described in Book I of *Metamorphoses*; this necessarily implies a comparison between the setting 'then', in the poem, and the world 'now' where it is being read. Vergil quite clearly used pastoral for the oblique discussion of matters political and moral as well as artistic and poetic, and the mode implies an absolute standard of judgement by which men of the Age of Iron are implicitly judged.

Renaissance pastoral, when it is more than merely pretty fooling, discusses much more than meets the eye. For one thing, it offered the chance to open up the perennially interesting question of the balance between Art and Nature, a central psychological, moral, political problem. (The problem is with us today, only we call it by different names).[4] Furthermore, it drew not only on Classical pastoral, but also on the development of it called 'bergerie' in the medieval vernaculars. *Bergerie* does use the real shepherds Theocritus treated with caution and Vergil kept in the background (and whom Petrarch and Pope would never have dreamed of including). For French and English writers saw in the real shepherd enormous artistic potential: he could be made a symbol of the good life: of the teacher, the priest, the prince, the lover, and Man; and even of Christ. (The delicious multilayeredness of Robert Henryson's *Robene and Makyne* depends on just this multivalency.) In this type of pastoral, the ideal is therefore not withdrawal to seek private wisdom (as it might have been in some of the Classical poets) – but social responsibility: the same sort of thrust we shall note in Renaissance ideas of education (see pp. 22f, 29). The duties of the good shepherd are real before they are metaphorical: Our Lord's injunction to St Peter to 'feed my sheep' affects all his successors. Naturally, this realistic treatment becomes itself a convention that can work in several literary genres, from plays like the Towneley *Secunda Pastorum* to the *Pastourelle*, from sermon to romance.

Influenced, then, by this medieval development, serious Renaissance pastoral has two principal subjects – religion and politics. Mantuan, hailed as a 'second Vergil', is particularly important in this redirection of the mode. He had an enormous reputation, and Milton certainly knew his work well.[5] His collection of eclogues, *Adolescentia* (finally completed and published in 1498), represents a convincing synthesis of Classical and medieval eclogue with *bergerie*. The Vergilian country poem became a contemporary form not just because it had topical potential but also because its characters and setting were recognizable in modern terms. For Mantuan, as for Boccaccio, the pastoral world may be an intimation of Heaven, but it can reach full perfection only there; here on earth the shepherd's world is realistic, and all Mantuan's eclogues are didactic.

In Elizabethan England political pastoral (in poetry, fête, entertainment and painting) concentrated mainly on panegyric of the Queen, though we should not see that panegyric always as mere sycophantic flattery of power, devoid of criticism, injunction and comment. Sometimes, too, religious allegory is present since Elizabeth was Head of the Church. The connection of pastoral with religion in the sixteenth century is indeed noticeable: from John Skelton's *Kepe Wel the Shepe* in the reign of Henry VII down to Spenser's *Shepheardes Calendar* and Sidney's Epilogue to *The Lady of May*. There is also a natural pull towards satire – the sort of thing Milton glances at in *Comus*, ll. 323 ff. William

Browne, for example, breaks off in the middle of Marina's adventures
– one has to admit they are hardly gripping – in *Britannia's Pastorals*
to describe the ills of society, including

> The prelate in pluralities asleep
> Whilst that the wolf lies preying on his sheep.
>
> (II. i. 869–70)

William Warner in the 1612 revision of his *Albion's England* (Ch. 91)
tells of the shepherd dreaming of Robin Goodfellow denouncing the
state of the Church. A number of eclogues at the turn of the century
take religious matters as their exclusive subject. The form's natural
suitability for satire against the pastors of the church is a part of its
recognized function which Milton exploited in *Lycidas*. And the pastoral
was probably the most commonly used mode for dirges and epicedia:
the *Epitaphium Damonis* and *Lycidas* could hardly employ any other
with decorum.

Number and Shape

It will already be obvious that a good part of the meaning of any
serious poem or play is expressed not simply in the verbal text but
also through the recognition of a 'hidden text', conveyed by the signals
of genre and convention. The audience must be alert in reading or
watching, ready to pick up clues that may often be given in coded
form. Indeed, it is no accident that several collections of poems in the
Elizabethan period address their prefaces not to readers but to 'under-
standers'; the art of poetry, like the art of painting, was an intellectual
game – a highly serious one very often, demanding skill and knowledge
not only of its producer but also of its consumer. He was expected to
look beneath the surface; to use his intelligence to see through the
veil. Extreme ingenuity and complexity in all the arts were expected:
even simplicity itself, whether asked for in prayer by George Herbert
in *A Wreath* or suggested by Ben Jonson in 'Still to be neat, still to
be dressed' (Clerimont's song in *Epicoene*, I. i), is paradoxically complex.

Attention to form and pattern as well as semantic content was expected.
For example, the shapes of many seventeenth-century poems can echo
a layer of meaning in the verbal text or reveal a further one – George
Herbert's *The Altar* and *Easter Wings* are instances that get into most
anthologies and selections. The practice is very common, particularly in
devotional poets like Francis Quarles. Less well known is the popularity
of acrostic poems: the initial letters of the lines in the poems of Sir
John Davies's *Hymns to Astraea* spell *ELISABETHA REGINA*. (What is
almost beyond understanding is how Milton, by then blind, built into

Paradise Lost at several important places acrostics that highlight the topic of the verse at that point.[6]

Or take the complexity of the canzone, which I discuss below in relation to *Lycidas* : here half the enjoyment for practitioner and audience is the ingenuity of the fitting of thought and expression to an arbitrary and rigid form: the summit of art is where what is extremely complex and artificial sounds simple, sensuous and passionate. In *Lycidas* we have exactly that mix: a highly elaborate and very carefully designed form which nevertheless gives so good an illusion of an extempore effusion of powerful feeling that the poem is deeply moving even when we know that Milton's relation to Edward King was nowhere near as close as the poem pretends. Nor is such practice purely an aristocratic literary taste. Among the bourgeois guilds of mastersingers in Germany, which lasted in several towns well into the seventeenth century, an aspiring member served a long apprenticeship to an established master, at the end of which he had to sing a prize song of extremely complex form. The 'master song' was divided into three, five or more *Gesätze*, or stanzas, each of which was subdivided into two strophes (*Stollen*) and an 'after song' (*Abgesang*). This is fearsome enough; but in addition, no line could have more than 13 syllables, and stanzas of 30 to 50 lines of varying length were common: no strophe was to have fewer than 7 or more than 100 lines. The rhyme schemes were often of extreme ingenuity. Thus, if we do not pay close attention to the form of a Renaissance poem, play, song or painting, it is odds on that we are losing a good deal not only of the potential pleasure in it but also of its meaning.

This complexity in art is no mere fashion, but a consequence of an understanding of the nature of the world and of man in it based on impressive philosophical grounds. It represents as genuine an attempt to deal honestly and fully with the paradoxes and problems of the human situation as any of the more modern artistic theories. At the root lies the Platonic understanding (see p. 32) of the phenomenal world as a shadow of the ultimate reality, as a clue to the real rather than the real itself. Then there is St Paul's assertion, certainly influenced by Plato, in Romans 1.20 that through the world we see we may begin to understand that which we do not see, the mind of God. (His remark that human perception on earth is 'through a glass darkly' (1 Cor. 13. 12) implies both this Platonic conception and the consequent fallibility of human language I mention below.) There is the concept, common through the Middle Ages and Renaissance, that God is an Artist, that the world is His poem, and that the activity of His creature, Man, in creating art is analogous to that Divine Art that created the world.[7]

So our ancestors expected that just as the world was filled with multiple meaning, serious art that attempted to describe the world would be, like the world, polysemous – that is, carrying many meanings; understanding, and informed pleasure, were the result of the effort to penetrate the veil of appearance. St Augustine's remark that 'that which is sought with difficulty is discovered with pleasure' (*De Doctrina Christiana*, II. vi. 7) not only repeated what his contemporaries believed but was also treated as prescriptive in later centuries. Dante, too, is quite clear that he expects his readers to work hard:

> O voi, che avete gl'intelletti sani,
> mirate la dottrina, che s'asconde
> sotto il velame degli versi strani.
> *Inferno,* IX. 63 ff.

('You who are of healthy understanding, mark well the teaching hidden under the veil of strange lines.') Thus, a poem attempting to deal with high and serious matters could not be true to its subject if it were not difficult, needing to be read on many levels using many techniques.

But there is a major dilemma in medieval and Renaissance theories of art. St Paul's dark glass reveals something Real, but we can know it only in part; as our minds are clouded, so the language in which we try to discuss Truth is fallible. Words, imprecise things, relate only problematically to the things they attempt to describe. It was believed that with the Fall of Man and the confusion of tongues at the destruction of the Tower of Babel (Gen., ch. 11) human language ceased to communicate perfectly or to describe exactly. Adam's speech had been an accurate expression of the nature of things as they were:

> My tongue obeyed and readily could name
> Whate'er I saw . . .
> I named [the creatures], as they passed, and understood
> Their nature . . .
> (*Paradise Lost*, VIII. 272–3, 352–3)

But the language of fallen men, even of poets, enjoyed no such power: it was (and is) a matter of everyday observation that even the simplest communication between two people is hedged with ambiguity, and that the verbal sign carries associations for the speaker that the hearer will share only approximately. A poem, the medium of which is words, is thus open to a potentially devastating amount of miscomprehension: the more serious, or religious the subject, the more dangerous the lack of full communication between artist and audience. But there were ways of limiting this.

Reading the Bible, the word of God, was the most important literary activity a man might engage in. Medieval and Renaissance readers were accustomed to reading it on many levels besides the literal: the tropological, the anagogical and the allegorical meanings depended on the ancient practice of extracting meaning through many techniques. One might recognize the typological fulfilment of the meaning of an ancient historical event, like the Burning Bush, in the New Testament event of the Virgin Birth; or one might see special significance in mathematical symbolism, for example in the central verses of chapters or books, or in the relationship between the numbers of the Blessed in Heaven, the Twelve Tribes and the Twelve Apostles – or in the 153 fish caught in the miraculous draught of fishes.[8]

Now the reader who expects so to extract meaning from the most important of all books may also be the poet who, in his own work, has to cater for a similar extraction. So, just as the will of God might be known through the proper analysis of both his Poem, the world, and his Word, the Bible, so in human art there grows to be a reliance on non-verbal means of communication as a check on the imprecision of verbal through the use of symbol, form, pattern and number.

For God was seen in Creation – an act, indeed, of words (Gen. ch. 1) – as an Artist who 'composed all things by number, proportion and weight' (Wisdom of Solomon 11.21 – an idea interestingly echoed in the last line of Andrew Marvell's *On Paradise Lost*). The ancient and modern Pythagoreans and Platonists saw number as the key not only to music but also to the universe, which was built on due harmony and proportion. As Boethius put it (*De Consolatione Philosophiae*, III. met. ix), 'tu numeris elementa ligas' – 'you bind together the elements by numbers'. Through the study of mathematics and its cousin music (from which it cannot be separated) the mind could be raised to the contemplation of the Divine beauty: St Augustine had written in *De Musica* that 'the soul is truly better when it turns from the carnal senses and seeks the divine numbers of wisdom'. Milton's contemporary, Sir Thomas Browne, talks of things being shaped 'according to the ordainer of order and the mystical mathematics of the City of Heaven'. Moreover, just as the study of mathematical harmony and proportion exalted the mind, so the use of it by an artist could affect his audience. I refer below (p. 63) to the political importance attached to music and poetry in certain French circles in the later sixteenth century; yet Baïf and his associates were doing nothing theoretically out of the ordinary in trying to affect men's political behaviour through music, as we see from Natalis Comes's discussion of the story of Philomel and Tereus (*Mythologiae*, VII. x):

> For there is this power in sounds, even the sort that carry no meaning, that they move us to happiness or sadness of mind. Because the soul of men is composed from number, as the Pythagoreans realized, it easily perceives the sound of harmony, and, as if by some titillation it is rapidly stimulated to either emotion even by voices and sounds that signify nothing

but which have regard to a certain ratio of numbers. This same ratio of numbers applies also to the faculty of speech, for more sluggish minds are aroused, and when aroused are kept in check, not only by what is said but also by the tone of the voice. Just so, poets in ancient times are said to have fired the minds of soldiers to war by the harmony of their songs, and many instruments of music were invented in military camps, by the noise of which soldiers might be incited to battle. (my translation)[9]

Milton's Penseroso is sensitive to music in this way, and in *At a Solemn Music* the poet unambiguously claims music and verse as capable of adjusting the 'proportion' of the human mind with a vision of heaven. The artist, therefore, who treated his art with high seriousness, as it is beyond question Milton did, would be very prepared to use mathematical proportion and symbolism to supplement the charge of his words.[10]

The belief in the close relationship between mathematics, music and the order of the Heavens which man's art strove to emulate led naturally to the employment of formal, numerical and structural patterns as an aid to communication. So, important ideas and areas of a work of art might be signalled by the convention of placing them at the triumphal centres, or climaxes (see p. 110ff), which often may be signalled by a shift in the level of language. Furthermore, mathematics added a (to us) yet stranger component of meaning. Over many centuries certain numbers had come to carry a fairly precise symbolism, with which it is clear most Renaissance artists were familiar. (The symbolism may seem arbitrary to us, but the many texts devoted to this topic make it clear that it was the result of much deep study of the Bible, of music, and of the theory of number itself.[11]

We shall see these techniques being used by Milton in the *Nativity Ode*, in *Lycidas* and (I would argue) in the structure of *Poems* (1645). *Paradise Lost*, whose subject is by definition, and by Milton's admission, beyond commensurate mortal utterance, employs 'triumphal' patterns, balanced structure, and number symbolism extensively.

A poem cannot transcribe reality: it creates a new one. The poem, not the desire to write it or the circumstance of writing it, is the only reality, strictly speaking, we readers can touch: it is not words on the page so much as their operation in the reader's mind controlled by the author's intelligent manipulation of what he assumes to be there. Hence Renaissance poems are not only outward-looking, focused on what they are talking about and what sort of language has been developed elsewhere for talking about their particular subject, but also inward-looking – aware of how they are doing it, and relying on our recognizing when they are making new and bold experiments, creating new amalgams of familiar elements. In reading Milton, particularly when he is unfamiliar to us, we need to keep in mind that he makes few concessions to our ignorance: he expects us to be alert to the symbols and allusions he is using and to bring to the composition before us a readiness to read it using several strategies simultaneously or consecutively. For there are examples – the *Nativity Ode* is one – where there is a layer of meaning that cannot be grasped until we have finished the poem and then turned round and looked at how we read it. Furthermore he expects us to be aware of the difficulties of his utterance: both the difficulties he has put there as the simplest means of conveying the complexity that his subject entails, and also his own creative problem of measuring his words in just proportion to the seriousness and magnitude of his subject.

With generations of editors, we have become used to thinking of the 1645 poems – the English ones, that is, for few now read the Latin that make up half the volume – as 'Milton's Minor Poems'. In the light of the massive achievement of *Paradise Lost*, the scale and ambition of which is paralleled in European literature only by Dante's *Divine Comedy* 300 years earlier, I suppose they are minor; but in 1645 *Paradise Lost* in its first published version was 22 years in the future. I want to try to recapture how a first reader, in January 1645/6, might have felt on reading the book – to read *Poems* (1645) on the terms Humphrey Moseley offered it to the public: as 'true a Birth, as the Muses have brought forth since our famous *Spencer* wrote', a major poetic collection of obvious importance. Part of the interest of *Poems* (1645) lies in the presentation in a collection of disparate poems of a voice that is already assured, of enormous resource, and of unusual authority; part lies in Milton's public committing of himself to the promise he fulfilled later.

By 1645, Milton was up to his neck in the political activities and the social and moral controversies of his day, and his handling of them altered the way his contemporaries and successors – including ourselves – could formulate them. He was on terms with many of the great; he had a considerable reputation as a controversialist, and on his travels abroad he had been welcomed – lionized, even – as the most learned of Englishmen. But he had little or no reputation as a poet, despite this being, as we shall see, his one constant ambition; his poetry in Britain, despite the praise of a few discerning spirits like Sir Henry Wotton, was out of step with fashion, and though we may well see *Poems* (1645) as a virtual redefinition of poetry, the book's modest first printing took over 15 years to sell out – unlike *Paradise Lost*, which sold out very fast. Yet the publication of this book by a man with such a high political profile both in England and increasingly in Europe in such a year – the year of the battle of Naseby – cannot have been without political significance and political intent. There are good grounds for seeing it as a poetic autobiography, as a manifesto, and as laying claim to an unprecedented moral authority in the commonwealth of what Milton called 'God's Englishmen'.

The autobiographical nature of the collection makes obligatory a short discussion of his life, reading and training – and how he thought about them: life and work are mutually illuminating. Milton is the first poet, perhaps, to reveal publicly so much about his inner thoughts and feelings – in both his poetry and his polemics – especially as they related to what he conceived of as his divinely appointed calling as a poet. He was much given to self-examination: so were many sincere Christians, Catholic or Protestant, in the turbulent century after the Reformation, when questions of the means, or the certainty, of salvation were endlessly and furiously discussed not only in pulpit and pamphlet but also in plays and poems and public houses. But within that context, the issue, which Milton simply cannot leave alone, of inspiration and the public duty of the poet is so important that it will need a full chapter to itself: what he meant, and what his contemporaries understood, by being a poet, by inspiration, is crucial to our reading of the poems.

Notes to Chapter 1

1. Hereafter I shall refer to the complete 1645 volume as *Poems* (1645).
2. Milton's Christian theology develops in very idiosyncratic directions, however: the first publication of *De Doctrina Christiana* in 1823 revealed opinions that many saw as frankly heretical – support for polygamy, salvation by works, limitations on God's power, and so on. (I raise these matters later.) His theology is often remarkably close to that of the group who have been dubbed the Cambridge Platonists (see p. 34).
3. *Ut pictura poiesis* – 'poetry is like a picture (and vice versa)' – is a much quoted phrase – for example, by Ben Jonson – that goes back to Plutarch and Horace. It follows that visual imagery (at least) in poems and plays needs looking at very warily by us moderns: it is going to work much more like the symbolic details in Renaissance painting than as straight description (see pp. 8, 12, 91). The relation of some verbal imagery to the emblem form I discuss in my *A Century of Emblems: An Introductory Anthology* (Scolar Press, 1989).
4. Cf. Shakespeare's use of pastoral in *As You Like It*, or *The Winter's Tale*, or *Cymbeline* to discuss this issue. This problem can also be a religious one: the nature of man's 'doctrine of ill-doing' (cf. Romans, ch. 7) and his stewardship of the world entrusted to him by God.
5. Milton seems to take the line 'The hungry sheep look up and are not fed' (*Lycidas*, l.125) from his *Falco*: this is an attack on the Roman Curia, and was much read in German and English Protestant circles. Spenser's *September Aeglogue* uses the poem too.

6. See my article 'A Note on Possible Acrostics in Paradise Lost', *Notes and Queries*, June 1988.

7. Cristoforo Landino, echoing Boccaccio, says 'the world is God's poem' (*Dante con l'espositione de Cristoforo Landino*, Venice 1564, sig.**3^V (1st edn, Florence, 1481). Cf. J. C. Scaliger, *Poeticae Libri Septem* (Lyons, 1561, vol. III). For the poet as subcreator, and poetry as analogous to God's creating activity, see M. C. Nahm, *The Artist As Creator* (Baltimore, 1956).

8. There exist printed Bibles from the Renaissance in which the central verses of chapters are marked. (The division into verses was a recent thing.) John Colet's statutes for St Paul's School, which he founded and Milton attended, specify that 153 pupils 'of all nations' are to be educated free: a neat symbolic emphasis, through the usual interpretation of the story in St John 21.11, on what he saw as the prime job of his school, education in Christianity.

9. Comes we shall meet several times in this book. His encyclopaedia of mythology, many times reissued and much expanded, enjoyed a huge vogue in the late sixteenth and early seventeenth centuries. It is inconceivable Milton did not know it.

10. Giles Fletcher's defence of poetry (Preface to *Christ's Victory and Triumph*, Cambridge, 1610) appeals to the poetic passages of the Bible, and the example set by the late Latin devotional poets 'sedulous Prudentius' and 'prudent Sedulius' both of whom composed using numerical patterns. (Milton echoes Prudentius a good deal in the *Nativity Ode*.)

11. Those interested in this area might start by looking at Isidore of Seville, *Liber Numerorum*; Honorius of Autun, *De Imagine* and *Speculum Ecclesiae*; Boethius, *De Arithmetica*; Rabanus Maurus, *De Numero*; Hugh of St Victor, *Exegetica*; and Pietro Bongo, *Numerorum Mysteria* (Bergamo, 1591). Modern discussions of the importance of these ideas in the Renaissance are in V. Hopper, *Mediaeval Number Symbolism* (New York, 1938); A. Fowler, *Triumphal Forms* (Cambridge, 1970); and M.-S. Røstvig, *Fair Forms* (Cambridge, 1975). J. D. North, in *Chaucer's Universe* (Oxford, 1986), has an interesting discussion of how that poet employed this tool.

2 'The Ceaseless Round of Study and Reading'

Mr. John Milton
Was of an Oxfordshire family: his grandfather . . . (a Rom. Cath.) of Holten, in Oxfordshire, near Shotover. His father was brought up in the University of Oxon, at Christ Church (his mother was a Bradshaw, Chpr. Milton (his brother, the Inner Temple barrister), and his gr. father disinherited him because he kept not to the Catholic religion (he found a Bible, in English, in his chamber); so thereupon he came to London, and became a scrivener (brought up by a friend of his, was not an apprentice), and got a plentiful estate by it, and left it off many years before he died. He was an ingenious man, delighted in music, composed many songs now in print, especially that of Oriana.

His son John was born in Bread Street, in London, at the Spread Eagle, which was his house . . .

So run the gossipy John Aubrey's first notes in his *Collections for the Life of Milton*. Milton has never lacked biographers since soon after he died: Aubrey, who tackled a good number of the illustrious literary figures of the first half of the century, was the first. The artist, be he poet or painter, had begun in the Renaissance to be an object of interest not only as contingent upon his art but also as a man: how, why, did such men create such works? Moreover, the spiritual challenges of Reformation and Counter-Reformation forced men and women to look inward to the state of their own souls in a newly urgent way: the individual quite suddenly has become deeply interesting to himself, and when he is one of those exceptional creatures in whom resides that larger-than-life quality the Italians called *virtù*, he becomes deeply interesting to others. Boccaccio's *Life of Dante* is the earliest example of the sort of biographical examination of the artist's values that we see as a major theme in, for example, Vasari's *Lives of the Painters*. Dr Johnson's *Lives of the Poets* similarly mixes biography with critical discussion to satisfy a public demand that rests on the relatively new perception that the man and his work reflect each other. Milton's importance as a poet, obvious at last after the publication of *Paradise Lost*, guaranteed him such attention: but he himself, in his interest in himself as a poet, anticipated his biographers.

He is perhaps the first Englishman, let alone poet, to say publicly so much about his life, his education, his values (and how they changed), and his ambitions. The turbulent middle years of the century threw him into international prominence; when he writes about the things nearest to him, which most men kept private, he is usually publicly defending himself against attacks which even by seventeenth-century standards were exceptionally vicious. As a result of this polemical intent, even in the sincerest and most moving passages there is inevitably a certain amount of editing so that he may appear to best advantage to himself, as well as to his audience: one of his favourite controversial roles for himself is as a sort of innocent infant Samuel, consecrated to a high service, but abused and attacked by the malice and wickedness of the world.[1] *Defensio Secunda pro Populo Anglicano* (1654) gives the fullest account of his life, self-training and ambitions; he also discusses his intimate feelings in another controversial work, the *Apology for Smectymnuus* (1641).[2]

It is not only in his prose works that he constantly returns to the examination of his values, motives and purposes; disguised, this is his major interest in his poetry, as *Lycidas* alone demonstrates. The delicately intimate Latin poem *Ad Patrem* (1637?) was originally written to his father as a justification (among other things) for his decision to devote his life to poetry, as a gentle pointing out that if the elder Milton was upset that his son had as yet found no gainful employment, he had only himself to blame for planting certain tastes and values in him as a boy. Yet even this Milton made public in *Poems* (1645).

In his contemporaries George Herbert, Henry Vaughan, or Francis Quarles, such interest in the self and its mental and spiritual state often springs from a deliberate discipline of meditation and self-examination that is part and parcel of a religious faith deeply affected by new devotional practices in both the Catholic and Protestant traditions. It is possible Milton was so affected. But where these other poets are most concerned with the exploration of an essentially private relationship with God – even Quarles, who wears his flaming heart on his sleeve – with Milton it seems to be his relationship to a holy role that interests him. Whatever the explanation, Milton offers his own life as a major key to his intentions and purposes as a poet: in his own words, 'He who would not be frustrate in his hope to write well hereafter in laudable things, ought himself to be a true poem, that is, a composition of the best and honourablest things' (*Smectymnuus*; cf. *Elegy VI*).

Home and Schooling

Like so many of his age, Milton's father was a first-generation Protestant. Nowadays, perhaps, it is only in contexts deeply divided on sectarian lines (like Northern Ireland) that we can glimpse anything of the horror a father might feel if his son went over to the other side. But there the resemblance stops: in Northern Ireland the division is tribal with merely the label of religion attached to it, whereas in sixteenth-century England the division was in the vast majority of cases between men and women who knew exactly what they were arguing about and did so bitterly in the belief that their immortal souls depended on it. That division of Milton from his father is an anticipatory symptom of the religious controversy that occupied so much time and energy in that and the next century, and which is one of the constant strands in Milton's own life and thought. (Milton's brother Christopher became a Roman Catholic – and a Royalist to boot.) If there is one single idea that dominates Milton's political life, it is the establishment in England of a Church and government that, freed of the corruption and tarnish of centuries, would reflect the newest gloss of Apostolic Christianity and, so far as was possible on a fallen earth, prepare the way for the Kingdom of God.

The home into which Milton was born in 1608 was comfortable and cultured. Milton clearly had a great affection for his lawyer father, who recognized and encouraged his precocious talent, and 'destined [him] from childhood to the pursuits of learning' (*Defensio Secunda*). He gave him the best education available: he not only sent his son to St Paul's School, where he progressed at an exceptional rate (reading often, even at the age of 12, until midnight), but also provided teachers of languages (notably French, Italian and Hebrew) for him at home. One was Thomas Young, the 'TY' of *Smectymnuus*, with whom Milton remained friendly for many years – until Young decided that wordly advancement mattered more than principle. These are the years when the foundations of Milton's extraordinary learning were laid.

St Paul's had been founded by John Colet early in the previous century. The statutes he drew up for its government are interestingly specific about the curriculum – which in essentials was unchanged under Alexander Gil the Elder, High Master in Milton's time – and its purpose. Colet was dissatisfied with the education provided in the cathedral schools of his day, and his aim was to provide an easier, more specifically Christian way to the active encouragement of a good life with good learning: the ideal product of the school would combine Christian wisdom with Roman eloquence. His curriculum is remarkably short on the giants of the pagan past – Vergil, Cicero, Sallust and the rest are named in the statutes but not specified for study; on the other hand, he specified as core authors an interesting collection of late Latin writers: Lactantius, the Church Father who by general agreement wrote the most Ciceronian Latin; the fourth-century Christian poet Prudentius; Proba, the fourth-century authoress of a Vergilian cento; Iuvencus, the early fourth-century Spanish poet much influenced by Vergil; the fifth-century poet Sedulius; and, finally, the late fifteenth-century Italian poet Mantuan. Traces of all these, and especially of Mantuan, appear in Milton's own writing, and coping with Lactantius must have early developed not only his stylistic polish but also his ability to argue on matters moral and theological. A boy could not plough through such an author and merely learn Latin: he would learn a lot of Church history and a lot of theology as well. The Latinity the school encouraged – it was not unusual in this – was that of Cicero in prose and Vergil in verse, and there was a strong emphasis on the pupils' mastery of the art of rhetoric. By Milton's time, the study of ancient poetry was much more readily accepted[3] – as a guide to life, hidden under the veil of the literal sense (see p. 14); and ancient history, especially Livy, whom it is clear Milton knew very well, gave practical examples of the precepts of philosophy. Gil and Colet, a century apart, had the same view of the main aim of Renaissance education: the creation of good men and active citizens, fit to take their part in the running of the commonwealth.

Milton here acquired written and spoken fluency in Latin – then still a living language, the international medium of scholarship, controversy and diplomacy, as well as of much good poetry. He would certainly have read, and reread, the major Latin writers, especially Ovid and Vergil, whose influence on his writing in both Latin and English is very marked. St Paul's had long had a reputation for the teaching of Greek, and it is entirely possible that before their teens were fairly started many boys would have read substantial amounts of Homer and other Greek writers in the original. His grounding in rhetoric through such texts as Erasmus's *De Copia* and the pseudo-Ciceronian *Rhetorica ad Herennium* – the commonest school texts – is very likely to have been supplemented through the study of English poets, especially Spenser. Gil, an original thinker who seems to have been a gifted teacher as well as a tireless flogger of his pupils, was a great admirer of Spenser. His *Logonomia Anglica* (1619), urging the reform of spelling, is full of examples from that poet, used exactly as a teacher would use them.[4]

Finally, Milton was grounded in the art of logical argument – that is, not in the mere forceful expression of opinion that today so often passes for argument and discussion, but the recognition and understanding of the rules and formulae – which have a lot in common with certain areas of mathematics – that allow sound conclusions to be deduced from premises, principles and evidence. In fact, the school provided an excellent grounding in the three Arts that formed the medieval *trivium* of grammar (language and literature), rhetoric and logic. Before he left for Christ's College, Cambridge, in February 1625, he tells us he was 'instructed in various languages, and had a great taste for the sweetness of philosophy' (*Defensio Secunda*).

St Paul's, attached as it was to the cathedral, offered other advantages too. Old St Paul's was one of the most beautiful Gothic churches of northern Europe, and the reaction of the narrator at the end of *Il Penseroso* (ironic as it may be – see p. 139) perhaps recalls how sensitive Milton was to its architecture. It had a fine musical tradition, wedded to the beauty of the Anglican liturgy, and we know Milton was extremely sensitive to music. Moreover, Milton was at school while John Donne was Dean; to read Dr Donne's sermons today can still give us some pale glimpse of what it much have been like to hear them, and he was only the most notable of the many fine preachers who occupied that important pulpit or stood under the preaching cross in the churchyard. Several important foundations for the later development of Milton's mind can be discerned here.

Cambridge

Milton was at Christ's from 1625 to 1632 – the seven years necessary to complete the courses leading first to the baccalaureate and then to the Master of Arts degree. His career at Cambridge was brilliant – he graduated *cum laude* in July 1632 – and he left it (he says later) with some regret on the part of the senior members of the College. This period of Milton's life is of great importance for the development of his mind and ideas, and it seems to have been his disappointment with the complacency of the system there, and with the people who accepted it, that pushed him off onto his own lonely and individualistic path.

The majority of men who went to Oxford and Cambridge at this period would have expected eventually to take holy orders: the two universities were the main training ground for the clergy of the Established Church of England, and Roman Catholics and other Dissenters were not admitted. To become a Fellow of a College it was necessary to be ordained (as indeed it was until the mid-nineteenth century). There is no doubt that when Milton entered Christ's, eventual ordination was in his, and probably his father's, mind: it was, after all, then the natural road to public service and private advancement for a man of Milton's temperament, background and accomplishments. But it was while at

Cambridge that he began to have serious doubts.

The religious dissensions of that age were nowhere more acridly argued than in the universities, and the two were divided against each other and within themselves. The 1620s was a period of acute and increasing controversy. There was a major division between the Calvinists and the Arminians, and the political power of the latter's most vociferous champion, William Laud, was patently growing: first, President of St John's College, Oxford; then, Bishop of St David's (1621); then, Bishop of Bath and Wells (1626); next, Bishop of London (1628); and, finally, Archbishop of Canterbury (1633). Now, as it happens, Milton was throughout his life much closer to an Arminian theological position than a Calvinist one; but Laud and his party, to the horror of many besides the extreme Protestants, also rejected the dour distrust of any form of decoration or ceremonial in churches and services and encouraged the installation of stained glass, paintings and occasional statues; and, when they had the power, they obliged incumbents to celebrate Communion in a particular way. Opponents saw this as galloping Romanism, and the move towards a stronger clergy as a return to the bad old pre-Reformation days of a priestly class who could exploit power and wealth to their own advantage. With that, Milton would have no truck.[5]

Of the two universities, Oxford was more ready to accept the position of Laud's party; Cambridge, always the more Puritan and radical, was generally very opposed to them. Certain colleges were noted for extreme Puritan positions, to the extent of implicitly rejecting the status quo of the Church of England and its services. A young man contemplating ordination could not avoid taking sides in these disputes. To take his degree in 1632, Milton must have subscribed to the Thirty-nine Articles of Religion,[6] but it is clear that by 1628 he already had no great respect for many of the young men he saw in Cambridge who were to be ordained, as well as that distrust of a venal clergy which would eventually draw his attacks in *Lycidas* and partly lead to his decision not to be ordained.[7] His growing distrust of the government of the church by bishops, a government which the Thirty-nine Articles insist upon, would not in all conscience allow him to accept employment in a church so governed.[8]

Moreover, though the universities were long on controversy, they were intellectually pretty stifling at this time: most of the really original scholarly work was being done outside them, and Cambridge, particularly, had a bad record in not making room for the ideas proposing a reform of logical thinking and what we would call analytical science that had been offered by men like Pierre de La Ramée, Francis Bacon and John Dee. At Cambridge there was still great stress on the basic Aristotelian subjects – logic, ethics and physics (the study of nature, not what we call physics) and metaphysics. There was also endless, compulsory grammar, even at the most basic level of understanding the language, which any product of St Paul's under Alexander Gil would have thoroughly mastered before he was in his teens. 'Aristotelian', or 'Scholastic', logic, with its relentless and nit-picking deductions from 'authorities' and accepted premises – of sometimes questionable truth – was still the usual academic method of argument and study. Milton evinces growing impatience with this system, and eventually proposed its complete abolition (see p. 30f); but he had no alternative but to accept it while an undergraduate despite his misgivings and inevitable boredom.

The university curriculum had developed from the medieval framework of the Seven Liberal Arts. The three arts of grammar, rhetoric and logic constituted the *trivium*, which as a whole was preliminary to the four-year course of the *quadrivium*, which had a predominantly mathematical content. Arithmetic led on to the study of music, and then geometry led on to the study of astronomy. These names suggest quite different – and much more restricted – topics to us than in fact they were. Arithmetic was what now might go by the name of pure and applied maths: our ancestors, like the ancients, saw mathematics as the key to the understanding of the structure and nature of the universe, and besides its teaching of basic techniques this was a subject with a high philosophical content. It was – and still is – closely related to music, which for the Renaissance student was not just making noises – that was the business of the *cantor,* the performer – but of understanding the proper physical, mathematical and mystical relationships between those noises: that was the business of the *musicus.* Music was, after all, a reflection on earth of the music of the spheres: the mathematical relationship of those spheres expressed itself as musical tones and notes which men could not hear because, as Milton says in *At a Solemn Music*, they expressed a God-given perfection man's sin did not allow him to hear (see p. 120). Geometry introduced another technique of mathematical thinking, and finally astronomy used the principles of music, geometry and arithmetic to examine the nature of the heavens and the way they affect the earth and all that is in it.[9]

And when a man had mastered these disciplines of words and number, had digested the literature and learning of the distant as well as the recent past, he might be ready to tackle 'the Queen of the Sciences', theology herself.

The system is neat: so neat as to be self-justifying as long as you do not look outside it. Once upon a time it had served Europe excellently as a means of organizing and interrelating the sum total of human knowledge. It also had profound effects on the perception of reality: not only would a man who had mastered – as Milton largely did before he left St Paul's – grammar and rhetoric (for example) by reading and studying deeply most of the poets, historians and orators of Greece and Rome have a mind furnished with antique culture whose value neither he nor anyone else doubted, but also this culture would form his values, standards, expectations and taste. While the arts of the Renaissance and after are certainly modern and deal with modern problems, the perceptions that made them are affected by the experience of the literary remains of antiquity. Those perceptions condition how an issue or an object can be formulated and communicated, and indeed reference to or imitation of an accepted or well-known antique idea, poem or statue may be a most effective and economical way of communicating with a contemporary audience. Where we see mere imitation, Milton's contemporaries saw a modern idea as being like a ball bounced off an antique wall and deriving greater force from its bounce.

The study of grammar and rhetoric continued to fill a useful role for many years after Milton – though he must have found it irksome to be compelled at Cambridge to go through elementary linguistic material that he had already mastered. But Cambridge, as we have seen, spent a lot of time on the third of the 'trivial' arts, logic, the science of argument. The formal techniques of the elenchus, the enthymeme, the syllogism, the sorites and other monsters that lurk on the boundaries of discourse are indispensable tools, but the way it was taught made the tool more important than the material it was supposed to shape. The art is concerned with the correct derivation of conclusions from premises; it was not primarily concerned with those premises or first principles themselves. And precisely for that reason it had gathered over the centuries a carapace of formal patterns that turned the sinewy racehorse of the Greeks into a lumbering armadillo that rooted among rubbish. Milton was not alone in recognizing that this formal logic, the empty shell of what was once the most exciting and controversial academic tool of the medieval universities,[10] was getting in everybody's way: the extremely influential French educationalist and philosopher Peter Ramus (Pierre de La Ramée) defended a thesis at the Sorbonne that 'All the Opinions of Aristotle are wrong', and proposed, in *Dialectique* (1555), *Scholae in Liberales Artes* (1559) and *Grammatica* (1559), that things rather than books be looked at, and the disciplines of argument and rhetoric be overhauled and simplified. Francis Bacon, much in debt to Ramus, wrote *Novum Organum* (1620) as a manifesto for an alternative method of research, and its very title (echoing Aristotle's *Organon*) was a challenge to the dominant position Aristotle held in the academic curriculum. The fundamental criticism was that the logic of Aristotelian scholarship might be fine, but it looked too much to written authority for its initial material, and not enough to things as they really were.

Milton was not unusual in a growing impatience with this system. He had to accept it while an undergraduate, but he was not very happy in Cambridge where he '[found] almost no real companions in study here' (*Letter 3*, 1628). At one point, in 1626, after some unspecified quarrel with his tutor, he left the place and went back to London: in Elegy I, addressed to his greatest friend, Charles Diodati (see p. 37), he says he does not miss Cambridge at all:

> Iam nec arundiferam mihi cura revisere Camum
> . . . .
> Nuda nec arva placent, umbrasque negantia molles,
> Quam male Phoebicolis convenit ille locus!

('At the moment I do not care to see again the reedy Cam . . . Those naked fields, which deny all sweet shade, do not attract me – how badly that place suits those who would worship Phoebus [god of poetry and wisdom].') Though much later he does speak very affectionately of 'those courteous and learned men, the Fellows of [Christ's] College' in *Smectymnuus*, he and his tutor, William Chappell, seem not to have got on at all. One cannot help feeling a little sympathy for poor Chappell: brilliance is never comfortable, and his very superior, cruelly witty pupil never suffered fools gladly. Chappell was merely trying to do his job according to his limited lights. (If it is Chappell, as some have suggested, who is glanced at as 'old Damoetas' in *Lycidas*, it is no surprise to find that Damoetas in Vergil is the most clownish of shepherds.) Trying to put Milton through the usual hoops must have been worse than trying to persuade a seal to wear water wings.

When he did return, he attacked Scholastic philosophy in the *Third Prolusion*, and said he would persuade his fellow students not to open those huge tomes of the 'so-called subtle doctors' by which neither is the mind delighted nor any common good promoted. True enjoyment is not to be got from them; if they have a place on Parnassus, the Hill of Apollo and the Muses, it is as a thicket of brambles at the bottom. He is scathing elsewhere, too, about the usefulness of the dialectical method as taught at Cambridge. He pokes learned academic fun at it: his *De Idea Platonica* (1628–30) was written as a college exercise, and, like the *Second Prolusion* 'on the Music of the Spheres' (also a college exercise), is ironic about Aristotle and Aristotelians. One of the reasons for his rejection of Aristotelianism may have been his growing attraction to the Idealist philosophy of Plato and his interest in Pythagorean mathematics and what it implied about the structure and nature of the world and all that is in it (see p. 32). Whatever the reason, the rejection was serious and final, one more step on the way to the thorough radicalism that marks his maturity – a radicalism the fundamental principles of which are that human institutions should serve men, and not the other way round, and a basic concern for the liberty of the mature and responsible individual.

His dissatisfaction eventually bore fruit in a most interesting and revealing pamphlet. *Of Education* (1644) gives a lot of clues not only about his own practice as a schoolmaster – evidently, according to his nephew Edward Phillips, one of his pupils, a most excellent one – but also about his ideals for education and, by implication, his dissatisfaction with his own. He was far from alone in recognizing the need for radical reform of the educational system. This was not simply a desire of change for change's sake, as can so often be the case in periods (like our own) when people have lost confidence in old ideas and structures, intellectual or political. Rather, there was a reasoned recognition by many that neither the system nor what was taught in it was serving at all well individuals or the society of which they were a part. Milton shared the view of many that educational reform, which ultimately had a religious as well as a social purpose, was the final necessary step in the Protestant Reformation of England.[11]

The last years of the sixteenth century and the first half of the seventeenth, in England and France, saw a number of proposals for the setting up of new academic institutions outside the control of the old universities. Some remained theoretical: for example, Humphrey Gilbert's *Queene Elizabeth's Achademy*,[12] or the description of Solomon's House in which, in the *New Atlantis* (1626), Bacon exemplifies the structural implications of his proposals in the *Advancement of Learning* (1605); some did actually happen, like François I's Collège de France, with its aggressive independence of the University of Paris, or, in England, the founding of Gresham College, which was to become much later the nucleus of the Royal Society (chartered by Charles II in 1662). Much divides Milton from Bacon, but in their recognition of the purpose of education, and concern for its utility, they sound the same note.

Both held the common view that before the Fall Adam possessed 'a pure light of natural knowledge' (Bacon, *Works*, ed. Spedding and Ellis, III, 219, 'Of the Interpretation of Nature'; cf. *Paradise Lost*, VIII. 342–54). But with the Fall and the confusion of language at the destruction of the Tower of Babel (see p. 14) this perfect language and knowledge were lost. Bacon and Milton, and many others, agreed that the end of all learning should be, as Milton says in *Of Education*, 'to repair the ruins of our first parents by regaining to know God aright, and out of that knowledge to love him, to imitate him, to be like him, as we may the nearest by possessing our soul of true virtue, which being united to the heavenly grace of faith makes up the highest perfection'. But whereas Milton's first principle remains theological and devotional, the practical minds of Peter Ramus and Bacon saw a more immediate benefit in the restoration of man's control over nature, lost at the Fall. Bacon saw the end of knowledge as also the 'effecting of all things possible', and devised a new analytical method to achieve this. (The scientific methods of observation and thought that we take for granted descend directly from him.)

Of Education

The practical consequences that Milton saw as implied in his vision of the purpose of education is best seen in his pamphlet, which he wrote in the form of a letter to the indefatigable Samuel Hartlib.[13]

He does not speak, as too many would-be educational reformers did then and do now, either having got safely away from a strenuous job they found too much for them or from a position outside education altogether, but from the committed and experienced standpoint of a teacher himself: from 1639 he had been running a school in his house in London. Milton attacked the customary procedure of first teaching grammar, rhetoric, and logic, with the traditional texts as material, and then proceeding to arithmetic, music, geometry and astronomy: he recognized the silliness of demanding that young people learn to write verses, manipulate logic and make speeches before they have any serious and solid knowledge in their heads to talk about.[14]

The results of 'misspending our prime youth at the schools and universities . . . in learning mere words or such things chiefly as were better unlearned' are lawyers who care nothing for justice; parsons who know and care little for the true calling of a priest, politicians 'unprincipled in virtue and true generous breeding' who are a prey to flattery and tyranny, and, finally, men who waste their lives in a self-indulgence no good either to them or their fellows. Milton offers a fairly detailed and awesomely comprehensive programme as an alternative: he proposes the abolition of the universities and schools as separate entities, and suggests that each town should have an establishment of some 150 youths aged from 12 to 21 who would follow a programme which is a remarkably attractive mixture. Its fundamental principle is of learning through pleasure. Carefully ordered reading would ensure that the most accessible books and subjects preceded the much more difficult with which, all too often, students were forced to tangle at a quite unsuitable age; bodily exercise (including individual proficiency in fencing and corporate practice in military manoeuvres, both mounted and afoot) was given its proper place.

Attention to teaching the rudiments of the Classical languages properly would make the acquisition of other languages like Italian, Hebrew and Syriac relatively painless – it still can – and the young men so educated would have a thorough grounding in most of the important and practical matters of life. They would also have a skill in and knowledge of music, and have developed, through wide reading, a cultured taste for poetry, which Milton saw as 'more simple, sensuous and passionate' than rhetoric.[15]

His views on poetry (see pp. 58ff) and its important function in society make it clear that literary taste is not a question of mere polish; it would lead to true discrimination, and recognition of where the high moral and spiritual value of poetry lay. This cultured taste, which we may be sure Milton felt himself (with good reason) to possess, 'would make them soon perceive what despicable creatures our common rhymers and play-writers be, and show them what religious, what glorious, and what magnificent use might be made of poetry both in divine and human things'. Such a 'complete and generous education' would, Milton claimed, 'fit a man to perform justly, skilfully, and magnanimously all the offices, both private and public, of peace and war . . .'.

It is ambitious, but it is not a foolish programme, and might be tried with profit even today. (It might even be fun.) What is so significant about it, however, is the insistence throughout on the power of words: misused, throughout an education inevitably based on books, they weaken the understanding and vitiate the mind, substituting for the real thing – the Ideas, in a Platonic sense – that should be the object of attention, the conventional sign by which the real is recognized; used properly, words can ultimately lead not only to the recognition, under-standing and exploration of public and private virtue, but also to the wisdom whose beginning, so the Biblical book of Proverbs reminds us, is the fear of the Lord. For if the ancients in the darkness before the revelation of God in Jesus had developed, by proper learning and teaching, 'old admired virtues and excellencies', how much more, 'now in this purity of Christian knowledge', could not those virtues 'redound mightily to the good of this nation . . .'

Critical as he was of the university's programme of study, Milton nevertheless got some considerable benefits out of being in the place. He found a good deal of enjoyment in out-of-the-way areas of scholarship. He found and apparently read some of the Anglo-Saxon manuscripts that Archbishop Parker had collected in the reign of Elizabeth; some of them he annotated. Milton pursued his interest in the history of Britain, as told by Geoffrey of Monmouth and those who, like Malory,

Spenser and Drayton, followed Geoffrey's version, and he considered seriously the stories of King Arthur he found there as a possible subject of the great national poem he was even then contemplating (see pp. 60–61). He read deeply in Spenser, Shakespeare, Ben Jonson and Philip Sidney, making himself thoroughly conversant with the distinct tradition of English poetry and fiction. (That is not to say, of course, that that tradition did not draw deeply on Classical writing.) He also read people of whom he came to disapprove, and tuned his already inestimable gift of a good ear: through much experience of the 'best and elegantest authors' he 'could measure a just cadence and scan without articulating, rather nice and humorous in what was tolerable, than patient to read every drawling versifier' (*Smectymnuus*). He explored books of natural history, travel and theoretical geography: the evidence of this eclectic, omnivorous reading is scattered throughout all the poems.[16]

Most important for the development of his mind, however, was the fact that he drank deep at the wells of Classical poetry, philosophy and historiography, and, especially, deepened his reading of Plato. One task regularly given to undergraduates at Cambridge was the translation of Plato into Latin and (probably) Cicero into Greek:[17] the aim was primarily to increase linguistic competence, but, of course, the business of translation requires that the text be throughly understood. Reverence for Plato's philosophy at Cambridge was patchy, but not unknown, and there were those of Milton's generation who were exploring its application in exciting ways (see p. 34). Indeed, it is not to overstate it to claim that it is impossible to understand Milton's mature attitude to words (and poetry), to virtue, to the nature of existence, and to reality itself without some grasp of Plato's ideas, and so a brief explanatory digression is necessary.

Plato and Platonists

In *The Republic* (vii. 514a–521b) Plato suggests that reality is not simply that which is quantifiable by the senses, but is something much more complex. To illustrate how he thinks we human beings know reality, he uses the famous Allegory of the Cave. Suppose that men are like prisoners living in a cave, so chained that they can look only at the back wall. Suppose, too, that outside the cave is a fire burning, its light reflected on the back wall. Now suppose further that other people pass between the fire and the mouth of the cave, some silent, some talking, some carrying different sorts of objects: their shadows will be cast onto the back wall of the cave, their voices will echo so that they seem to come from the shadows, and those shadows are all that the prisoners can know of the real things and people outside. The shadows are not real themselves except in a limited sense, but are evidence of and depend on a hard reality that the prisoners can never know directly. Thus, the perception of the prisoners both has real value as a road to Truth and is irretrievably partial and inaccurate. The application of this allegory to human cognition is so clear as to need no explanation. Such an understanding of human cognition and the possibility of knowledge relates closely to Plato's Theory of Ideas or Forms, which, perhaps, is his principal contribution to philosophical thought (*Republic*, v. 474–80). The Idea or Form of a thing – like a chair, or the Good, or Chastity – has an existence outside the world of sense; it is the unchanging reality behind the changing appearance by which we men, limited by time and consciousness and sense, recognize individuated splinters of it in the comfortable chair on which we sit, in a good meal, a good poem, or a chaste man or woman. The supreme Idea is that of the Good. As did his teacher Socrates, Plato maintained that virtue was tantamount to knowledge of the supreme Idea, such knowledge implying the effort to make it real in ourselves. This perfect virtue, though, is given to very few; ordinary practical virtue consists in behaving in accordance with man's true nature, as developed by education.

The matter is not, so to speak, merely academic: the subject is the very nature of the world we live in and how human beings relate to it. Plato's ideas are an attempt to understand the human condition to which late twentieth-century men as well as fourth-century BC Greeks are subject: the agenda has not changed. A. N. Whitehead, the distinguished philosopher, once remarked that the whole of European philosophy is a series of footnotes to Plato, and Plato has never lacked followers or opponents from his own day to ours. For Platonism offers a theory of the mind and knowledge which accepts the provisional nature of our understanding but allows it a real value and some measure of a truth not merely that of logical and linguistic coherence. It breaks out of the vicious circles of empiricism and scepticism, where we can know only what the senses reveal to us – and never know that the word one man uses means the same to another man – and know that we do not know. It offers, too, a viable *model* of a relationship between a world limited by time and the fallible perception of sense and the existence of an Absolute, a Creator, a God. It also places a great deal of weight on the importance of human moral choice and effort. But, like all philosophical theories, its nature is such that proof is impossible from where we sit in the cave.

Milton's Platonism eventually went very deep indeed. Several of the college exercises and Prolusions indicate a growing commitment to it not just as a standpoint from which to attack the Aristotelians. Later it comes to provide some of the ideas by which he understands himself as a poet (see Chapter 3). Moreover, it is a philosophy that easily lends itself, even leads to, Christianity: St John, St Paul and St Augustine – to go no further – show its deep impress on their thought. The late fifteenth-century Italian humanists, like Pico della Mirandola and Marsilio Ficino, had restressed the idea that Christianity and Platonism were closely allied.[18]

Milton's beloved Philip Sidney and Edmund Spenser had revered Plato too, and in the *Apologie for Poesie*, Sidney provided one of the main arguments for the moral, social and religious justification of the beautiful lie that is fiction and poetry. Neoplatonism had been vastly influential in Renaissance art: the paintings of Botticelli, or Titian, Spenser's *Faerie Queene*, and the very way Queen Elizabeth dressed[19] all show Plato's direct influence and assume in the audience a sophisticated acquaintance with him.

As I have said, Platonism was not the dominant philosophy at Cambridge while Milton was there, nor did it become so later. The seventeenth century is, generally speaking, a period when materialist philosophies, like that of Hobbes, come to dominance. But there was a group of men in the university, one of them Milton's contemporary, who rejected the advancing materialism and restated a form of Christian Platonism in terms that are ultimately revolutionary. Milton was never one of the Cambridge Platonists, but the work of his maturity has much in common with theirs. It is most unlikely he did not know Benjamin Whichcote (1609–83); Henry More (1614–87) was all his mature life a Fellow of Christ's, and Cudworth (1617–88) eventually became Master. Following the tradition of Erasmus and Hooker, they tried to promote a Christianity that was wholly rational. They maintained that sense reveals only appearance, reality consisting in Forms. Their main idea was to argue that revelation from God, the rational order of the universe, and human reason were all in harmony, so that to search for Truth was to search for God: an idea that Milton clearly expresses in *Areopagitica* (1644). Furthermore, they rejected the Calvinist view of an utterly corrupt human nature, redeemable only by divine grace, and saw man as able to advance to perfection through the imitation of Christ and the pursuit of reason. Milton's independent, even heterodox theological thought that appears in *De Doctrina Christiana* has a lot in common with these ideas, especially in the notion of God's limiting of his own power in order to give man free will: a position exactly that of Cudworth.[20]

It would be easy to imagine Milton at Cambridge as a rather dour fellow, the natural butt of the seventeenth-century Hooray Henries who dubbed him 'the Lady of Christ's' because of his delicate appearance.[21]

In fact, it is quite clear that he had a real sense of humour, a not unattractive, if donnish, frivolity, which enabled him to make very good jokes and get his own back publicly on those who teased him.[22]

In some of his verse he deploys a mock solemnity which is curiously tender and moving, as in the poem written at 17 on the death of Richard Ridding, the elderly beadle of the university, whose gait he describes as 'alipes' ('wing-footed') – when he has to summon to assembly the 'Palladium . . . gregem', 'the host of Pallas Athene' – that is, the undergraduates, who were no more Palladian than they have been since. (The joke, of course, lies in the incongruity of the *expected* transposition of the Greek and Latin poetic conventions to a context wholly inappropriate to them.) The humour of *In Quintum Novembris* (1625/6) is unpleasantly (for us) anti-papal, but we can be sure a contemporary audience would have enjoyed the wit of remarks like that of lines 52 ff., where the Pope 'carries about his bread-making gods' ('Panificosque Deos portat', l. 56), or Milton's describing him as heir of Hell and an adulterer (ll. 74 ff.). Even we can see the comedy of Satan's appearing – as in *Dr Faustus* – in the likeness of an old Franciscan friar. The overstatement, inevitable in a poem of this type, rejoices in its own ingenuity. The two English poems on the death of Thomas Hobson, the university carrier, play wittily with a series of puns and conceits based on Hobson's profession; yet the downbeat, jokey couplets do communicate an affectionate sense of a down-to-earth, practical and rather rough-hewn personality which, by all accounts, is what Hobson was. Milton was also popular enough – and recognized as an able enough poet – to be invited to contribute *Lycidas* to an anthology of Cambridge poems marking the death by drowning of Edward King in 1637.

It is also often claimed that Milton hated women. This simply cannot be true. His own marriage was apparently unhappy to start with, though how much Mary Powell's return to her family is a result of its being on the other side of the political fence from Milton is often not considered: civil war, particularly over matters of religion and honour, has a way of dividing families. She did, after all, return to him and bear him children.[23]

But not to get on with a wife – if he did not – does not imply that he hated women: he enjoyed the society and friendship of a number of aristocratic ladies, like Lady Margaret Ley and Lady Ranelagh, and his second wife he adored. The unfallen Eve, in all her majestic beauty and innocence, he calls 'God's last *best* work'. His depiction of the relationship between the unfallen Adam and Eve has a nobility and a generosity in it that those who sneer about hierarchy and authority miss, to their great loss. He seems, in fact, to have been a perfectly normal man of his time, and more gentle, thoughtful and respectful of women than most, recognizing that the sexual morality that is binding on a woman is even more demanded of a man (*Smectymnuus*). He was, certainly, perfectly normally constituted: he had an acute sensitivity to female beauty, shown not only in the late portraits of Eve and Dalila but also in early poems. *Elegy I* may (or may not) be just literary pastiche – we do not know when Milton was 'Cupid's captive'. It still shows a delight in feminine beauty and a loving re-creation of it in allusive verse. (So, too, in *Elegy VII*, ll. 54 ff.) It has been claimed, from internal evidence, that the series of Italian sonnets, written long before he went to Italy, were addressed to, and welcomed by, a lady who had a facility with languages and music, and who may have been called Emilia. This is a perfectly tenable – and, so far as I know, unprovable – hypothesis, and it is attractive to entertain a picture of a young Milton madly in love writing sonnets to his mistress's eyebrows. But poets do not have to stick only to personal experience and feeling when they write. Many have written love poems where no lady existed, as a witty, sometimes ironic exercise. Other poets, like Spenser or Wyatt, translated or built on the love poems of Petrarch, and any lady they refer to lay between sheets of paper quite as probably as she did of linen. It is entirely possible that Milton is here writing Petrarchan pastiche, and doing it well enough to create the illusion of the passionate lover: which is what the game is all about. But what ultimately matters is that these are good poems on a subject which no misogynist would have ever bothered to write about.

Hammersmith, Horton and Italy

By the time he left Cambridge, the decision not to be ordained seems already to have been taken. This rejection of the expected career presented no financial problems, for Milton's father was neither poor nor ungenerous, but, reading between the lines of *Ad Patrem*, we infer that he seems to have been disturbed by his son's readiness to continue a course of intensive study and let the business of regular employment be. In a rather old-fashioned way, Milton seems to have looked around for a patron to maintain him, and, to some extent, to have found one in Anne, Countess of Derby.[24]

But the four years at Hammersmith, and then two at Horton, were mainly spent reading the Greek and Latin authors, occasionally visiting London to buy books or to learn something new in mathematics or music, 'which then gave me much of my amusement' (*Defensio Secunda*).

His visits to London would allow scope for his delight, too, in the theatre: while in *Elegy I*, written in 1626 during Milton's brief absence from Cambridge, the delight in theatre seems to be a solitary literary delight in Classical tragedy and the ancient comedies of Aristophanes, Plautus and Terence, he clearly liked the work of 'learned' Jonson and 'sweetest Shakespeare, fancy's child', as *L'Allegro*, which probably dates from the beginning of this period, calls them. (The enjoyment of and admiration for Shakespeare was not new: in 1630 or thereabouts he wrote the lovely lines 'On Shakespeare' which appeared in the Second Folio [1632] of Shakespeare's Works, and were reprinted in *Poems* [1645].)

This was apparently a very happy period. He seems to have had a number of cultured friends, many of them of power and influence. We easily forget that simply because there were a lot fewer people in England then, it would be perfectly possible for all the men and women of taste and influence (even in London, which then passed as a large town) to know each other. Anne, Countess of Derby, who had been Spenser's patroness, stood in a somewhat similar relationship to Milton for a time: through her, Milton was linked to the great intellectual families of the turn of the century and just after – including the Herberts, the Haringtons and the Sidneys – within whose orbit came John Donne, George Herbert, Edmund Spenser and Shakespeare himself. The Egerton family – John, Earl of Bridgewater, was Anne's grandson – both were politically powerful and had long had a tradition of patronage of the arts: the first version of *Comus* was written for them as part of the Michaelmas night celebrations at Ludlow Castle in 1634, and Anne was the focus of the little masque *Arcades* (1632) (see p. 176). Milton was friendly, too, with people like the Lawes brothers, two of the most distinguished musicians of the day; with John Selden, the antiquarian and jurist; and with the distinguished connoisseur Sir Henry Wotton, Provost of Eton, one-time ambassador to Venice, and secretary to the Earl of Essex. Wotton himself wrote some exquisite verse. Milton's high connections and growing reputation made it very easy for him to move in similar circles when he decided, as increasing numbers of young men – like his near contemporary John Evelyn – were beginning to do, to set out on what came to be called the Grand Tour. The object of this was not mere enjoyment: it was the coping stone of a man's education, when he went to the birthplace of European culture, saw the remains of antiquity for himself (there were no museums in England then), and became proficient in the modern languages through frequenting the society of learned and cultured men.

Wotton encouraged Milton in his decision, giving him advice on his route and on how to avoid danger: 'I pensieri stretti, ed il viso sciolto'

– which translates roughly as 'Be friendly to everyone but keep your thoughts to yourself'. (The letter was printed in *Poems* [1645].) He travelled with only one servant – most gentlemen would have taken more. At Paris Milton was introduced by the English ambassador to the Dutch polymath Hugo Grotius: this man virtually invented modern international law, but was a theologian, poet and dramatist of note as well. Indeed, his play *Adamus Exsul* was widely regarded as a work of genius, and it is just possible that it gave Milton the first idea for *Adam Unparadis'd*.[25]

Then he passed rapidly to Florence, staying there two months and becoming familiar with all the leading poets and scholars of the city. His unusually wide learning made him very welcome among men who valued learning in the humanist way, and he was in any case a pleasant and witty companion. To a man of Milton's cast of mind and culture Florence was above all the city where so many of the men he admired had worked – the great humanist scholars like Lorenzo Valla and Guido delle Collonne, Politian, the philosophers Marsilio Ficino and Pico della Mirandola; it was the city of Dante, whose *Divine Comedy* is arguably the greatest European poem since the *Aeneid* (if it does not surpass it), and of Petrarch, who not only gave the European lyric poem a new voice and a whole new set of ideas, but also recovered and restored much ancient literature and offered a serious theory of poetry that Milton was able to build on (see Chapter 3). In the academies of Florence, where learned men gathered to discuss philosophy and the arts, and to read their own compositions, Milton made many friends; and it is ironic that he found in Catholic Italy the intellectual stimulus and really deep learning that Protestant Cambridge had never been able to provide. He made no secret of his Protestant views either there or later in Rome, but received only courtesy. Several members of the academies with whom he became very friendly became Catholic priests, and it is useful to remember that Milton, who was doggedly opposed to the Church of Rome, could relate to its members, here and later in Rome and Naples, with respect and affection. So much did he enjoy Florence that on his return journey he again visited the city, being welcomed back as an old friend. It was on this second visit that he met Galileo, he who had scanned the secrets of the heavens, now blind and forced to recant his views by the Church: an object lesson of what a triumphalist church could do to scholarly pursuers of truth.[26]

Florence was also, thanks especially to the patronage of the Medici family, stuffed with a wealth of visual delight: the work of Michelangelo and Botticelli particularly.[27] Botticelli was not just a painter: he had made himself a learned man, several of whose paintings – like the familiar *Primavera* and *The Birth of Venus* or the *Mystic Nativity* –

were designed to express by a complex language of symbolic figures aspects of that Neoplatonic philosophy developed by Marsilio Ficino. Milton's interest in Platonism, already considerable, would have allowed him to move freely into the pictorial discourse of Botticelli's allegorical painting; and in return, that painting would reinforce, emotionally and visually, philosophical principles that were already in his mind.

Rome, where again two months were spent in learned society, offered even greater richness of culture, and in addition the ruins of the city of the Caesars, then, as John Evelyn tells us, just beginning to be the tourist trap they have been ever since. Milton clearly enjoyed the culture, including music, that city had to offer, and was welcomed even at the English College, the seminary for exiled English papist priests, where he dined. Here again he made no secret of his hostility to papal claims, but this did not stop him from becoming friendly with the Pope's nephew, Cardinal Francesco Barberini. Then he moved on to Naples, where he was welcomed by Giovanni Baptista Manso (Mansus), Marquis of Villa, the patron of Tasso the poet and himself a considerable scholar and writer. With most of the men he met, Milton seems to have struck up a friendship going beyond the mere conventions of congratulatory letters and poems. Later, indeed, he wrote what must be one of the most distinguished 'Thank you' letters ever – 100 lines of excellent Latin verse, celebrating not only Mansus's generosity and his patronage of Tasso, but also outlining Milton's own poetic ambitions. To another Italian friend, Salzilli, when he heard he was ill, Milton wrote 41 lines of 'Get well' verse whose Latin limps along, wittily echoing the gait of a sick man.

Milton had ambitions to extend this tour by crossing over to Greece, then in Turkish hands. Not very many Englishmen had done this, and there is some intrepidity in the plan. (He was, in fact, greatly interested in travel as a liberal education, and read travel books voraciously.) But 'melancholy tidings from England' – the outbreak of the Bishops' War in Scotland, caused by Laud's trying to impose the new liturgy on the Scottish Church – stopped this: 'I thought it base that I should be travelling at my ease, even for the improvement of my mind abroad, while my fellow citizens were fighting for their liberty at home.' So he returned to Rome, despite the hints he was given that the English Jesuits in that city were plotting to trap him because of the freedom with which he upheld a Protestant religious position. He ignored this warning, and spent a couple of months there speaking quite openly: this must have taken some courage, for the prisons of the Inquisition were not pleasant places and Milton was not immune from them. Afterwards he returned to Florence for another two months; then he proceeded to Venice, where he thoroughly explored the city – then still a sovereign republic remarkable for its art, its architecture, its libraries and its printers. Here he almost certainly met Claudio Monteverdi, the composer. He had bought many books in Italy and arranged for them to be shipped home from Venice. The return journey took in Geneva, the republic organized by John Calvin in the previous century on uncompromisingly Protestant lines, where he spent time with Charles Diodati's uncle, the professor of divinity. Then he returned home through France. The English Civil War finally broke out in 1642.

In several texts – *Mansus* is one – Milton recalls the visit of Chaucer to Italy, drawing an implicit parallel with himself. We can never know whether he recognized, as we do, the convulsive change Chaucer's Italian journeys stimulated in his mind and art; but something similar seems to have happened to Milton. The scale of his mind and interests was already European, in the sense that any man of culture from any part of Europe had grown up using the Latin that was the international medium, had read the books that all other Europeans of similar education had read, and looked back to ancient Rome as both the mother of Europe and a mark for moderns to aim at in their own endeavours. But to be freely welcomed and to win distinction in the way Milton did wherever he went cannot but have made him realize that the stage on which he was to play was a European one. One reason for his unease at the choice of English for *Paradise Lost* was that the poem would thereby be closed off from Europe (the irony is that within ten years of its appearance it was translated into French and internationalized in Latin). Milton's Latin poetry itself has a considerable place in the tradition of European Renaissance Latin poetry, which includes Dante, Petrarch, Mantuan, Pontano, Sannazaro and Buchanan – all authors he read and admired and from whom he occasionally borrowed. In his diplomatic and polemical work, his audience was Europe: the influential people whom he might have met and whose work he knew.

All this is obvious enough. But Italy is rather a special place and does odd things to people. It is not only beautiful: it is the wealth of painting and ancient and modern architecture – the sheer depth of the layers of human culture – that is so extraordinary. The importance to Milton of the visual experiences must be hard to overestimate while it is impossible to quantify: for no Englishman who had not travelled abroad could have had any substantial experience of the exciting and radical developments in composition, subjects and treatment that painters and sculptors in Italy had mastered, for in the England of Milton's youth the visual arts, though not without their own subtlety and sophistication, were singularly out of touch with what was happening on the Continent.[28]

The depiction of the human form (particularly the nude), even in the 1640s when Rubens and Van Dyck were doing magnificent work in England, was, in England, still largely a matter of portraiture. But to see the work of Raphael and Poussin in Rome, Botticelli in Florence, and Mantegna, the Bellinis and Titian in Venice would have opened a window in the mind in a quite remarkable way. While there can be no argument about Milton's strong visual sense – his writing is full of it – how the experience of the visual arts on Italy affected his poetry is more problematic. But in the painting and sculpture of the Italian Renaissance there is exactly that same readiness Milton shows to use Classical subject matter to explore modern philosophic, moral and political concerns; the picture of Eve tending her flowers in Book IX of *Paradise Lost* is composed with the same sort of spatial patterning as Italian painting, and the phrase 'her hand / Soft she withdrew' introduces a careful change of our perspective view from close to long focus. The similes that qualify her are all composed with detailed visual reference to common mythological subjects treated allegorically in painting. The Renaissance and Classical cliché that 'poetry is like a picture' should make us take seriously the readiness with which the compositional techniques of a painting may be transferred to the creation of a scene in a poem. Perhaps we should look at the painterly qualities of the composition and detailing of his poetry as readily as we accept the literary content in Renaissance painting.

The Italian journey seems to have had one other peculiar effect: a sense of the 'specialness' of England. Several times in his prose works Milton talks of God 'revealing himself to his Englishmen, as his manner is', and it seems that Milton genuinely saw in the upheavals of the middle of the century the hand of God at work. Italy, its culture and the intellectual society he found there he obviously loved, but his response to them is deeply qualified by his Protestantism. There, indeed, might have been found the perfect human society, if only the darkness of unreformed religion were to be lightened.[29] The blind Galileo becomes the ultimate symbol: the man who saw into the heavens no longer able to read his own work and imprisoned by the Inquisition. But if, on the other hand, an England where true religion and virtue flourished could take from Italy her intellectual magnificence and riches, then indeed she would be the lodestar of Europe, a 'noble and puissant nation rousing herself like a strong man after sleep, and shaking her invincible locks' (*Areopagitica*). In that rousing, education could play a great part, and any pupils who had followed the regime offered by *Of Education* would have taken their places worthily both in the academies of Florence and in the government of God's Englishmen.

Civil war is the most terrible of conflicts. Milton, patriot as he was, and committed to the idea of men living harmoniously in a just and godly commonwealth, felt deep pain at the war. He several times mentions its disruptive effects on the family and on the life of the mind.[30]

His energies were now bent on his prose works, and, after the establishment of the Commonwealth, consumed by the onerous post of the Latin Secretaryship – a sort of one-man Foreign Office and Ministry of Information. Apart from a few sonnets and minor verses, the man whose whole life had seemed to lead him in the direction of being the 'new poet' seems to have written little for the best part of 15 years.

Milton and European Tradition

Milton was perhaps exceptional in the rigour with which he put himself through a strenuous course of intellectual training and reading, but the assumption behind his so doing was not unusual. Like most of his predecessors and contemporaries, he saw himself as an heir of the entire European poetic and philosophical tradition: serious new work was part of, and an organic growth from, a tree first planted in antiquity. Indeed, the structure of medieval and Renaissance education itself, which we glanced at above, presupposes a view in which the present is continuous with and dependent on the learning and literature of the past.

The growth of the vernacular languages and literatures of Europe did nothing to weaken this stance: Latin remained a living and powerful language of great resource, and (particularly in the Renaissance) there was a deliberate attempt to lift the national vernaculars to the level of dignity and achievement reached in Greek and Latin.[31] Thus any new author would expect his audience to be as familiar with both the antique and modern background as he was himself.

It will therefore be useful to glance at Milton's inheritance from, and response to, three main areas: Latin poetry, Italian, and the native English tradition. But there is no point in Milton's life at which one can finally say, 'This was his response': his reading continued, his mind continued to think and feel, and his ideas – as our own do – were constantly developing. The debt he owes to Ovid at the time of writing the poems that made the 1645 volume differs considerably from the debt to Ovid in *Paradise Lost*; yet the one developed out of the other.

Latin

In *Smectymnuus*, Milton makes this very point: he read the 'grave orators and historians' given him at school with pleasure, but 'as my age then was, so I understood them'. The 'smooth elegiac poets', such as Ovid and Propertius, he imitated, delighting in their 'pleasing sound' as well as in their matter – 'No recreation came to me better welcome.' Yet as he matured, so did his appreciation: 'If I found those authors anywhere speaking unworthy things of themselves, or unchaste of those names which before they had extolled, this effect it wrought with me: from that time forward their art I still applauded, but the men I deplored.' The critical judgement develops from pleasure in the texture of the writing to an understanding and appreciation of the total economy of the work, allowing discrimination between good and bad features: and it is interesting that his criticism is ultimately moral.

Above we looked at what was on the curriculum at St Paul's and at Cambridge. There is, in fact, very little Latin literature that Milton cannot be shown to have read, but he had his preferences. In Vergil, somewhat surprisingly, he seems to have spent less time with the *Aeneid* than with the *Georgics* and *Eclogues*: it is the last-named especially that had a great influence on his earlier Latin and English verse and against which he often bounces his own poems – *Lycidas*, for example. Yet no epic poet is not in some substantial degree in Vergil's debt, as Vergil was in Homer's: the grand sweep, the huge and greatly important subject, the exalted and complex language, and the 'folded in' time scheme that are the main conventions of the epic, and that recur in *Paradise Lost*, were defined by Vergil's poem for all its successors.

Propertius, of the generation of Vergil, offers several parallels to Milton's early work, particularly in Latin. His verse can be laboured and artificial, overladen with mythological ornament, but even so it is passionate and personal. His masterly use of the sonic potential of the elegiac couplet cannot have escaped Milton's good ear, and particularly in Milton's verse letters and elegies the echoes of both the good and the less than good characteristics of Propertius, as of the elegance of Ovid, are many. Milton's *Epitaphium Damonis* recalls in several places Propertius' lament for Cynthia.

It is Ovid to whom Milton seems to owe the most detailed poetic debt, in forms, language, structure and, indeed, concepts. Early imitation gave Milton a naturally easy voice in Latin verse, and his fondness for Ovid (and Própertius) as a model is clear in the verse letters. Ovid's masterly handling of the reciprocating movement of the elegiac couplet, his carefully crafted detail, and the denseness and allusiveness of his poetry, where every line is Technicolor, are everywhere apparent as a stylistic influence. The schoolboy's imitations of Ovid, part of the rhetorical exercises in any school, gave the young poet a rich epistolary and elegiac voice, where remembered phrases and even lines are both allusion and a means of thinking afresh; eventually the epic author transformed the Classical model. For in *Paradise Lost* he revalues and transforms Ovid's *Metamorphoses*. The *Metamorphoses* is a huge poem, sustained with scarcely a dull moment over 15 books, dealing with and seeking to understand change, mutability and decay, both cosmic and detailed, and in the end offering a coherent view of the nature of the universe: Milton's interest in this grave and weighty subject is hinted at in *Lycidas*, and glanced at in Comus's rout of monsters, but receives its fullest treatment in *Paradise Lost*. The relationship between Ovid and Milton is as significant as that between Vergil and Homer.[32]

English

In the English writing of his own day Milton was exceedingly well read. He was certainly influenced by Elizabethan and Jacobean drama, especially in the handling of speech that is at once highly rhetorical and completely vivid and colloquial. Oddly enough, it is often in his prose that one hears these echoes: of Fletcher or Middleton, of Marlowe or Jonson or Shakespeare. Shakespeare – 'my Shakespeare' – he clearly loved, but it seems to have been the Shakespeare of *A Midsummer Night's Dream* or *As You Like It*, rather than of the tragedies, who deeply affected him – despite their common drawing (like the works of Michael Drayton) on the traditional history of England. Yet, when the speaker of *L'Allegro* hears Shakespeare 'warble his native Wood-notes wilde', we must, I think, judge that love not to have been uncritical: the implication is that Milton's attitude was, like Ben Jonson's, of great admiration for the man's natural talent, but not much for his construction, finish or polish.

We easily forget that there was a great deal of very subtle and informed discussion about the nature and practice of poetry in English in the years before Milton. In the controversy between Gabriel Harvey and Thomas Campion over the decorum of the use of rhyme, Milton eventually came down on Harvey's side; the endless discussion over whether English verse could or should be written in quantitative metres, to give it the dignity of a Classical language, were largely over by Milton's day, but the issue was not quite dead; and George Puttenham's *Arte of English Poesie* is a thorough discussion of the techniques and qualities of verse that illuminates the sophisticated ways in which contemporary poets looked at their craft. Furthermore, no serious poet could ignore Sidney; we know that Milton admired him greatly. Sidney's *Defence of Poesie* offers one of the finest and most original syntheses of the philosophy of poetry, drawing (both directly and through the Italian critics) on Aristotle, Horace and Plato. This synthesis clearly coloured Milton's own understanding of poetry as a fictive presentation of an ideal to engage the audience by pleasure and emotion and fire them to virtuous action and living. Sidney's influence elsewhere is slighter: the sonnet sequence *Astrophel and Stella* influenced Milton more by what he does not do than what he does: he breaks the formula of the English sonnet sequence as a narrative either overt or hidden, and establishes the individual sonnet, rather as Tasso had done with the Italian, as a freestanding and uniquely authoritative form. Moreover, the moral concerns of Sidney's prose romance *Arcadia*, like those of *The Faerie Queene*, have a considerable bearing on Milton's conception of the seriousness of pastoral and on the quest motif in *Comus*.

The debt to Spenser, however, is the greatest. Spenser is a poet of the same kind as Milton, a literary craftsman who had a lot of the same interests, ideals and purposes. According to Dryden, Milton said Spenser was his 'original'; by this he probably meant Spencer anticipated him in the ideal of a learned poetry dedicated to high spiritual and national ends, for Spenser set himself to rival and 'overgo' the poetry of the Renaissance abroad, and had adopted some French and Italian methods of emulating Greek and Latin. He might also have been referring to the enormous intricacy of the verse music in *The Faerie Queene*, for Spenser is the only English poet who anticipates Milton in this way. The parallel between the two poets was obvious to Humphrey Moseley.

Milton must have very early come across Spenser not only as a poet but also as a technician and rhetorician, for Alexander Gil made much use of Spenser in his teaching of English grammar and rhetoric. Milton would have been taught to analyse Spenser's poetic diction[33] and memorize the examples: he would have been led thereby to see the care with which Spenser had tried to devise ways of writing in English which would correspond to Vergil's style in Latin. For one of the chief technical problems of vernacular verse in the epic, in the view of some Renaissance critics – for example, Giovanni Della Casa (1503–56) – was to 'express by the quality of the verse the subject with which it was concerned'. Those who have read Vergil will recognize that he was deservedly the acknowledged master of such writing.

Italian

The importance of Italian literature for Milton is abundantly clear. It is a major determinant of his poetic practice: he not only frequently acknowledges this (and it shows in his work), but in *Of Education*, which he wrote just after his return from his travels, he gives Italian a very important place in his scheme for the reformation of manners and the education of useful citizens. It is the only modern language to be set beside ancient Greek, Latin and Hebrew. The pupils in his ideal system are to study Italian – and, for that matter, Classical – poetry in the light of the work of sixteenth-century Italian critics – like Julius Caesar Scaliger, Ludovico Castelvetro, and Torquato Tasso – in response to the study of the Aristotle's *Rhetoric* and *Poetics*, Horace's *Ars poetica* and Cicero's *De inventione*. This programme would give them a true understanding of what great poetry is, and 'what glorious and magnificent use might be made of Poetry both in divine and human things'; it will also teach them to see 'what despicable creatures our common Rimers and Playwrights be'. That contempt of much of contemporary English literature is something we can glimpse in *Lycidas*: it is sobering to realize that the group Milton condemns would probably have included some of the authors in the period we most admire now, like Donne.

Milton attained fluency in Italian while still a very young man. His Italian sonnets date from around 1630, while he was still at Cambridge; and when in *Smectymnuus* he outlines his reading he stresses his delight in and respect – on moral grounds as well as poetic – for Dante and Petrarch. Clearly, he not only read widely in their works, but was also thoroughly familiar with later poets like Sannazaro, Rota, Della Casa, Tasso and Guarini: the last-named of these he met. He knew the works of the historians and the scholars, too. His Italian journey was in a sense a going home: for it was from Italy that the New Learning of which Milton was the conscious heir had spread to alter the mind of Europe for ever.

Despite Italy's troubles in the sixteenth century, it remained the fountainhead of new ideas in art and learning until well into the seventeenth century. The country where the recovery of the literature and philosophy of antiquity had largely been accomplished (we still rely on texts established or rediscovered by fifteenth- and sixteenth-century scholars) was, even in Milton's youth, still an intellectual powerhouse: it was thence that the Classical style of architecture spread across Europe; it was thence that the subtle and philosophical art of garden design revolutionized the appearance of the landscape of northern Europe in the seventeenth century; it was thence that the science of hydraulics and mechanics spread;[34] and it was thence that new styles in art and poetry arrived to alter the way we see and the way we express things even today.

Italy was also, as it had long been, in the forefront of literary criticism and scholarship, and the place where the practice of literature and poetry had in modern times first been put on a serious and systematic philosophical basis. The *Poetics* of Aristotle had been recovered and edited in Italy: Milton knew not only this work but also the important commentaries on and responses to it by critics such as Ludovico

Castelvetro and Julius Caesar Scaliger. Their critical ideas in turn influenced the work of Englishmen like George Puttenham and Sir Philip Sidney, who gave their own twist to the discussion. The influence of Italian critical theory on Milton is thus both direct and indirect, and the same can be said for the influence of poetry: the work of Petrarch particularly had a huge effect on English lyric poetry[35] generally and on Milton's mentor Spenser in particular. This influence through at least two routes of the Italian tradition needs to be kept in mind; it is exactly of a piece with the type of influence Latin and Greek exercised on Milton, as he both responded directly to the originals and to those later works that depended on them.

Through all the vicissitudes of his troubled century, Milton remains a man of the later Renaissance. In this respect, even after the world had changed, he stayed the same, both as a thinker and as a poet. More connects *Paradise Lost*, in conception and execution, with the epic poetry of Dante and Tasso than with the only slightly later work of Dryden or Pope. His ambition to write a work in English that would equal the epic and the tragedy of antiquity in value and importance, as well as in beauty, made natural his turning to those Italian poets who had attempted the same in their vernacular. What he found in the Italian of Petrarch, Dante, and Torquato Tasso (1544–95), as in no other modern language, was not only a grandeur of conception of subject matched by an appropriately resourceful expression. He could also examine a variety of verbal and metrical devices which had been worked out over a long time by the deliberate transference of idiom and pattern from Latin and Greek to Italian – thus vastly extending the range and subtlety of what *could* be said. Their poems were useful to Milton because they were in a modern language, and in a tradition of prosody which had already been explicitly shown to be capable of extending the range, beauty and flexibility of English verse.[36]

Indeed, in *Paradise Lost*, it is clear that though his prime models obviously remained the Greek and Latin epics, and his very peculiar idiom was designed to reproduce the dignity and weight of, and stand direct comparison with, the verse of Vergil and Homer, the Italian influence on his epic verse was very strong. It has been demonstrated that there is a close technical relationship between the verse of Tasso in his two epics, *Gerusalemme Liberata* and *Sette Giornate del Mondo Creato*, and that of *Paradise Lost*.

It was not, of course, merely to pick up metrical hints that Milton read Tasso – or Dante or Petrarch, for that matter. After all, these poets are greatly to be enjoyed, and at the lowest level Tasso's two big poems are sheer good narrative – the recovery of Jerusalem by the First Crusade and the Creation of the World. But the scope of these subjects, like the scope and ambition of *The Faerie Queene*, indicated a confidence in the seriousness of the vernacular as a literary language, and set up a mark to aim at. Reading Tasso, moreover, offered Milton not only demonstration but also theory: in his critical essays, the *Discorsi del Poema Eroica*, Tasso allows the reader to take his style to pieces, to isolate and judge the effect of certain principles as they work in the poems.

This self-consciousness is a reflection of the seriousness with which the Italian Humanists had thought about their literature and their language. The first theoretical discussion had been Dante's *De Volgari Eloquentia*, which I find it inconceivable that Milton did not know. Dante's discussion ranges widely, but key ideas in it are that the vernacular, properly modified and beautified, can be just as high and serious a language as those of antiquity. If the vernacular is consciously developed by extension of vocabulary and the deliberate naturalization of useful idioms and structures from Latin and Greek, it can give identity to the nation, creating the community by allowing the discussion of matters of the highest philosophical, political and theological importance (cf. p. 68) – aims that are by no means far from Milton's mind, especially in *Paradise Lost* and *Paradise Regained*.

Dante's *Divine Comedy* was the poem that exemplified these principles; but in the century and a half after he died there had been no poets like Dante, and the gracefully serious verse which his near contemporary Petrarch had taught his admirers to use had degenerated into a fashionable mannerism of only marginal importance to the intellectual and spiritual life of the community. It was in an attempt to correct this, and again to set up principles for a truly noble national language that at the beginning of the sixteenth century the humanist Cardinal Bembo wrote his *Prose della Volgar Lingua* (1525). Every serious Italian poet afterwards is in Bembo's debt, and Milton, directly or indirectly, is too.

Bembo's dialogues – the form itself imitated Dante's *Convivio*, as well as Classical precedent like the *Noctes atticae* of Aulus Gellius – set up the Tuscan writers of the fourteenth century (Dante, Petrarch and Boccaccio) as the standard of correct literary usage, for modern writers to imitate in Italian.[37] But the dialogues also encouraged the emulation in this literary and no longer spoken language of the glories of Classical Greek and Latin. The result is an unnatural, yet highly polished, mode of utterance, the language being moulded into grammatical patterns quite alien to its natural bent. The verse of *Paradise Lost* and, to some degree, of *Lycidas* is exactly like this.

There is of course plenty of poetry in Italian in the years immediately before Bembo. It is, however, mainly what one might call social poetry, of transitory and topical effect. The craze for writing Latin and Greek with the accomplishment and assurance of the best writers of antiquity led men who could have written high poetry to write in Latin verse of Augustan polish: a 'high style', therefore, just had not developed in Italian, since what needed saying was being written in Latin for those cultured men and women who mattered. Bembo's great achievement, whose effects ultimately spread far outside Italy, was to end this artificial divorce between Classical learning and vernacular writing. Bembo supported and encouraged Ludovico Ariosto, whose great romantic epic *Orlando Furioso* attempted to unify the popular tradition of adventurous and chivalric romance and the New Learning; Bembo himself was an accomplished writer of elegant if rather cold poetry, and practised and gave theoretical justification for the Italian poetry of the New Learning. Further, he rescued the Petrarchan tradition with all its disciplined artifice from the trivial repetition of standard images, conceits and situations into which it had sunk, and gave Italian verse the means of setting out on new and ambitious experiments.

The value of all fine writing, says Bembo, ultimately depends on *gravita* (seriousness) and *piacevolezza* (pleasure); of Dante and Petrarch, it is only the latter who fulfils these perfectly, for while Dante is serious, he is not as pleasurable. Bembo's enormous authority is thus thrown behind the sixteenth-century rediscovery of Petrarch, which deserves a book in itself.[38] Bembo also provides a set of detailed critical principles to help poets and readers discriminate between good and bad writing, and a terminology for the appreciation of verse. Indeed, he initiates that great sixteenth-century quest, from which no country of Western Europe would have wished to be free, for *latinita in volgare* – 'the resources of Latin in the vulgar tongue'.

Without the examples of Bembo's followers, particularly Giovanni Della Casa and Tasso, Milton would never have succeeded as he did in forming his epic diction, in which he uses all the varied texture and registers of English words but works them deliberately into an un-English structure. There is a very precise relationship between Milton's grand style, as it develops from *Lycidas*, through the 'heroic' sonnets to the epic, and the verse of Della Casa and Tasso. Tasso acknowledged his great debt to Della Casa's experiments within the narrow limits of the sonnet; Milton's own sonnets indicate that he took as his prime models those of Della Casa, not Tasso's imitations of them.

The influence of Italian literature on Milton, then, was as profound as that of the Classics. He not only was able to move with freedom in what was arguably the most developed literature and language in Europe, but also learnt from it the tools and the principles to help shape his own.

Notes to Chapter 2

1. Though a man of unusual charm and humour, in controversy he was every bit as lacerating and scurrilous as his opponents, and was not above mere name-calling and abuse – as in his attacks on Bishop Joseph Hall.

2. Whence the title of this chapter is taken: 'Thus from the laureate fraternity of poets, riper years and the ceaseless round of study and reading led me to the shady spaces of philosophy . . .' He was writing to support a tract, 'An Answer to a Book entitled "An Humble Remonstrance"' (1641) by five Presbyterian ministers whose initials were formed into the name 'Smectymnuus'.

3. There had been, and were to be again, those who would have banned the reading by Christians of any pagan writers at all.

4. Milton's own spelling is clearly influenced by the phonetic arguments of Gil, and the variations in spelling he uses between, say, 'me' and 'mee' are not immaterial: they signal the stress and length of vowel Milton wanted both for sense and versification.

5. We had better clear up the business of Calvinism and Arminianism. (The issue is closely related to that of Grace and Works, on which see p. 124.) The essence of Calvin's theological position is that (a) the Bible is the only rule of faith; (b) after the Fall, human free will ceased to exist; (c) Man is justified by faith alone. (These three tenets he has in common with Luther.) Calvin sees that saving faith as the unsolicited gift of God's grace, and added (d) that some men are gratuitously predestined to salvation and some to damnation.

   Jacob Arminius (1569–1609) (a) challenged Calvin's doctrine of predestination; (b) asserted that Man had real free will despite the sovereignty of God; and (c) held that Christ died for all men, not only for the 'elect' (Calvin's 'saved').

   Laud's programme as Bishop of London and Archbishop of Canterbury was in essence very sensible: he was determined to equip the Established Church with a clergy that were properly educated – shepherds who really could guide the sheep through the wilderness and graze them safely on good doctrine – and who had adequate financial support.

6. Few nowadays read these – they are printed at the back of most editions of the 1662 and 1928 versions of the Book of Common Prayer – but it is extremely useful to do so. They represent the doctrinal position of the Church of England agreed upon under Elizabeth I, and state clearly the nature of the state's authority *vis-à-vis* the church. It would come as a surprise to most Anglicans today to realize that the basic theological position is a Calvinist one – that is, that men and women are elected, foreordained, to salvation or damnation by God's grace alone, and that they cannot affect the matter one way or the other. A grasp of these articles is *invaluable* as background for reading the literature and understanding the history of the sixteenth and seventeenth centuries.

7. He writes to Alexander Gil, son of the High Master of St Paul's, that the academic performance of his contemporaries at Cambridge causes fears 'of our clergy's falling gradually into the popish ignorance of former ages' (*Letter 3*, 2 July 1628, pp. 7–8 in P. B. Tillyard, *Milton's Private Correspondence and Academic Exercises*, Cambridge University Press, 1932).

8. There seems also to be a perception that God might be calling him to poetry rather than the ministry – he seems to see the world as his parish. (*Reason of Church Government*; *Letter to a Friend*: see p. 72, note 12)

9. The world-picture all this implies, and depends on, is now virtually forgotten – though all the languages of Europe today are deeply affected in vocabulary and concepts by it. A brief summary of it is in Chapter 2 of my *Shakespeare's History Plays: 'Richard II' to 'Henry V': The Making of a King* (Penguin, 1988).

10. The name 'Scholastic' usually given – disapprovingly – to it derives from the 'Schoolmen', the medieval scholars who grasped the significance of the recovery of Aristotle's logical and philosophical works from the Arabs in the thirteenth and fourteenth centuries and with them revolutionized the mind of Europe. Their vast labour of editing and commenting is one of the foundations of the modern world; but by Milton's time, the work had been digested and its mere repetition was useless and stultifying. Hence Milton's dislike of it and distrust of its place in the educational system.

11. Cf. John Hall, *An Humble Motion to the Parliament of England Concerning the Advancement of Learning and Reformation of the Universities* (1649).

12. Before 1583; printed from the British Library MS Lansdowne 98 by F. J. Furnivall, Early English Text Society, London, 1869.

13. A lot of the ideas and values of the pamphlet make their first public appearance in the *Seventh Prolusion*, delivered in the chapel of Christ's College, probably as part of the requirement for Milton's proceeding to the degree of MA in 1632. The influence of Bacon's *Advancement of Learning* is clear.

   Hartlib made his home in England in 1628. He was recognized as an authority on agriculture, religion and education, and wrote incessantly on these topics. He was in contact with the great Isaac Comenius, and, like those of Comenius, his values in his work were less humanist and more utilitarian than Milton's. Milton's pamphlet was a response to Hartlib's translation of one of Comenius's educational blueprints, *A Reformation of Schooles* (1642).

14. Cf. the scorn he pours on the misuse of logic in the *Seventh Prolusion.* He wrote a textbook of logic for his own pupils, *Artis Logicae Plenior Institutio*, which is a development of the principles of Peter Ramus.

15. Note that Milton is thus characterizing poetry relative to rhetoric. He is *not* saying this is all poetry should be, as he is so often misquoted as doing: he was much more rigorous in his examination of the philosophical basis of poetry: he knew his Horace and Aristotle; see p. 46.

16. It is often forgotten that Milton was a serious historian, geographer and grammarian as well as everything else. In the 1640s he began a *History of Britain*, which eventually appeared in 1670. He also wrote a short *English Grammar*, and a *Brief History of Moscovia*, which he disarmingly claims to have put together to show how historical or geographical books should be written.

17. At Trinity College, every undergraduate had to possess copies of Plato, Demosthenes, Aristotle, Cicero and the Greek Testament or be sent down. I do no know whether Christ's had a similar rule, but it is not impossible.

18. Ralph Cudworth, Milton's younger contemporary and eventual Master of Christ's (1654), also stressed the link between Pythagoreanism, Platonism and Christianity.

19. See R. Strong, *The Cult of Elizabeth: Elizabethan Portraiture and Pageantry* (Thames and Hudson, London, 1977) and F.A. Yates, *Astraea* (London, 1970).

20. The best recent work on these men is C. A. Patrides, *The Cambridge Platonists*.

21. It has been suggested that his feminine appearance, as well as his eventual blindness, was the result of a malfunction of the pituitary gland.

22. Unfortunately, for most of us, the only humour of Milton's that we come across is the grim irony surrounding Satan or the biting scorn and sarcasm of the polemics. Most of the delightful fooling is locked away in the Latin works.

23. The passage in *Defensio Secunda* about Mary's return to her family is certainly bitter, and written long after the event: 'The mother of the family was in the enemy's camp, threatening death and ruin to her husband'; *Paradise Lost*, x. 899–908 is traditionally taken as referring to Milton's marital unhappiness, and most people have argued that his divorce pamphlets are a rationalization of something he wants for himself rather than a disinterested seeking of the common good.

24. The writing of 'obituary' poems, of which he produced a number at Cambridge – e.g. those on Lancelot Andrewes, the Bishop of Ely, the Marchioness of Winchester, and others – was a standard way of getting noticed then, and indeed much later. Wordsworth's uncle was 'mortified' when he learnt that on the coffin of the Master of St John's 'stuck over by copies of verses English or Latin' there was nothing by his nephew: 'it would have been a fair way of distinguishing yourself'.

25. Later, in Florence, he saw Andreini's absurd comedy *Adamo*, in which there are several motifs that seem to reappear in *Paradise Lost*.

26. Milton, of course, does not in *Paradise Lost* (or anywhere else) use the Galilean cosmology: his is basically the old Ptolemaic, geocentric system. But he is writing poetry and myth, not a textbook on astronomy.
    Galileo's trial is still contentious. It has recently been argued that the condemnation of Galileo's cosmology was a way to avoid having to charge him with a much more serious heresy that attacked the doctrine of the Eucharist – for which he could have been cruelly executed – and the Church authorities were therefore acting as gently as they could. See Pietro Redondi, *Galileo: Heretic* (London, 1988).

27. How far he was able to enjoy the detail of their work is open to question for his eyes had never been of the strongest.

28. See L. Gent, *Picture and Poetry: Painting in England 1580–1640* (Leamington Spa, 1981).

29. There is a similar ambivalence towards Italy in the attitudes of other Englishmen before and after Milton. John Evelyn's account in his diary suggests an attitude similar to Milton's and the corrupt Italy of play-settings was also the Venice that might, just possibly, embrace Anglicanism. (See R. Strong, *Henry, Prince of Wales and England's Lost Renaissance*, Thames and Hudson, London, 1986, pp. 75–6.)

30. *Letter 10* [Mary Powell] 1647): see also *Defensio Secunda*: 'She, the mother of the family, was in the camp of the enemy, threatening slaughter and destruction to her husband.' Cf. *Paradise Lost*, x. 899–908. The second strophe of *Ad Ioannem Rousium* complains at the disruption to the life of the mind the war is causing.

31. See p. 48. This could include not only the modelling of modern writing on ancient genres, but also attempts to make the modern languages, where versification is most naturally stress-based, accept quantitative metres based on length of syllables. In the late sixteenth century in England there was a lively controversy over whether a language could be truly dignified if it could not be written in the metres of Classical poetry. Several poets (including Sidney) tried their hand at quantitative verse in English.

32. R. J. DuRocher, *Milton and Ovid* (Cornell University Press, Ithaca, 1985), points out that Milton largely ignores the traditional Platonic and Christian allegorical reading of Ovid's *Metamorphoses*.

33. Spenser's poetic diction is a deliberately constructed language, quarried and adapted mainly from Chaucer, such as no man ever spoke. The reasons for creating it are complex, but may be briefly summarized. First, the creation of a poetic language in the vernacular paralleled the distinct poetic languages in Classical literature, and by its very distinctness was intended to signal the authority of what was being said. Second, a language which demands thought and attention because it is not a spoken one encourages close attention to the poem, and to the ambiguities and subtleties of its language. Third, by creating a language of special meaning that is not and never will be spoken, the poet does something to escape that wearing down of his meaning by the passage of time and slow linguistic change through use. The constructed poetic language of *Paradise Lost* may be approached on these terms as well.

34. Roy Strong, *The Renaissance Garden in England* (London, 1979).

35. Petrarch's influence on Sir Thomas Wyatt and (to a lesser degree) Henry Howard, Earl of Surrey, in the reign of Henry VIII was decisive for them, but they had few immediate heirs. The publication of *Tottel's Miscellany* in 1557 marks the real turning point in English poetry, when the influence of Petrarch began, as it were, to get into the woodwork.

36. The process starts with Chaucer, whose response to Italian poetry was almost as profound as Milton's. He is the first English poet to attempt something like the complex forms of *terza rima* and *ottava rima* developed by Dante and Petrarch from troubadour poetry. Wyatt, Surrey, and especially Spenser and Sidney are further examples: Spenser while still at Merchant Taylors' School was translating Petrarch's canzoni, and his *Amoretti* sonnet sequence is very indebted to Petrarch.

37. Anyone who doubts that imitation can be an extremely powerful way of writing should read Horace's *Epistle to Augustus* (*Epistles*, II. i), then read Pope's *Epistle to Augustus*, and then think about how Pope's poem would have been read by the members of the court of George II. Imitation can be dynamite.

   Originality in our sense would have completely mystified our forefathers. Surely, they would have said, we aren't reduced to making up new stories? There is lots of life in the old ones yet.

38. Cf. L. Forster, *The Icy Fire: Studies in European Petrarchism* (Cambridge, 1969).

3 'Himself a True Poem': The Poetic Vocation, Inspiration and Orpheus

When we look back over the whole of Milton's career as a poet, it falls into a clear shape that has a noticeable similarity to the careers of other great poets whom he admired and took as his models. Vergil's poetic career is the model that many later poets who took their work really seriously seem to have adopted for their own, as a sort of training programme: his earliest work is the pastoral *Eclogues*; his career's climax the epic *Aeneid*, which set out to analyse the identity and values of the Roman people; to hold up ideals to be followed and to criticize tendencies that were all too apparent in the rule of Augustus. This poem was indeed, in Milton's words about his own epic-to-be, 'doctrinal and exemplary to a nation'. No serious poet at any time in the Middle Ages and Renaissance is untouched by Vergil's influence.

During the Renaissance, however, the Vergilian model takes on a new importance. For, as we have seen (p. 48), men began to feel that they were no longer stumbling on crutches in the paths of the giants of antiquity, but had digested what antiquity had to say to them and could go on to heights of achievement that would rival the great work of the past. Rome had its Vergil: why should not the vernacular cultures of Europe have their own great epic poems which would express and examine a sense of nationhood? More than a few poets, many now forgotten, attempted something like this. In nearly all cases, the same progress from pastoral – serious discourse under the swags of hawthorn blossom – to epic is noticeable. For example, the great Torquato Tasso[1] moved from love lyric and sonnet to pastoral drama (*Aminta*, 1562), and finally to the epic *Gerusalemme Liberata* (published in authorized form in 1581). Spenser moved from love lyric and sonnet to the accomplished and serious pastorals of the *Shepheardes Calendar* (1579), and then on to the *The Faerie Queene* (Books I–III, 1590; IV–VI 1596), where as he says in his prefatory letter to Sir Walter

Ralegh, 'the twelve private morall vertues, as Aristotle hath devised . . .
[and] the other part of polliticke vertues' were to be displayed in the
person of Prince Arthur.[2] Samuel Daniel on his visit to Italy met (in
1579) the poet Guarini, the greatly influential author of a pastoral
drama, *Il Pastor Fido*. Daniel himself wrote a fine sonnet sequence
(*Delia*, 1592), and then turned to tragedy and epic: *The Civill Wars*
(I–IV, 1595; I–VIII, 1609). Milton's poetic career begins in just this
way, with the pastoral poems and lyrics in Latin and English, before
the grand undertaking that was to be *Paradise Lost*.[3] After Milton, we
notice a similar pattern in other poets who single-mindedly dedicated
themselves to that extraordinary career. Pope starts with pastoral; then
he translates Homer's epics (which made his fortune); and finally he
produces his own mock epic, *The Dunciad*. Keats, deeply influenced
by Milton and Vergil, died while he was engaged on *Hyperion*. All
these poets had a firm conviction of the national importance of their
calling, and a recognition that the life of a poet was exacting, a
continual reaching forward and going into training for the next great
work.

Milton is explicit about his high purpose and his sense of duty. It
is pretty clear that his father did not always entirely approve of his
full-time devotion to poetry; the probability of some such opposition
indicates just how early that great ambition was formed. The reply, if
such it be, to his father in *Ad Patrem* contains in essence all Milton's
thought on the nature and function of poetry and the seriousness of
the poet's calling. The true poet's song, Milton says, is heavenly in
origin. It not only shows the unrivalled glory of the human mind, which
originates in God himself, but also preserves some spark of the Pro-
methean fire: that is, just as Prometheus stole fire from heaven out of
pity for men and gave them its great benefits, so the poet is a public
benefactor. He urges his father not to ignore the importance and dignity
of sacred poetry:

> Nec tu vatis opus divinum despice carmen,
> Quo nihil aethereos ortus, & semina caeli,
> Nil magis humanam commendat origine mentem,
> Sancta Prometheae retinens vestigia flammae.

(ll. 17 ff.)

('Do not despise poetry, the holy work of the poet: nothing more
powerfully reminds us of our heavenly birth, of the seeds of heaven:
retaining some traces of the Promethean fire, nothing by its origin more
powerfully graces the human mind.') Milton points out that his father
was himself a fine musician, and this art is closely related to poetry.
It was, too, his father who was responsible for the growth of his interest
in poetry: he had had him taught Latin and Greek, and had urged the

acquisition of French, Italian and Hebrew. The divine origin of poetry; the public benefits it could bring; the necessity for learning and study on the part of the poet: all these are ideas that we meet repeatedly in Milton's work.

In 1628, before a large college audience, Milton had to deliver a long speech in the Latin enjoined by university statute. The *Sixth Prolusion*, however, breaks with academic precedent and statute by ending with the English lines usually printed on their own as *At a Vacation Exercise*. The whole performance is not without a certain humour: Milton in the Latin gets his own back on those men who gave him his unfortunate nickname of the 'Lady of Christ's', and plays with Scholastic logic to demonstrate that enjoyment may not be too disruptive to academic studies. The English poem is a long and learned joke; what is important at the moment is that he makes an open statement of his high poetic ambitions. Addressing his 'native Language', he reveals his ambition to use English in 'some graver subject',

> Such as may make thee [Language] search thy coffers round,
> Before thou clothe my fancy in fit sound

– a poem that will deal with the great matters of heaven and earth (ll. 35–52) in a language which there were still those who, for one reason or another, felt was neither up to the job nor appropriate for it. Milton seems already to have had a reputation in the university as an extremely learned and witty man; nevertheless, one wonders what the audience's reaction might have been to such huge ambition.

Language, Truth and the Choice of English

We need in passing to glance at that determination to write in English. It was not one easily taken. When he was travelling abroad, he was shocked to find how great was the reputation of (the now nearly forgotten) George Buchanan compared with that of his admired Spenser: Latin gave the one free access to the world, English restricted the other to Britain. And Milton could write Latin poetry that connoisseurs said was as good or better than Vergil's: Salzilli, for whose illness Milton wrote a witty and flattering get-well poem, said just that in verse that was printed before the Latin section of *Poems* (1645). But if the great poem was to be, as he was coming to think it must be, a national poem, it had to be in English: when he wrote *Elegy VI* to Charles Diodati in the Latin in which they seem to have habitually communicated, he apologizes for keeping him waiting for the promised *English* poems. That choice, though, raised problems of its own about the capacity, range and validity of English.

The relation of language to reality exercised many men's attention, as we have seen. This was no new worry – it had been acutely discussed by Classical as well as medieval philosophers – but it acquired a new urgency as a result of the various movements which, lumped together, we call the Reformation. A central doctrine of the reformers was the prime importance of the Word of God: Luther went so far as to say that 'the most holy Word of God [that is, the Bible and the Christian's inner voice] is the only thing necessary for Christian life, righteousness and freedom'. This was one of the reasons for the Protestant Churches' insistence on the Bible's being available in a tongue 'under-standed of the people' rather than clerical Latin. Yet to insist on this central principle necessarily implied that the Bible, in both its original languages and in those into which it was newly translated, was literally true in an absolute sense such as no scholar would accept any other text to be. It implied that the translator was, in fact, the mouthpiece of the linguistic versatility of the Holy Spirit.[4]

But the Word of God, the Platonic Logos, is also the Son, by whom all things were made. Now prelapsarian Nature, created by the Word, was a visual and material expression of Supernature, and postlapsarian Nature necessarily, to some degree, so remains. So it became possible to argue that fallen humanity comes to redemption through the Word in Jesus only after it has come to know God through the creating Word, the speech of God in Nature and in the Bible,[5] while the inadequacy of human words and perception (especially when their referent is divine) has still to be admitted. Yet those inadequate words are indispensable in pointing people to the knowledge of God, a knowledge which, because it is necessarily gained through language perpetually imperfect, offers the opportunity for the joy of unending discovery.[6]

Yet the problem about the existing languages of men would not go away. Some extreme Protestants, aware of the problems of verbal language, distrusted words and reason so much that they heeded only the inner Word, the inner promptings of conscience. The seventeenth-century rationalists, on the other hand, tried to re-establish the integrity of prelapsarian language, deliberately setting out to create a universal language which would perfectly express reality.[7]

But Milton and others were aware that just as speech necessarily fell with the Fall, so it must have been redeemed with the Redemption. Modern human speech is no longer the speech of Adam in Eden, isomorphous to reality, but neither is it damned; indeed, if as part of man it shares in the Redemption it has the potential – *O felix culpa!*

– for yet greater glory. The poet has a job to do in redeeming language, knowing that what he makes will not be an unfallen one. (This issue is quite important in *Paradise Lost*.)

If Milton really believes himself to be inspired, as we shall see he did, he consequently has to believe that his poetic utterance can relate organically to reality. *At a Vacation Exercise* may be a joke following the attack in the *Sixth Prolusion* on Scholastic logic, but it is one with serious implications. In it Milton, appearing as himself, as a poet, presents the Aristotelian Ens, or Absolute Being, and his ten 'sons' (played by other young men), the Ten Categories – that is the first Category, substance, and the nine by which it is made manifest: quantity, quality, relation, time, place, possession, posture, action and passion. (For example: one cat, which is tabby and which is mine, this afternoon, in the study sat and purred as it was stroked.) Now the point is implicit that categories can not have being themselves, but, equally, the being, or substance, cannot be perceived except through a combination of categories. Yet the primacy of Substance is clear, and Milton is making the Aristotelian strategy carry a Platonic point (Cf. p. 28 above). When Language is addressed in the first part of the playlet, there is the clear implication that thought is prior to articulation in words, that meaning is merely *clothed* in words – 'clothe my fancy in fit sound'. There is the implication, too, that through and beyond words the mind may search the secrets of Heaven and Earth (ll. 32 ff). The problem, with English – or, as we saw, with Italian – is finding a language resourceful enough to do the job of communication. The poem thus asserts Milton's poetic ambition, affirms the potential of English for the 'graver subject', and declares firmly where he stands on the vexed matter of language, its relation to truth, and the capacity of poetry to reach beyond the stars.

Many young men have extraordinary ambition, but few have accepted its implications as seriously as did Milton. He recognized that to be a great poet required not only unceasing study – study which, as he said, ruined his eyes; he also felt that it demanded moral commitment and self-discipline. The *Apology for Smectymnuus* (1642) and *The Reason of Church Government* (1642) contain illuminating accounts of his conception of himself as a poet. Both were written, of course, in the heat of controversy, and in reply to those of his opponents who, using the smear tactics beloved of seventeenth-century polemic, had accused him of all sorts of depravity; both were written when Milton was already in his mid-30s and are thus inevitably a reconstruction in his memory of his earlier feelings and ideals. Nevertheless, the earlier letters give support to the ideas that are spelled out in detail in these later works, and so do poems like *Lycidas* and *At a Solemn Music*. Milton argues in *Smectymnuus* that the job and power of the poet relate closely to the virtuous life, and that 'he who would . . . write well hereafter . . . ought himself to be a true poem . . . so how he that should be truly eloquent who is not withal a good man, I see not.'[8]

Smectymnuus also contains, as a refutation of the charges of immorality brought against him, a theologically based defence of the virtue of chastity as an imperative for both men and women – even more for men – that throws interesting light on the values he embodied in the Lady in *Comus*. And although Milton knew more than most men about the art of rhetoric, of making words work hard and effectively, *Smectymnuus* states unambiguously that 'true eloquence I find to be none but the serious and hearty love of truth'.

The public duty of the poet is expressed equally strongly. In *The Reason of Church Government* Milton stresses the duty of all learned men to speak out and defend right religion and virtue. The poet is in a situation analogous to those prophets of ancient Israel who were mouthpieces for God Himself, recalling a backsliding nation to its true duty and its true self, holding up before it the values it had denied. It is not – and never was – a pleasant job: Milton implicitly compares himself to the prophet Jeremiah, who, however reluctantly and, with however much unpopularity, had to speak out, becoming 'a man of strife and contention'. He compares himself, too, to Sophocles' Tiresias (in *Oedipus Tyrannos*), who knew more than other men and felt the terrible burden of that knowledge.[9]

Nevertheless, 'when God commands to take the trumpet and blow a dolorous or jarring blast, it lies not in a man's will what he shall say or what he shall conceal'. Milton clearly felt the writing of prose polemic – the 'cool element of Prose' – to be a tiresome burden, and a diminution of the powers he felt himself to possess in the 'empyreal [i.e. fiery] conceit' of verse; nevertheless, it was part of God's job for him, his duty to speak out on behalf of true religion:

I should not choose this manner of writing, wherein knowing myself inferior to myself, led by the genial power of nature to another task, I have the use, as I may account it, but of my left hand.[10]

This defence turns into a vindication of his poetic powers and a manifesto for his future career. He reminds his readers of the welcome he was given by Italian poets and scholars, and the unusual distinction he won for his learning and his youthful Latin poetry ('composed at under twenty or thereabout', i.e. most of the material in *Poems* [1645] in a country whose literati only reluctantly honoured foreigners. This praise, and 'an inward prompting which now grew daily upon me', led him to think 'that by labour and intent study . . . joined to the strong propensity of nature, I might perhaps leave something so written to aftertimes, as they should not willingly let it die.' He had perceived that he could write to the glory of God by creating something for 'the honour and instruction of my country'. But, as we saw with the *Sixth Prolusion*, that meant writing in his native tongue, lifting it to equal dignity with the great Classical languages: 'What the greatest and choicest wits of Athens, Rome, or modern Italy, and those Hebrews of old, did for their country, I in my proportion *with this over and above of being a Christian* [my italics], might do for mine.' The implication is that if the people that walked in darkness created such great moral poems, the man who walks in the light of Christian revelation ought to be able to do even better. As yet, the form of the great national work, though not one of its possible subjects (see p. 00), was still unclear to him: he admits his difficulty in choosing between epic poem or tragedy and imitating in English the grand odes of Pindar or Callimachus. Few men engaged in controversy can ever have so frankly revealed their deepest ambitions and given their enemies so many opportunities for sneering.[11]

The Reason of Church Government also indicates plainly that Milton thinks the prophetic power of the poet to be divine in origin, and the function of the poet to be related to that of the priest and preacher. The gifts of true poetry are 'rarely bestowed', but they come from God. They 'are of power beside the office of a pulpit to inbreed and cherish in a great people the seeds of virtue and public civility, to allay the perturbations of the mind and set the affections in right tune, to celebrate in glorious and lofty hymns the throne and equipage of God's almightiness and what He works and what He suffers to be wrought with high providence in his church. . . .'[12]

The poet has a peculiar power since his moral teaching gets under his audience's skin by working – as Spenser had implied in the Letter to Ralegh – through the pleasure of poetry. Conversely, bad poets and artists can be thoroughly dangerous for the same reason. He points to the immorality of much contemporary writing, art and behaviour, and of course returns to this theme in *Lycidas* (see p. 156, and cf. the parallel argument in *Of Education*, p. 30). With magnificent scorn, he stresses that his future great work is

> not to be raised from the heat of youth or the vapours of wine, like that which flows at waste from the pen of some vulgar amorist or the trencher fury of a rhyming parasite, nor to be obtained by the invocation of Dame Memory and her siren daughters [the Nine Muses], but by devout prayer to that eternal Spirit who can enrich with all utterance and knowledge, and

sends out His seraphim with the hallowed fire of His altar to touch and
purify the lips of whom he pleases: to this must be added industrious and
select reading, steady observation, insight into all seemly arts and affairs . . .[13]

The confidence this argument shows is partly a consequence of the
occasion of its expression: he was fighting. Milton was not proof against
self-doubt, even while the faith in God's ultimate purpose for him never
wavered. It is in private letters to friends like Diodati that one glimpses
this. In *Letter* 7 (1637), to Diodati, he half-jokingly tells him he is
thinking of 'immortality . . . And what am I doing? I am growing wings
and thinking about flying, but, to date, my Pegasus lifts himself on
feeble wings' (my translation). Pegasus, whose hoof struck the ground
and released the well of poetry, is still not strong enough for the 'no
middle flight' that *Paradise Lost* demanded. Yet while the *power* may
be doubted from time to time, the *ambition* to achieve the great work
never seems to have wavered. In the splendid *Epitaphium Damonis*
(1640), he reveals in a poem to Diodati's memory what he had no
chance to tell him in life: the pipe of pastoral poetry in which he had
so distinguished himself had burst asunder under the weighty strains
of more serious verse: he is contemplating a grand work on the mythical
history of Britain, its settlement by the Trojan Brutus, and its glorious
history down to King Arthur (ll. 161 ff). His interest in this mythical
history as a basis for a moral poem is of course identical to that of
Spenser, and for a long time – certainly until the writing of *Mansus* –
it was his preferred subject (ll. 81 ff.). References to it abound in the
poems of his early maturity – *Lycidas* and *Comus*, for example – and
he refers again to its eventual dismissal as his preferred topic in *Paradise
Lost* (IX. 25 ff). This was indeed an appropriate national topic for the
national poet – as the Trojan War had been for Homer, or the wanderings
of Aeneas and the founding of Rome had been for Vergil. For Milton,
as a man and as a poet, is nothing if not a patriot, believing that in
what many saw, through the Civil War, as the second and final stage
in the Reformation of the Christian religion that would recover the
purity of the first centuries of Christianity, England had, like ancient
Israel, a divinely appointed part to play:[14] 'Methinks I see in my mind
a noble and puissant nation rousing herself like a strong man after
sleep, and shaking her invincible locks. Methinks I see her as an eagle
mewing her mighty youth, and kindling her undazzled eyes at the full
midday beam' (*Areopagitica*); 'Let England not forget her precedence
of teaching nations how to live' (*Doctrine and Discipline of Divorce*).
In that rousing and teaching he saw a part for himself, and hurried
home from his Italian journey to take part in the great events: 'I thought
it base that I should be travelling for pleasure abroad, while my fellow
citizens were fighting for their liberty at home' (*Defensio Secunda*). That

determination to involve himself in the struggle led to his being at the centre of political events, to the extent that some of the more excitable of his opponents accused him, in the pamphlet *The Cry of the Royal Blood*, of being second in evil only to Cromwell.[15]

He certainly kept a high profile, and his polemical writing must have been a thorn in the sides of his adversaries both domestic and foreign. But his involvement completely suspended his poetic ambitions in favour of polemical and diplomatic work, cost him his eyes and eventually nearly cost him his life.

The appearance of *Poems* (1645) in the middle of the most acrimonious years of the Civil War is a matter we shall have to return to (Chapter 4). It was preceded by Milton's radical tractates on divorce; by his anti-episcopal writings; by *Of Education*; and by *Areopagitica*, a major discussion of the place of letters in a godly and supposedly free society. It was followed by *The Tenure of Kings and Magistrates* (1649), which argued that the authority of rulers was dependent on contract with the ruled, and by *Eikonoklastes* (1649), which attacked *Eikon Basilike* (published as having been written by the recently executed Charles I). *Eikon Basilike* made the king out to be a saint and martyr, and his opponents blasphemous murderers.[16] In 1651 and 1654, respectively, appeared the two Latin *Defences of the English People* in which Milton attempted to justify the republican cause before the bar of foreign opinion. Those books (particularly the earlier ones, as we have seen) elucidate in passing Milton's certainty of his calling as a great national poet: and given this context, and the fact that he had had to put his ambitions for the great poem into cold storage for the time being, it is hard not to see *Poems* (1645) as his personal manifesto. Here the poet announces himself with a demonstration of what he can do and has done, laying claim to high purpose and even higher quality. It is certainly revealing that Milton prefaces the Latin poems with commendatory verses from his Italian friends, and by a complimentary letter from Sir Henry Wotton. Salzilli (cf. p. 56) ranks Milton as a poet above Homer, Vergil and Tasso.

Behind all this lies a view of poetry as an activity that is clearly miles away from our own: it demands examination. In the first place, behind Milton's conception of the poet's responsibility to his society lie ideas of how poetry and music affect reality which, if not commonplace, at least were fairly common in Renaissance Neoplatonic thought. It might seem very odd to us to argue that poetry and music could so alter men's minds and dispositions that a civil war might be averted.[17]

It is, however, a fact that in the sixteenth century serious attempts were made to do just that. The most notable example is the Academy of Poetry and Music set up by the poet Jean-Antoine de Baïf in France, with the patronage of Charles IX, in the months before the Wars of Religion broke out. By the joint practice of the arts, it was hoped that the Catholic and Huguenot nobles who participated would find a unity beyond their differences; and experimental work was done to examine how music and rhythm affected men's moods, attitudes, and even heartbeat. If the soul of the universe, the way it was made and the way it worked, was musical and mathematical, by music and mathematics men might be brought into tune and harmony with it.[18]

Such a view of the poet and musician, still current in Neoplatonic philosophy in the next century and in Hermetic philosophers like Thomas Vaughan, goes part of the way to explain how readily Milton could accept in himself a sense of public mission. Ideas like this are the fabric of *At a Solemn Music* (see p. 120); and in the *Third Prolusion* Milton says 'truly divine poetry is able to lift the soul with its rind of earthly dirt and place it in heaven . . . to fill it with heavenly bliss, whispering to it of undying joy'.

Secondly, perhaps we are wrong to use the word 'ambition'; for to us the word implies personal glory, whereas, for Milton, any 'Fame' he might win is specifically – for example in *Lycidas* – linked to doing what is pleasing to God – the only fame that matters. The last thing he is talking about is mere popular esteem. Finally, Milton believes it quite possible that the poet who trains himself in the rigorous and ascetic way we have noticed is literally inspired by God with what to say and how to say it. He is not unique in this: Spenser, in the October Eclogue in *The Shepheardes Calendar*, says pretty much the same, and had good precedent for it in Boccaccio, Dante and Petrarch.[19] Marsilio Ficino, in his influential commentary on Plato's *Symposium* (180; cf. Plato's *Phaedrus*, 244), had developed the idea of the four 'madnesses' – poetic, Bacchic, prophetic and erotic – as means whereby the soul rises to the contemplation of God, and Richard le Blanc, in the preface to his translation of Plato's *Ion* in 1546, had equated the gift of the poetic madness, the *furor poeticus*, with divine grace. Such an understanding of how poetry works demands that we now examine Milton's view of the inspiration that fired his poetry.

Inspiration

The fullest statements of Milton's belief that God in the Person of the Holy Spirit directly inspired his work are to be found in *Paradise Lost*. This is not surprising: that poem deals with matters, as Milton knew, as far beyond human language and human utterance as it is possible to go, and the poem could only be validated for both himself and his readers by claiming that it is inspired. But those statements are in fact expansions in detail of ideas that remain consistent throughout his career, for the first dim intuitions glimpsed in letters and early poetry imply exactly this view of sacred poetry. And though Milton is unusual in the openness with which he refers to the literary abilities of the Holy Spirit, we should recall that his contemporaries would have seen nothing inherently improbable in the idea of human utterance being guided in the very act of speech or writing by God Himself. Every preacher in every church would hope to claim as much.

It was one of the conventions of ancient and modern epic that at the beginning, and at points when the narrative took on new seriousness (as, for example, at *Aeneid*, VI. 263, when Vergil is about to begin the description of Hades), the poet should appeal for the inspiration of one of the Muses. Milton does just this at the beginning of *Paradise Lost*; but his appeal is to the

> Heavenly Muse, that on the secret top
> Of Oreb, or of Sinai, didst inspire
> That Shepherd [Moses], who first taught the chosen Seed.
>
> (I. 6–8)

– the Creating Word of God Himself (I. 19–26). It was an article of faith to Milton and his readers that God had spoken through the prophets to fallen men; and Milton's linking of the Creating Word that inspired Moses with that power which inspires him claims not only a high authority, moral, spiritual and political, for his poem, but also that the construction of the poem in all its extraordinary detail is an analogue, as well as necessarily a part, of that world – called by Boccaccio 'God's Poem' – in which St Paul stresses we may read the mind of God Himself (Romans 1.19 ff).[20]

When Milton, in the opening lines of Book VII, where he prepares to soar 'Above the flight of Pegasean wing' (i.e. far beyond, in importance of subject, all previous poetry; cf. I. 14–16), invokes the Muse Urania, he makes quite clear that behind the Classical name of this most serious of the Muses he is invoking the 'sister' of 'Eternal Wisdom' (VII. 9) which, according to the Apocryphal book of the Wisdom of Solomon, 'created all things by number, proportion and weight' (Wisdom of Solomon 11.21).[21]

Urania would not have suggested a pagan Muse (despite her ancestry) to Milton's readers. They could already have met her as the Muse of the Heavens and Heavenly Song whom Du Bartas invoked in the *Devine Weekes and Workes*, and whom Spenser appealed to in *The Teares of the Muses* (11. 499 ff) since she gave knowledge

> of the world's creation,
> How in his cradle first he fostred was;
> And judge of Natures cunning operation,
> How things she formed of a formless mas.

In one of the emblems (symbolic illustration plus pithy motto and verses)[22] which Henry Peacham applies to himself in his *Minerva Britanna* (London, 1612), he pays homage to Urania and the superior claims over all others of divine and devotional poetry (p. 177). Milton's Muse, then, would have been recognized by his contemporaries. And when he claims that she 'deigns'

> Her nightly visitation unimplor'd,
> And dictates to me slumb'ring, or inspires
> Easy my unpremeditated verse,
>
> (IX. 21–4)

he is obviously sincere.

These are high claims, and to us look extraordinary, almost deranged, at first sight.[23] But there is no doubt that in his ideas, and especially in the prayer in *Paradise Lost*, III. 52–4, Milton is expressing perfectly the Renaissance theory that great poetry can be written only by men who *deserve* and *are granted* divine illumination. Many other poets of Milton's period invoke divine guidance: Francis Quarles, for example, in the Invocation to his extremely influential and popular *Emblemes* (1635), prays for divine illumination so that his music may be, to use Milton's words in *Lycidas*, l. 87, a 'strain . . . of a higher mood'. An age much better versed in its Bible than our own would be perfectly happy with the notion of God's inspiration of His chosen witness, and the only thing that might have worried contemporaries would have been finding that they disagreed with what Milton had to say! The claim to authority as high as this is unusual merely in its earnestness and confidence, not in its conviction. And even towards the end of his life, when old, blind, bitter and contemplating an England in which everything he despised and hated seemed to be triumphant, when he was writing *Paradise Regained* (1666–70), his old confidence in the guidance of the Holy Spirit remains: 'Inspire, / As thou art wont, my prompted song, else mute' (I. 11–12).[24]

The work of his early manhood frequently refers to the 'enlightening' (*Church Government*, 1642), 'illuminating Spirit' (*Doctrine and Discipline of Divorce*, 1643); he frequently suggests that he is led by God and is doing God's work in his controversial writing (*Judgement of Martin Bucer, concerning Divorce*, 1644). The *Nativity Ode's* (Christmastide, 1629) third and fourth stanzas ask for the help of the 'Heavenly Muse' and suggest that the present poem's 'Voice' might be joined 'unto the Angel Choir' that sang at the Nativity: and that voice must be touched, like the unclean lips of Isaiah, with 'hallowed fire'.[25]

We can get an interesting crossbearing on Milton's idea of inspiration from one of the early Latin elegies, *Elegy V* (1629). Its theme is the return of Spring, and it is exquisite in its evocation of the new flowering of the earth. Yet it is an evocation not so much of real soil, real rain and real flowers as of those things transmuted into symbolic art: Milton's spring, lush, tactile, vivid as it is, is the spring of a Poussin painting, or of Botticelli's *Primavera*, with its gods and nymphs, and its formal yet abandoned movement of bodies through space. It is a greatly interesting, even brilliant, poem, particularly when set against the handling of landscape in *L'Allegro* and *Il Penseroso*, or the depiction of Eden in *Paradise Lost*. But it is precisely its conventional, baroque artificiality which makes its opening 24 lines, on inspiration, so helpful to our present discussion. For the poem, however good it is, must in some sense be pastiche – pastiche of Vergil, of Theocritus, of Ausonius: the reality it touches is a reality seen through many lenses of art, and the lenses are in some sense the real subject of the poem – *how* our pleasure is being created is as of much interest as what that pleasure is. So the first lines are not, as in the other instances we have looked at above, Milton talking about inspiration as Milton, but Milton adopting the mask of being a Classical poet using Classical conventions to describe a set of supernatural beings in which he had no belief whatever.

The lines turn on the inspiration of the god Apollo and the gradual taking over of the human breast by his power. This clearly is not the prophetic inspiration, but the *conventional* inspiration of this class of poem – the sort of thing any competent Latinist could cut off by the yard. Yet the real point is not that; it is the vocabulary Milton uses in what is after all an elegant neo-Latin poem on an altogether hackneyed theme. The vocabulary and the description it creates of the process of inspiration remind us forcefully of the experience of the Cumaean Sibyl in Book VI of the *Aeneid*, who with pain and struggle submits to the overmastering power of Apollo, and in her 'lofty strains', her 'holy frenzy' (the poetic madness, *furor poeticus*, that Horace, and Plato before him, described), sees visions of the heights of Olympus and the deeps of Tartarus. Now, Milton had a completely free choice whether or not to include this passage; he also had many models to go to. The fact that he went to the inspiration of the Cumaean Sibyl, who guided Aeneas through Hades in the *Aeneid*, suggests that even at the age of 20 in a pastiche, school-theme poem he simply could not get away from the idea of serious visionary poetry, the utterance and quality of which was dependent on supernatural power.

An understanding such as this of the role of the sacred poet and the source of his utterance entails, necessarily, a recognition that it is not merely bad taste but actually sinful to write bad, meretricious verse – the 'barbarous dissonance'

> Of Bacchus and his revellers, the race
> Of that wild rout that tore the Thracian bard [Orpheus]
> In Rhodope, where woods and rocks had ears
> To rapture, till the savage clamour drowned
> Both harp and voice.
>
> (*Paradise Lost*, VII. 33 ff)

Milton is often scathing about bad writing, insisting on the need to educate men to distinguish it from good: the so-called digressions in *Lycidas* deliver a broadside at those, who should know better, who merely 'sport with *Amaryllis* in the shade, / Or with the tangles of *Neaera's* hair', and write 'lean and flashy songs [which] / Grate on their scrannel Pipes of wretched straw' (cf. *Of Education*; p. 31). Bad poets are not merely false to their calling: they dismember the body of Orpheus, the archetype of the poet.

The figure of Orpheus could, with only slight exaggeration, be argued to be the key to the whole of this discussion. In Renaissance understandings and uses of his story the issues of truth, inspiration, knowledge, understanding, and the relation of art to reality are constantly raised. He recurs constantly in Milton's writing[26] – which is what we should expect since he is a central figure and symbol in the literature and philosophy of the previous 200 years. So I make no apology for filling in a little background.

The Greek story of Orpheus reaches back to the very earliest times. Orpheus was the son of the Muse of epic poetry, Calliope, and was so skilled a player on his lyre that all the wild things forgot their nature and were spellbound by his music. He was one of the Argonauts,[27] and the power of his music contributed materially to their success. After the expedition returned, he lived in Thrace, civilizing its wild inhabitants. His wife, Eurydice, was lost when she was bitten by a serpent;[28] he followed her to Hades, putting the raging Cerberus to sleep with his music and song and giving relief to those, like Ixion, Tantalus and Tityos, who were enduring eternal punishment for their crimes. His music so charmed Pluto that he was allowed to have Eurydice back on condition that he did not look back at her when they were ascending to the upper world. But, of course, he did, and she was lost for ever. The bereaved Orpheus separated himself from the society of mankind, and as he wandered alone, mourning, a troop of maenads[29] came upon him and tore him to pieces. His head was thrown into the river Hebrus, and, still singing 'Eurydice', was carried down to the sea. Some legends relate that the Muses collected the fragments of his body and gave them burial, and that Zeus placed his lyre in the heavens as the constellation Lyra.

The story is much used, altered and interpreted by Classical, post-Classical and Renaissance writers. The power of Orpheus' poetry and music, and his activity in civilizing men and taming the wild and inhuman, became the ultimate metaphor for the way the sacred poet works among men, civilizing, winning man by the sweetness of his voice to a common consent and cooperation in goodness that allows society to exist. That poets did this is a commonplace which Milton repeats in the *First Prolusion* : the ancient Greek poets 'won glory and honour because they taught men to settle in fixed dwellings, when they had previously been like wild beasts ranging the forests and mountains; they founded states and by divine inspiration taught all those arts of which we are today the heirs – teaching by presenting them pleasurably in the disguise of poetry' (my version). Similarly, Henry Peacham (*The Compleat Gentleman*, 1634, p. 79): 'What were the songs of Linus, *Orpheus, Amphyon, Olympus*, and that ditty *Iopas* sang to his harp at *Dido's* banquet, but Naturall and Morall Philosophy, sweetned with the pleasance of numbers, that Rudenesse and Barbarisme might the better taste the lessons of civility?' Both merely echo – though, we may be sure, with complete conviction – Cicero's remark in *De inventione* that the poet had the power to create, to give corporate identity to, a community.[30]

Vergil's Aeneid is premised on the same ideas; in the fourteenth century, Petrarch's pupil Salutati pointed out the close connection between rhetoric, poetry and government. The symbolic figure of Orpheus, therefore, elicits important expectations when he appears in Milton's poetry or anyone else's.

But Orpheus was not just a character in a story. He was supposed to have left poems behind him: some dating from the fifth and sixth centuries BC, now almost completely lost, were known to Plato, who treated the story as a myth of the power of the mind and its relation to virtue and matter. The poems are said to have embodied the doctrines of the mystical religion known as Orphism: the Orphics taught that man had a divine origin, that he could expect retribution for his evil in a future life, and that he could be liberated from the evil that was part of his nature by observation of strict purity. A further body of Orphic writings grew up in the early centuries of the Christian era, largely as the product of Christian grammarians and philosophers of the school of Alexandria. Until the early years of the seventeenth century, these were accepted as genuinely Orphic writings. The frequency of printed editions – before Milton's birth, editions in 1517, 1519, 1540,

1543, 1566 and 1606 are known to me – is evidence of the considerable interest in them, and there are several important early Renaissance reworkings of the Orpheus story which discuss very important theological and philosophical matters.[31]

Throughout the Middle Ages there had never been a complete lack of interest in the Orphic material, but it is at the end of the fifteenth century that it suddenly takes on much greater importance. Two figures are especially important – Marsilio Ficino and Pico della Mirandola – and it is certain that Milton was much affected by their ideas.

Orpheus finds a place, of course, in all the multitude of handbooks to mythology and symbolism published in the Renaissance. (He also is a frequent subject of emblem pictures – as in Geffrey Whitney's *A Choice of Emblemes*, 1586, p. 186.) For example, in Natalis Comes's (Natale Conti) *Mythologiae* (VII, xiv), Orpheus is declared to be the first interpreter of the physical and spiritual secrets of hell, a man most learned in divinity: since Milton seems to have known this book, it is not surprising to find a reference to the '*Orphean* lyre' in *Paradise Lost* (III. 17) in terms similar to this. But Ficino and Pico went much further. They remembered the opinion of Proclus, Plato's fifth-century follower who influenced Boethius, that all theology among the Greeks had sprung from the mystical doctrine of Orpheus: the first to develop this doctrine was Pythagoras, and then Plato took it over from Pythagoras and the Orphic writings (Proclus, *In Platonis theologiam*, I. vi; an idea repeated by Marsilio Ficino). They recalled, too, how the great Augustine himself had said that Orpheus was among the earliest theological poets, antedating the Hebrew prophets of the Old Testament (Augustine, *De Civitate Dei*, XVIII. 37; cf. XVIII. 14). Their profound belief in the love of God for the World he had created made it inconceivable that he should have left generations of men in hellish ignorance until the revelations to the Hebrews. Thus, they postulated that the revelations to the pagans in the Orphic hymns and poems constituted a revelation of parallel importance to that in the Bible – a *prisca theologia*, or early theology, which modern men, who as Christians could see the whole picture, could attend to with profit. It was claimed, for example, that the Orphic hymns contained anticipations of the central doctrine of the Trinity.[32]

An element of sound religious doctrine was thus imparted by Pico to classical myth – an extension of how Boccaccio in *De Genealogia Deorum* had seen those myths as fables in which truths about the world were concealed – and, reciprocally, an element of the obscurity of poetic discourse was imparted to the canonical doctrine of the Bible.[33] Nor was this heretical: Pico quotes Augustine's remark that the real thing, now called Christian religion, was with the ancients and the human race from the beginning of time to Christ's appearance in the flesh: the true religion, which already existed, only then began to be called Christian (*Retractationes*, I. xiii; cf. Acts 18.28). So Orpheus becomes a prophetic figure: even, in his attempted redemption of Eurydice and the breaking of his body by the sins of appetite symbolized by the maenads, a *figura*, an anticipation, of Christ himself.

But Orpheus, theologian or symbol, remained a poet – *the* poet – and his power a model of that of the poet in all states and times. What was attributed to him gave clues about the nature of true poetry, and how it was conceived. In *An Oration of the Dignity of Man*,[34] Pico claims that like the ancient theologians, Orpheus interwove the mysteries of his doctrines with the texture of fables and covered them with a poetic veil, in order that anyone unworthy to profit from reading his hymns would think them to contain nothing but the merest tales and trifles. The idea of the poetic veil concealing truth is one that is wholly familiar to Dante, Petrarch and Boccaccio: serious poetry is thus not something that yields its meaning easily, but engages us through its pleasure and beauty so that if we are worthy we work through its fable to its inner significance. Serious poetry is thus deliberately difficult, even obscure: its audience is the elite, those who can understand (cf. Chapter 1). This deliberate difficulty must be remembered as we read Milton, for despite the fact that in the great work, *Paradise Lost*, he set out to write a poem 'doctrinal to the nation', his intended audience, in his pamphlets defending the Commonwealth as in his poetry, was never a general one. He wrote for the learned few – the people Humphrey Moseley appeals to in his preface to *Poems* (1645) – 'men of mature and manly understanding', as he says in *Christian Doctrine*, who would influence and guide opinion. For the unlearned mob he had nothing but contempt: 'fit hearers' for what Urania inspires him to write were 'few' (*Paradise Lost*, VII. 31).

The number of times Milton uses Orpheus throughout his career to put down a marker for his own activity as poet is very striking. Clearly, he is using him as a defining analogy to what he is himself hoping to do. Yet there is in this an irony: it is clear that Milton saw Orpheus as only a reflection of the Truth, not the Truth itself. Urania is a Heavenly Muse, whereas Orpheus' mother Calliope is 'an empty dream' (*Paradise Lost*, VII. 39). Nevertheless, though all Orpheus won was an interim, not a final and harmonious reordering, he sang the world into order and harmony. He was a healer, a raiser of the dead. The figure of the poet Orpheus, who through his music founded and ruled cities and gave laws, yet was eventually torn to pieces by human beings who had abandoned their rational nature under the influence of impulse and sensuality, is sobering: the poet – like Milton – may sing a high and noble song, but may be destroyed by those who cannot or will not hear its call to harmony. When, after the Restoration, Milton wrote the lines with which I began this outline of the importance of Orpheus, everything he had worked for lay in ruins; he was solitary, blind and calumniated, and all that he thought worst had the ascendancy in the England he loved. Bacchus' rout now dominated court and taste, just as his son Comus's rout of monsters had seemed to dominate the common taste in the days of Charles II's father. Behind the conviction of his calling and the awareness of its religious importance, I think there lay, as he grew older, increasing pessimism. Orpheus had been dismembered, like Osiris, and all the poet could do was search the world to try to fit the pieces of the truth together.

Notes to Chapter 3

1. His epic, and his critical works – *Discorsi dell'Arte Poetica* and *Discorsi del Poema Eroica* – influenced many in England, including Samuel Daniel, Giles and Phineas Fletcher, Milton, Cowley, Dryden, and so on.
2. Cf. also 'The generall end therefore of all the booke is to fashion a gentleman or noble person in vertuous and gentle discipline.' *The Faerie Queene*'s success led the publisher, Ponsonby, to issue Spenser's juvenilia and minor verse in 1591. It is interesting to speculate whether Milton and Moseley published the juvenilia in the 1645 volume in imitation of Spenser and Ponsonby, on the principle that the minor work of a great poet – even one as yet only promising the goods – is of inherent interest.
3. Milton's subjects for the anticipated great work were always epic in scale – first, nothing less than the whole of (supposed) English history, culminating in Arthur (the influence of *The Faerie Queene* and Drayton's *Polyolbion* is obvious); later, the awesome subject of the Fall of Man and the Creation of the World. But he was for a long time undecided whether the noblest form for them would be tragedy or an epic poem. One further influence on his choice may have been the epic on the Creation, *La Semaine* (1578), by Guillaume du Bartas, translated into English in 1605 by Sylvester as *The Devine Weekes and Workes*.
4. This idea clearly would have made it much easier for contemporaries to accept claims that poets could also be so inspired; see p. 65.
5. Cf. St Paul's idea of knowing God through his Creation (see p. 13), and the influential Augustinian idea of the Two Books, of Nature and of the Bible, through which men may know God.
6. The paradox is exactly comparable to that of the Fall: the old phrase, *O felix culpa! O felix peccatum Adae!* – 'O happy fault! O happy sin of Adam!' – points out that without the Fall the Incarnation of God as Man and the taking up of Man into glory would never have happened. (The idea is fundamental to the *Nativity Ode*.)
7. Some people (like Isaac Comenius) tried pictures or hieroglyphics; others tried to create a verbal language from scratch. For a summary of the discussion, see Chapter 11 of my *Shakespeare's History Plays: 'Richard II' to 'Henry V': The Making of a King*. See also R. Entzminger, *Divine Words: Milton and the Redemption of Language* (Pittsburgh, 1985).

8. Cf. *Elegy VI*, addressed to Diodati: the poet is sacred to the gods, and needs to purify himself for his task.

9. When he had himself gone blind, he again compares himself to the blind Tiresias and the blind Homer, whose outer blindness concealed an inner vision: *Paradise Lost* III. 35–6.

10. This idea of his duty to abandon poetry at the beginning of the political crisis is stated more fully in *Defensio Secunda* (1654): 'I realized that if I ever wanted to be of use, I ought not to fail my country, my church, and my fellow-Christians in a time of such danger. I decided, though my mind was full of other subjects [just after the Italian journey], to transfer the full strength of my talents [to polemic].'

11. In the dark days 'When the assault was intended to the city' (Sonnet VIII, 1642) Milton reminded the 'Captain or Colonel or Knight in Arms' who might threaten his house that just as Alexander the Great had spared the house of Pindar in Thebes, and the memory of one of Euripides' choral odes had restrained the conquering Spartans from razing Athens, so his house, the 'Muses' Bower', might be spared: the self-identification with these great poets is revealing. Compare *Mansus* (1639): the mention of Chaucer (under the name of Tityrus, which Spenser gave him in *The Shepheardes Calendar*) in l. 34 returning from Italy in the same breath as Milton refers to his own return cannot avoid linking the great poet of the past with the young poet of the present. (Milton also wonders whether someone will write his own biography as a great epic poet as *Mansus* did Tasso's: *Mansus*, ll. 70–100.)

12. This idea is a development from its expression in *The Letter to a Friend* (1632?). He replies to the friend's reproaches that he spends all his time in retired study, not doing very much of significance. Milton equivocates about his future: the letter employs the parables of the talents and of the vineyard, and could be read as implying that he is still thinking, but with increasing misgivings about his fitness for it, of the Church as a career – 'having thus tired you singly, I should deal worse with a whole congregation'. But the letter is usually taken as meaning that he sees the poet as pastor and the readers as his parish. At the end of the letter he includes *Sonnet VII*, 'How soon hath Time, the suttle theef of youth', written some months earlier, in which he expresses a firm faith that God, his 'great task-Master' will lead him to the right job at the right time.

13. Notice the echoes of St Paul and of Isaiah 6.5 ff (repeated in v. 4 of the *Nativity Ode*); cf. note 23. The polymathic knowledge here demanded might be gained by following the prescriptions in *Of Education*.

14. See pp. 79,88. The equation of England – Protestant England – with Israel when throwing off the yoke of Pharaoh in Exodus is commonplace in the period. See my discussion of the Psalms, p. 115.

15. Dr Johnson's *Life of Milton* is less than just to Milton on this matter: 'Let not our veneration for Milton forbid us to look with some degree of merriment on great promises and small performance, on the man who hastens home, because his countrymen are contending for their liberty, and, when he reaches the scene of action, vapours away his patriotism in a private boarding school.' That period was one of intense work and serious thought about how, through a reform of Education, the polity itself might be reformed.

16. Milton's case rested on his assertion that the book was wholly misleading:

he 'prefer[ed] Queen Truth to King Charles' (*Defensio Secunda*).

17. Though if we recall how music and rhythm can affect our individual moods, and how martial music has a profound effect on group morale, it might not seem so strange.

18. See Chapter 1. The issue has been explored by Frances A. Yates in *The French Academies of the Sixteenth Century*, Warburg Institute Studies, (London, 1947). It also throws an interesting light on *The Tempest*. Prospero's manipulation of illusion and music – art like that of the dramatist or poet – eventually resolves the pain and evil of the past into a new reconciliation and harmony.

19. The most emphatic statements of Dante's view are to be found in several places in *Paradiso*; Boccaccio, in the *Vita di Dante* and the *Difesa della Poesia*, says that the poets were the first theologians, and that Dante was a sacred theologian; and Petrarch, in *Invective contra Medicum* (III), equates what the ancients called the inspiration of the Muses with the inspiration of the Holy Spirit.

    Milton's respect for Dante and Petrarch was on moral as well as poetic grounds, as *Smectymnuus* makes quite clear.

20. The structure of *Paradise Lost* is too big a matter for this present book; suffice it to say that the architecture of the poem is of a complexity that is matched, perhaps, only by that of Dante's *Divine Comedy*, and is deliberately, as in good Renaissance critical theory it should be, a metaphor of the creation of the world itself. See the discussion of cosmic metaphor in S. K. Heninger, *Touches of Sweet Harmony: Pythagorean Cosmology and Renaissance Poetics* (Huntington Library, San Marino, Calif., 1974).

21. Rabbinical tradition, in which Milton was well versed, had it that the universe was made by Wisdom and Understanding – the last-named is possibly how Milton understood Urania. The text from the Wisdom of Solomon, much quoted in the Middle Ages and Renaissance, is important to our understanding of contemporary attitudes to art, be it music, poetry, architecture or painting (see Chapter 1).

22. The small form of the emblem was of immense importance in the Renaissance, and deeply affected the painting of pictures, the writing of poems, and the staging of masques, plays and pageants. See my *A Century of Emblems*, pp. 1–32.

23. The claim that the poem was 'dictate[d]' obviously should not be taken too literally: the idea of Milton as some sort of personal secretary is ludicrous. *Paradise Lost* clearly came into its present form only after years of planning and trying things out. Nevertheless, anyone who has wrestled with the creation of a piece of writing from the intractable rubble of words will recognize that the final version often appears to arise, without warning, fully fashioned from below the level of the conscious mind. One's problems may even be helped by prayer. Milton's invocations to Books I, III, and VII are themselves genuine prayers.

24. Dr Johnson in his *Life of Milton* repeats John Aubrey's report of the statement of Milton's nephew Edward Phillips that Milton's 'vein [of composing, when writing *Paradise Lost*] never happily flowed but from the Autumnal Equinox to the Vernal'. This conflicts somewhat with the fear Milton expresses elsewhere that the cold climate of England may not be conducive to poetry (*Mansus; Reason of Church Government*). I think we should see this more as a common seventeenth-century recognition that

the best poetry had come from the South of Europe than as genuine fear that cold would prevent poetic endeavour: Milton, in *Mansus*, reminds himself of the example of the excellent Chaucer. *Elegy V*, firmly within the Theocritean/Vergilian pastoral convention, follows that precedent in making the coming of spring the occasion for the return of inspiration.

25. See Isaiah 6.1–10, especially 6.5 ff:

    'Then said I, Woe is me! for I am undone; because I am a man of unclean lips, and I dwell in the midst of a people of unclean lips: for mine eyes have seen the king, the Lord of hosts.

    'Then flew one of the seraphims unto me, having a live coal in his hand, which he had taken with the tongs from off the altar:

    'And he laid it upon my mouth, and said, Lo, this hand hath touched thy lips; and thine iniquity is purged away, and thy sin purged.'

    Milton stresses the devotional nature of the *Nativity Ode* in *Elegia VI*.

26. For example, *Paradise Lost* in several places, *L'Allegro and Il Penseroso* (see p. 135), and *Lycidas*, ll. 58–63.

27. It is worth recalling that later interpreters, including several Renaissance ones, saw the story of the search for the Golden Fleece as an allegory of the search for wisdom. This interpretation lies behind Shakespeare's use of the Argonauts' voyage as an important point of reference in the imagery of *The Merchant of Venice*.

28. Vergil seems to be the earliest writer to introduce the figure of Aristaeus, who attempted to violate Eurydice; fleeing from him, she trod on the fatal serpent.

29. Priestesses who were the habitual companions, inebriated and ecstatic, of Bacchus (Dionysos). (Rather like the irrational followers of certain pop singers.)

30. This may well be true even today. Television – which absorbs a lot of talented people who in other times might have been poets or preachers – and its ersatz, ephemeral mythology have demonstrably altered moral and social standards and given a common point of allusive reference to the vast majority of people.

31. One of the finest as well as one of the most profound is the poem by Robert Henryson, *Orpheus and Eurydice*, written about the beginning of the sixteenth century. It has been excellently edited by Denton Fox in his edition of Henryson (Oxford, 1980), and would well repay consultation by those who wish to grasp for themselves how profoundly this story could be used.

32. This is hardly surprising if these hymns did indeed originate among Christian scholars in Alexandria.

    The concept of a *prisca theologia* extended to the understanding of Egyptian mythology as well (see my *A Century of Emblems*, p. 6). It is interesting, given the dismemberment of Orpheus, how Milton in *Areopagitica* uses the myth of Osiris. ('The good Osiris' was cut up by Typhon, and his wife Isis scoured the world collecting the bits.) This becomes a myth of the reformation of religion: 'Truth indeed came once into the world with her divine Master, and was a perfect shape most glorious to look on . . . [but then] a wicked race of deceivers, who as that story goes of the Egyptian Typhon . . . how they dealt with the good Osiris, took the virgin Truth, hewed her lovely form into a thousand pieces, and scattered them to the four winds . . . To be still searching what we know not, by what we know, still closing up truth to truth as we find it (for all her body is homogeneal and proportional), this is the golden rule in theology as well as in arithmetic.'

33. One interesting idea developed by Ficino is that the Tables of the Law and the instructions on religious observance given to Moses on Mount Sinai were merely the outer shell, the written summary, of the wisdom God imparted to him during his stay of 40 days on that Mountain. What was not written down was passed down in Hebrew tradition by word of mouth, constituting the cabbala, in which Renaissance philosophers were much interested. Milton knew a good deal of this rabbinical material.

34. Essential reading for anyone who wants to grasp Renaissance ideas about man. It has been made available in translation in *The Renaissance Philosophy of Man*, ed. E. Cassirer, P. O. Kristeller, and J. H. Randall, Jr (Chicago, 1948).

Part Two
THE POEMS PUBLISHED IN
1645

4 'Twin Book':
The Presentation of the
1645 Volume

In January 1645/6, in the middle of a major political crisis, Humphrey Moseley[1] published from 'his true Copies' the 'Poems of Mr John Milton, both English and Latin, Compos'd at several times'. The English Civil War was already over three years old. In the crucial battle of Naseby, fought in June 1645, Fairfax and Cromwell routed the King's forces and captured all his state papers: the King's headquarters at Oxford surrendered in June 1646. Some – like Milton – saw in the King's defeat the hand of God Himself, fighting as he had done for ancient Israel against the Amalekites and other unsavoury Old Testament characters; others saw in it the culminating blasphemy, revolt against the Lord's Anointed Vicar on Earth, the final mark of England's apostasy from the path of true religion and virtue. And between these two extremes were the vast mass of honest, troubled people, who responded to an increasingly perplexing situation with a mixture of pragmatism and perception of their own advantage. But no Englishman could be unaware that the world would never be the same again: this civil war finally gave the *coup de grâce* to the customary and venerable ideas of the relationship between Crown and people which had been increasingly under threat since well before the beginning of the century.[2]

The war split families – Milton's, as we saw, as well – and friendships, disrupted the business of trade, and threw into confusion all Britain's relationships with other states. Living in Britain in the years after Naseby must have been as disturbing and frightening as living in France in the years after 1789, in Russia after 1917, or in Iran after 1978. Some of the pain Milton himself felt, and some of the disruption to the life of the mind, may be guessed at from lines in the Latin poem he enclosed in a replacement copy of *Poems* (1645) he sent in 1647 to the librarian of the University of Oxford:

Modo quis deus, aut editus deo,
Pristinam gentis miseratus indolem –
Si satis noxas luimus priores,
Mollique luxu degener otium –
Tollat nefandos civium tumultus,
Almaque revocet studia sanctus,
Et relegatas sine sede Musas
Iam paene totis finibus Angligenum,
Immundasque volucres
Unguibus imminentes
Figat Apollinea pharetra
Phineamque abigat pestem procul amne Pegaseo?

('What god, or man descended from a god, will pity the ancient nature
of our race – if we have paid sufficiently for earlier offences and our
degenerate idling in soft luxury – and will relieve us from these wicked
civil wars? What holy one will call back sweet scholarship, and the
Muses, who are now left with hardly a single place to dwell in the
whole of England? Who will use the arrows of Apollo to shoot the
filthy birds that threaten us with their claws, and drive the pest of
Phineus [a prophet who abused his calling] from Pegasus' river?')

To pull a system to bits is relatively easy; to know what to do with
the bits when you have done so is not. It is certain that neither side
had deliberately planned either the war or its outcome: they had been
forced into it by the logic of small event following on small event, and
were, like most of us, walking backwards into a future they could not
foresee and could not comprehend.[3]

Ironically, the majority on both sides appealed for support for their
cause to ancient precedent and what they saw as the ancient rights
and duties of Crown and people. The English Civil War, which, with
hindsight, we now see as the great divide between the medieval world
and the modern, grew out of fundamentally conservative attitudes. Yet
both sides were aware that they had entered a new world where the
old landmarks were indistinct or gone; there was an urgent need for
a new understanding of the obligations and relationships that allowed
men to live together in a society. For some, this was exciting: the later
1640s and the 1650s saw an astonishing proliferation of people and
groups offering various nostrums, political, social and religious, for the
problems of the age: on the one hand, there were what we might
(tendentiously) call early forms of communism, like the Levellers and
the Diggers, and, on the other, the apparently inevitable consequence
of all such cataclysmic upheavals in human societies, military dictatorship
and military government.

These were Milton's most active years. Over the centuries, he has
become very much an Establishment poet, and it is easy to forget that

he was what nowadays would be called a revolutionary; indeed, it is only to exaggerate mildly to call him a sort of Trotsky, the intellectual of the English republican movement – he was certainly its major propagandist from the earliest years of the open breach with the Crown. His activity in the 1650s, when in the important government post of Latin Secretary, put him on the Cavalier blacklist: it was only the intervention of powerful friends that saved him from execution by the restored Charles II in 1660. By 1645 he had published some ten substantial prose works on topics political, moral, and religious: the common central concern is liberty, and all are marked by a willingness to think dangerously and to kick sacred cows out of the way. He had a reputation as an experienced controversialist quite prepared to publish, if necessary, in despite of Acts of Parliament.

So the publication of what is tantamount to a *Collected Poetical Works* by such a man is an event that itself demands attention before we can go any further. An author lacking in either confidence or some measure of fame would neither have been asked by Moseley to collect the poems nor have complied to the extent of including most of his very early poems. And for a man of his reputation to publish such a collection in the year of Naseby is itself a political act: the poems that over the years have been disinfected in anthologies and emasculated in exam papers should be seen not just as Minor Poems – the all but inevitable title speaks worlds of assumption about Milton and his work – but also as adventurous, dangerous and provocative works.

Moseley's preface, 'The Stationer to the Reader', and the way the volume is presented by its title page and frontispiece, make very high claims indeed. the Preface stresses that these poems, both English and Latin, offered to the reader's 'exactest perusal', had already enjoyed the 'highest Commendations and Applause of the learnedst Academicks, both domestick and forrein', among whom was the learned Sir Henry Wotton.[4] Milton's 'peculiar excellency in these studies' was the immediate cause of Moseley's soliciting a manuscript for printing. He emphasizes that these are not easy poems, and his suggestion that perhaps the reader may be pleased better by 'more trivial Airs' indicates that he saw them as dealing with serious and important issues. Nevertheless, he claims to be 'bringing into the Light as true a Birth, as the Muses have brought forth since our famous *Spencer* wrote'. The linking of Milton with Spenser is acute, and draws attention to a number of issues we have already met. What is easily missed is that the comparison with Spenser ('whose poems in these English ones are as rarely [i.e. remarkably well] imitated, as sweetly excell'd') indicates that a reader, *as distinct from*

Milton himself, was ready to make claims for Milton's importance of no small order. For on the appearance of Spenser's *Shepheardes Calendar* in 1579, contemporaries had recognized that English had found a new poetic voice, that the practice and language of poetry would never be quite the same again. *The Shepheardes Calendar* was, moreover, a work which, through pastoral, looked hard at a lot of moral and political issues. Moseley's comparison therefore demands that we test what is in front of us against the acknowledged magnificence of Spenser in terms both of rhetorical and linguistic competence and of high moral – ultimately political and religions – seriousness. Milton's reverence for Spenser needs no further emphasis, and the ghost of *The Shepheardes Calendar* haunts many of Milton's pastoral poems; but there is no question of mere imitation in our modern sense. Rather, Spenser gave Milton a language in which to say what he alone could say. He also gave him a precedent and a mark to aim at. For Spenser was to go on to write (but not complete) what is arguably one of the most brilliant works of the Renaissance, *The Faerie Queene,* and the last remarks of the preface hint (to us) at a future which we know Milton never left off contemplating: the creation of the great poem that eventually appeared as *Paradise Lost.*

Prefatory engravings and title pages in this period are always significant.[5] Almost universally they serve as a sort of summary of the themes of the book, alerting the reader to things to look for. Replacing the motto on the title page, the lines 'Baccare frontem / Cingite, ne vati noceat mala lingua futuro' ('Bind on your brow fragrant plants, so no evil tongue may harm the poet who is to be'), in their context in Vergil's *Eclogue* VII, make a large claim for the poems that follow – and for the poet. The lines come from Thyrsis' speech in his singing contest with Corydon, and the whole speech runs:

> Pastores, hedera crescentem ornate poetam,
> Arcades, inuidia rumpantur ut ilia Codro;
> aut, si ultra placitum laudarit, baccare frontem
> cingite, ne uati noceat mala lingua futuro.

('You shepherds, crown me, your budding singer, with ivy, so that Codrus' bowels may burst with envy. Or, if that should praise me beyond what is acceptable, wreathe my brow with fragrant plants lest an evil tongue harm your bard to be.' (my translation) The 'poet to be' is implicitly laying claim already to a domination of the English poetic scene, and the word 'vates', which I have had to render as 'bard', carries religious and prophetic connotations as well as poetic. The frontispiece, too, is interesting, though its artistic merits are minimal. It is dominated by a dreadful engraving, apparently based on the Onslow portrait of Milton as a young man, and is certainly no compliment to one renowned for his graceful appearance. Milton must have seen and agreed to put up with it, for he wrote some very sarcastic Greek verses which were included on it.[6]

But the portrait is surrounded in the corners by representations of four of the Nine Muses: Melpomene, the muse of tragedy, Clio, the muse of history, Erato, the muse of love poetry; and Urania, the muse of astronomy and sacred poetry, Milton's 'Celestial Patroness' (cf. p. 64f).[7] This hints at the focus of the poems that follow, and so does the scene behind Milton's head: in it one shepherd sits piping under a tree while a shepherd and shepherdess dance. Here we glance into the artificial world of pastoral, a shepherds' calendar of delights, that provides much of the setting for *Lycidas, L'Allegro, Il Penseroso,* the Elegies, and the *Epitaphium Damonis.* But what is really significant is that the engraving purports to represent Milton not at 36 (his age when the volume appeared) but at 20: we are being offered what is tantamount to a poetic autobiography – whatever else it is – for most of the poems date from before 1630. Most of Milton's very early work, his juvenilia, in several languages, is included, even poems confessedly unsuccessful – for example, the poem on the Passion of Christ breaks off with 'This subject the Author finding to be above the yeers he had, when he wrote it, and nothing satisfi'd with what was begun, left it unfinisht' (see p. 116). What demands explanation is why Milton prepared an edition of what he knew was unsuccessful, for he was a hard critic of himself and, as we know from *Lycidas,* ll. 1–4, often reluctant to publish what did not wholly satisfy him. He was all too aware of how easy it would be to get a reputation, a typecasting, as a 'pretty', conventional poet writing pastorals and playing the sort of poetic organ he sneers at in Lycidas as a 'scrannel pipe of wretched straw': to be seen, in fact, as just one more of the elegant, witty poets we now lump together as the Cavalier Poets (even though several of them fought for Parliament). Indeed, it may be precisely because he recognized that danger that he decided to publish a poetic autobiography that not only would display his failures as well as his successes but also would declare firmly where he saw his poetic vocation to lie – and call attention publicly to the talent of which he never had any doubt.

The book is in two parts – it is a 'gemelle liber', or 'twin book', as Milton called it in his poem to Rous. The English poems are followed by the Latin, each group with its own title page. The poems show an astonishing technical range: there are free translations of psalms (see pp. 114–15) – some of which, like the first two in the book, were done from the Hebrew when Milton was only 15; there are sonnets, canzoni, blank verse, poems in elaborate metre and form, poems in Greek and Italian, and an assured and technically resourceful collection of Latin poems which stand comparison with any contemporary Latin verse. Besides failures, like *The Passion*, he includes Latin undergraduate exercises – often amusing. There is clearly some interest in how and why a man becomes a poet, and how he develops his authentic voice. The autobiographical poems such as *Ad Patrem* insist on a religious understanding of the poetic vocation, and offer an apologia for the poet and his craft. There is, too (e.g. in *Lycidas* and *Comus*), the implicit contention that the poet must be a moral mentor, a shepherd of the people, if he is not to betray his divine gift: we have looked at this in Chapter 3.

The volume as a whole has several further clear emphases. His dissatisfaction over many years with what was happening in England and his fear of the replacing of one type of tyranny by another crops up with some frequency.[8] *Lycidas* and *Comus* imply that in the 1630s Milton was worried by political and religious issues – these issues cannot really be separated – and anticipate the sustained attention given to those problems not only in the controversial writing but also in much later work like *Paradise Lost* and *Samson Agonistes*. And at the end of the Latin Elegies – a self-contained book within a book within a book – he added lines that reject the verse of the Muse Erato (conventional love poetry) as youthful 'error', stressing that his discovery of Plato taught him a higher purpose for his talent:[9]

> Donec Socraticos umbrosa Academia rivos
> Praebuit, admissum dedocuitque iugum.

('. . .until the shady Academy [where Plato taught] offered me its Socratic streams, and taught me to escape the yoke I had accepted'.)

At a time when the tide was setting against the Neoplatonism of much Renaissance philosophy, Milton publicly embraces Platonism. So *Poems* (1645) illuminates the development of a poet's mind and mission in a most interesting way, and, in the end, implies the coherent view of poetry I discussed in Chapter 3. And when we remember the Renaissance notion of the capacity of poetry and music to heal and reconcile divisions among men, and between men and God (see pp. 62–3), it is attractive to think that this notion may have been somewhere in Milton's mind as he published these poems in the middle of civil war.

Had Milton died in 1645, he would have left behind him a reputation as a major European Latin poet; and, as an English poet, he might have won later a reputation of genius untimely cut off – like that of Keats, whom he so strongly influenced and with whom he has many similarities.[10] The poems published in 1645 are minor poems only by comparison with what was still unwritten. They begin that career in which Milton radically altered the map of poetry in England for ever.

Moseley's volume did not, of course, introduce a wholly unknown poet: *Comus* and *Lycidas* had both been printed before (though without full attribution), and Milton had some reputation among the discerning, those who had an educated taste for poetry and an understanding of its theory. Among his English friends was one of the finest musicians of the day, Henry Lawes (whose brother William was killed fighting for the King at the siege of Chester in 1645), and as we have seen, among his contacts was the powerful Egerton family. The fact that he was asked to contribute to the Cambridge memorial volume for Edward King in 1637 shows that he was known as a poet in a university of whose system he had been highly critical. Yet *Poems* (1645) took nearly 15 years to sell out in its first printing, and, except for Moseley's and Wotton's praise, there is no evidence that the *generality* of his English contemporaries took much heed of him as a poet. Andrew Marvell, indeed, who followed him in the Latin Secretaryship, doted on Milton's work; but it was his prose Marvell admired; he attempted to get the *Defensio Secunda* by heart. It was only the surprising success of *Paradise Lost* in 1667 that finally made the English take real notice of him as a poet. His chagrin must have been intense.

The Structure of *Poems* (1645)

The order of the poems in the volume published in 1645 is not that of composition, as it might have been if a modern poet was producing his first *Collected Poems*, or if Milton's sole interest in the volume was simply to demonstrate his own development.[11] Nor did Milton include anything like all his early poems. The clever Latin ode Milton wrote to John Rous after Rous requested another copy of *Poems* (1645) to replace one that was stolen, indicates that Milton planned the book himself, including the separation of Latin and English poems into a 'Gemelle cultu simplici gaudens liber' – 'a twin of a book rejoicing in a single cover'. Either the order is entirely random, or there is some other principle than autobiography behind it. Randomness is unlikely, since the Latin poems are grouped in a separate section, and the placing of the two most substantial English works, *Lycidas* and *Comus* (which were originally composed in the reverse order), in a climactic position at the end of the English and Italian section seems to be deliberate. The most assured and ambitious Latin poem, the elegant and brilliant Neo-Latin *Epitaphium Damonis*, also is the climax of its group.

There are 22 English and 6 Italian poems in the first part of the book; 2 Greek and 24 Latin poems in the second. The book thus divides almost exactly in half between the modern and the ancient languages. The order of the poems, with their dates where ascertainable, is as follows: (The titles, except for 'English and Italian Poems' and 'Latin Poems', are those in *Poems* (1645). Material in square brackets I have added; quotes surround Milton's own first lines, or comments – e.g. about his age.)

English and Italian poems

1. *On the Morning of Christ's Nativity* [Elegy VI, ll. 79 ff. refers to this as in composition in December 1629]
2. *A paraphrase on Psalm 114* 'This and the following psalm were don by the Author at fifteen yeers old'
3. *Psalm 136*
4. *The Passion* [March, 1630]
5. *On Time* [1633]
6. *Upon the Circumcision* [1632/3]
7. *At a Solemn Music* [1633]
8. *An Epitaph upon the Marchioness of Winchester* [1631]
9. *Song: On May Morning* [1629–30]
10. *On Shakespeare* 1630
11. *On the University Carrier* . . . [1631]
12. *Another on the Same* [1631]
13. *L'Allegro* [1631?]
14. *Il Penseroso* [1632]
15. *Sonnet 1:* 'O Nightingale' [1630]
16. *Sonnet 2:* 'Donna Leggiadra' [1630]
17. *Sonnet 3:* 'Qual in colle aspro' [1630]
18. *Canzone:* 'Ridonsi donne e giovani amorosi'
19. *Sonnet 4:* 'Diodati, e te' l dirò.' [1630]
20. *Sonnet 5:* 'Per certo i bei vostr' occhi' [1630]
21. *Sonnet 6:* 'Giovane piano, e semplicetto amante' [1630]
22. *Sonnet 7:* 'How soon hath Time . . .' [1632]
23. *Sonnet 8:* [When the assault was intended to the City] 'Captain, or Colonel, or Knight in Arms' [1642]
24. *Sonnet 9:* 'Lady that in the prime. . .' [1645]
25. *Sonnet 10:* [To the Lady Margaret Ley] 'Daughter to that good Earl' [1645]
26. *Arcades* [1632]
27. *Lycidas* [1637]
28. *Comus* [including Wotton's Letter] [1634]

Latin Poems

ELEGIARUM LIBER PRIMUS

29. *Elegia Prima* [1626]
30. *Elegia Secunda* ('At Age 17') [1626]
31. *Elegia Tertia – in Obitum Praesulis Wintoniensis* ('At Age 17') [1626]
32. *Elegia Quarta* ('At age 18') [to Thomas Young, his teacher, 1627]
33. *Elgia Quinta – In adventus Veris* ('At age 20') [1629]
34. *Elgia Sexta – to Charles Diodati* [1629]
35. *Elegia Septima* ('At age 19') [1630]
36. *In Proditionem Bombardicam*
37. *In Eandem*
38. *In Eandem*
39. *In Eandem* [Epigrams]
40. *In Inventorem Bombardae* [1626?]
41. *Ad Leonoram Romae Canentem* [1639]
42. *Ad Eandem* [1639]
43. *Ad Eandem* [1639]

SYLVARUM LIBER

44. *In Obitum Procancellarii Medici* ('At age 16') (1626)
45. *In Quintum Novembris* ('At age 17') (1626)
46. *In Obitum Praesulis Eliensis* ('At age 17') (1627)
47. *Naturam non Pati Senium* (June, 1628)
48. *De Idea Platonica quemadmodum Aristoteles Intellexit* (1630)
49. *Ad Patrem* (1637)
50. *Psalm 114* (in Greek) (1634)
51. *Philosophus ad Regem* (in Greek) (?)
52. *Ad Salsillum, Poetam Romanum, Aegrotantem* (1638)
53. *Mansus* (1639)
54. *Epitaphium Damonis* (1640)

Some sort of pattern does seem to emerge from this. The first seven poems are all in some sense devotional or religious – even 'On Time', no. 5, deals with Time much as Donne deals with Death in his sonnet 'Death bee not proude'. I discuss *The Passion, The Circumcision*, and the *Nativity Ode* below as religious poems; *At a Solemn Music* – music, perhaps, such as Milton's Penseroso hears in ll. 160 ff. – closes with a prayer to be united to God's 'celestial consort' and takes as its subject the power of Voice and Verse to 'bring all heaven before my eyes' (*Il Penseroso*). The paraphrases of Psalms 114 and 136 from the Hebrew

follow exalted precedent, for many English Renaissance poets – Philip
Sidney and his sister, for example – tried their hand at recasting the
wonderful poetry of what is (among other things) the Hebrew hymn
book into fitting English verse, not just as an exercise, but as serious
devotional poetry (and of course the complete version of Sternhold and
Hopkins was regularly sung in Milton's day). Milton is here giving, with
no mean metrical skill, an example of what any serious poet might be
expected to do; he did, of course, in the 1650s write further translations
of the psalms; the matter clearly interested him. Moreover, both these
two psalms are psalms of deliverance, about Israel escaping from Egypt
and being given Canaan; it is a commonplace of Protestant thought
throughout Europe, but especially in Britain and Holland, that the
Reformed Church was the New Israel delivered, by the power of the
Lord, from the Egyptian or Babylonian captivity – that is, from the
errors of Roman Catholic doctrine and the corrupt rule of the Pope.[12]
Milton gives a Greek version of Psalm 114 as no. 50 of *Poems* (1645).
Both psalms lend themselves to tropological and allegorical application.
Furthermore, given the political circumstances at the time of the pub-
lication of *Poems* (1645), the psalms, to those of Milton's party persuasion,
could hardly not seem a triumph-song after Naseby.

A group of occasional poems, numbers 8–12, follows. These are on
a variety of subjects, and win a place merely because of their individual
wit and quality. But numbers 13 and 14, *L'Allegro* and *Il Penseroso*, the
middle poems of this English/Italian group, are of considerable philos-
ophical and moral interest (see pp. 128–31), analysing the types of
pleasure that may be explored in poetry as well as the need for wisdom
and *sophrosyne* (see p. 140) in the poet. They might be seen, perhaps,
as glancing both backwards and forwards over the collection and what
it shows of Milton's range, and perhaps even suggesting values on
which it might be judged. Then follows (nos 15–21) a group of love
poems, very much in the Petrarchan manner – indeed, despite their
assurance, they are rather trite, and it must be wondered whether they
are poems to a real lady or ladies, or are just pastiche (compare *Elegy
I* and *Elegy VII*). There are three love sonnets (one English and two
Italian); a centrally-placed canzone, the subject of which is the tension
between the desire for poetic fame and the need to write love poetry
in Italian; and then three more Italian sonnets about love. These can,
in fact, be read quite coherently as a little sonnet sequence, with the
self-referential canzone in the important central position. Then follows
the second of the English sonnets, no. 22. Although a copy of this was
sent in a letter to a friend who had accused him of dreaming away
his 'years in the arms of a studious retirement', and although it has a
clear bearing on Milton's understanding of his vocation as poet (see

p. 72), the sonnet acquires a new force here: coming after the Italian love poems, it reads almost inescapably as an ironic comment on them and on a young man's traditional devotion to love poetry, a wry apology for a delightful waste of time.

Three 'heroic' English sonnets (nos 23-25), in the manner of Tasso and Giovanni Della Casa, now follow, all of high seriousness, moral or political. The English/Italian poems conclude with the little masque entitled *Arcades* , then Lycidas , then *Comus*. The two last-named poems have considerable public and political reference, as well as moral and philosophical interest. *Arcades* not only is exquisite in itself, but may well have won him the invitation to write the much more searching *Comus*, which uses some of the same motifs.

The Latin poems also seem to have an order that is not random, for the 26 poems break down into some obvious groups. The seven elegies (see below) form a book within a book, as the Latin 'retractation' with which they conclude indicates. (It is indicative of Milton's attitude to the presentation of his own work that extremely polished examples of neo-Latin poetry are dismissed as 'nequitiae . . . vana trophaea meae' – 'the vain trophies of my foolishness'.) *Poems* 36–40 are all on the theme of the Gunpowder Plot; poems 41–43 are about the Roman chanteuse, Leonora. Poems 44–53 are gathered under the title 'Sylvarum Liber' – a significant title (' The Book of the Woods'), for it reminds us of all those other books of the period that appeared under titles like *Underwood*, or *Timber* (that by Ben Jonson, for example), in which heterogeneous (but not unimportant) material was gathered – unconnected thoughts and insights, sketches for poems, brief discussions of ideas. Such timber is the raw material from which the edifice will eventually be built. Such a title, therefore, paradoxically asserts Milton's own worth as a poet whose early work and development are worthy of study, and it suggests that the really important work is still to come.

In these 'Underwood' poems, Milton includes several things of interest. His embracing of Platonic philosophy is made public by *De Idea Platonica quemadmodum Aristoteles intellexit* (no. 48), originally a college exercise. Two obituary poems, those on the death of the Vice-Chancellor of Cambridge (1626) and of Nicholas Felton, Bishop of Ely (1627), are included, probably as examples of how stylishly he could handle the formal, exaggerated conventions of such public encomia which the death of any great man attracted in numbers: after all, they were one of the ways of getting noticed and attracting patronage. *Ad Patrem*, no. 49 (see p. 55), is a warm tribute to a loving father, but betrays a certain irritation that the older man cannot grasp that he must be still more patient: becoming a great poet is something that takes time. Milton insists on and offers an apologia for his religious vocation as a poet. But the elder John Milton must have been a little discomfited to find his son, still dependent on the father's investments and financial provision, offering as justification that the poetry that will in time be written will assure the father's undying fame as well as the son's! Milton, as we have seen, certainly had something to be proud about, but this cool, almost patronizing confidence is still breathtaking; so is the publication of what was originally private and intimate. The same confidence that his poetic ambitions can be achieved is apparent in the penultimate poem in the book, the elegant thank-you letter to Mansus. It might be argued, too, that the Greek epigram, 'Philosophus ad Regem', is a further expression of this confidence: it claims that if a king destroys a wise man like the writer, he will regret his loss for he will have destroyed a great protection to the state – the same sort of thinking that informs *Sonnet VIII* (no. 23): both poems claim special treatment for a great writer.

The volume finally closes with one of the finest elegies in any language, the *Epitaphium Damonis*, a tribute to Milton's greatest friend. Just as the vision of the divine perspective on human activity and art in *Lycidas* (see p. 156) both resolved the argument implicit in the English poems of the young poet that preceded it and prepared the ground for the highly philosophical poem of *Comus*, in which we have to view the narrative from a position as detached as Lycidas' now is (see p. 182), so the *Epitaphium Damonis*, the finest of the Latin poems, positioned as it is, is both a eucatastrophic vision of the resurrected Damon in a Classicized Heaven (as Lycidas was in a Christian one) and a farewell to the practice of Latin poetry. It can hardly be an accident that *Lycidas* is the 27th poem in the book, the Pythagorean number of the World Soul, or Christ as Creating Word, and the *Epitaphium Damonis* the 27th after *Lycidas* (see above, pp. 16,19.).

The Elegies

In numbers 29–35, the seven elegies, on a variety of subjects, Milton shows complete mastery of and fondness for Ovid and Propertius as models for love poetry and familiar letters in elegiac verse, and these seven elegies take a worthy place in the tradition of Renaissance Latin poetry, which includes Dante, Petrarch, Mantuan, Pontano, Sannazaro and Buchanan. These poems can all be dated: poems 29, 30, and 31 to 1626; poem 32 to 1627; poems 33 and 34 to 1629; and poem 35 to 1630. Elegies II, III, IV, V, and VII are preceded by a note of Milton's age when he wrote them, and there is little doubt that that note implies that the reader should both excuse youthful folly and admire the work of a prodigy.

These poems merit some attention. The first Latin poem, *Elegy I*, is addressed (like *Sonnet IV*) to Diodati, whose death elicited the last poem in the volume. It describes Milton's time in London while away from Cambridge (see p. 28). Playfully likening this absence to the banishment of Ovid to Tomi by Augustus, Milton exploits the poem's debt to Ovid's poems in *Tristia* and *Ex Ponto*. He describes his happiness with his books and the theatre: but rather than the contemporary English stage he seems to be talking about literary, Plautine or Terentian comedy, and Greek and Senecan tragedy (personified as in Ovid, Amores, III. i. 11–13); there is an interesting similarity to *L'Allegro* and *Il Penseroso* here (see pp. 134,137). Again like the two speakers in those poems, he delights in the countryside and the open air, and also in feminine beauty; but his interest in women looks very like literary pastiche. It is brilliantly if allusively sensuous, for all that.[13]

Elegy II (no. 30) is much shorter and lighter. Its subject is the death of the Beadle of the University of Cambridge, and the mock solemnity and open comedy, in which the old beadle is 'wing-footed' and the undergraduates 'Palladian' is oddly moving. The literary point is being made, of course, that the transposition of Greek and Latin pastoral conceits expected in such polite Neo-Latin verse can be merely ludicrous when brought sharply up against things as they really are, and not as they are in books. *Elegy III* (No. 30), another occasional piece, on the death of the Bishop of Winchester (the much loved Lancelot Andrewes), is handled with great assurance in a heavily mythological way, as allusive as Andrewes's own admired preaching. Like the elegy on the Bishop of Ely (no. 46), the basic structure is one of protest – 'Why did you have to go?' – leading to a vision of heaven (in terms very much those of a baroque painting!) and an assurance of resurrection that appears again in the climaxes of *Lycidas, Comus* and the *Epitaphium Damonis*.

Elegy IV (no. 32) is a verse letter on the theme of friendship, to Thomas Young, the anti-episcopal preacher, who was, at the time of writing, in Hamburg. Young, once Milton's tutor, was one of those controversialists whom Milton defended in *An Apology for Smectymnuus*. We can take Milton's youthful gratitude for Young's teaching (ll. 27 ff.) to be genuine; but, by 1645, circumstances had so changed that to publish such a letter was a nailing of party colours to the mast. (In lines 111f., moreover, Milton draws the parallel between the Protestants and the army of the Jews whom God protects – cf. p. 88.)

Elegy V and *Elegy VI* (nos 33 and 34) are best taken together as an important part of the discussion in *Poems* (1645) of the nature and calling of the true poet. They are in this respect the Latin counterparts of the *Nativity Ode, Lycidas, At a Solemn Music* and *Sonnet VII*. The theme of *Elegy V* (no. 33) is the coming of spring and the return of the capacity to write poetry. There is a good deal of pure pastiche in the sensuousness of the poem, particularly in the personifications – the Earth courting the Sun, and so on – and it is heavily allusive in the then fashionable manner. It is precisely such powerful allusiveness that Milton seems to have worked to transfer to the medium of English in *Lycidas*. However, while *Lycidas* speaks openly of the Christian poet's job and nature, this elegy through its literary decorum can deal with this important matter only through the image of the Cumean Sybil's being filled with the power of Phoebus. In *Poems* (1645), the two poems must contrast, and in that contrast one is tempted to see Milton implicitly giving his reasons for his eventual choice of English as his major language of poetic utterance: the decorum of Latin, however well handled, did impose restraints on what could be said.

Elegy VI, no. 34 (another poem addressed to Diodati), was seen by E. M. W. Tillyard as a 'serious self-dedication to poetry'. This is certainly an attractive way of looking at it, even when we allow for the playfulness of the opening 35 Ovidian lines and the fact that Milton is drawing on common ground in Renaissance theory in asserting (ll. 48 ff., 63 ff.) that the serious epic poet should pursue austerity of character; he who wants to deal with high and noble themes, as opposed to the man who writes comedy and love poetry, cannot indulge in the enjoyment of food, wine, music and feminine beauty. (In the last elegy, *Elegy VII* [no. 35], lines 46 ff. once again suggest very convincingly the attraction women held for him, but this is a last play on the traditional Ovidian theme of the poet's conquest by Cupid.) The ghost of Ovid dominates these elegies, but Milton was coming to reject the practice of such poetry – which could have won him no mean reputation – under the influence of his reading of Plato. For, following *Elegy VII*, separated from it only by a thin rule, are ten lines of Latin verse, dated usually to 1630, which reject the collection:

> 'These are the vain trophies of my foolishness . . . evil error led me astray, and my headstrong youth was a corrupt teacher: until the shady Academy offered me the Socratic streams, and taught me to escape from the yoke I had imposed on myself. Thenceforward, the flames were put out, and my breast has been firm, bound in thick ice; Cupid himself fears its cold for his arrows, and Venus herself fears my Diomedean power' (my translation).

To include such an editorial comment in *Poems* (1645) would have drawn attention, back-handedly, to the excellence of Milton's Ovidian poetry at the same time as it restated the collection's central theme: the seriousness of the poetic vocation and Milton's Platonic understanding of it.

We can pass rapidly over the miscellaneous collection that makes up the remainder of the volume, but a couple of points are worth a glance. The republication in 1645, some 20 years after they were written, of numbers 36–37, four short poems in elegiacs on the Gunpowder Plot, and of *In Quintum Novembris* in *Sylvarum Liber* (no. 45), can hardly be without some sly significance even though there is nothing openly anti-Royalist in them. They were the sort of thing that undergraduates and schoolboys were often given to do, and they look like school exercises, though they show a precocious wit and command of language. They are conventionally and violently anti-papal – they could hardly not be[14] – in a manner the authorities found useful, clearly implying that the Roman Church was behind the plot, when, in fact, it obviously was not, as wiser spirits knew. But for many in the 1640s the Pope was even more the Antichrist than he had been in 1605, and Parliament, though militarily successful, saw itself as under attack from both Royalist at home and Catholic abroad.

In no. 47, *Naturam non pati senium* – 'That nature is not subject to Old Age' – Milton again makes his philosophical and cosmological principles clear, and must have known he was courting controversy. I have already mentioned his embracing of Plato at a time when Platonism both had most able followers and was under severe attack. Another controversy was that between those who argued that the world was running rapidly down to dissolution and decay, and those who held to a sort of 'cosmic optimism' the Puritans, for example, hoping for their religious and political hopes to be fulfilled in the beginning of Christ's reign on earth. In *Naturam non pati senium* Milton may have been writing on an academic subject he did not choose; but he did choose to publish, and he comes down firmly on the optimistic side.[15] This poem is indubitably a political statement, dividing Milton from members of the parliamentary coalition of interests he supported as well as from its opponents. It is also a theological declaration, and goes hand in hand with his conception of the poet's job as the mentor of a country, showing it not only what to think but what to do.

The Epitaphium Damonis

This, the last poem in the book, is also one of the newest: written in 1639, it is later than *Lycidas*. Its subject is the death of Charles Diodati, and Milton, as he did with Edward King, exploits the parallel in interests and taste between himself and the dead man (see p. 153f). Like *Lycidas*, this poem works from the tradition of pastoral lament, drawing especially on Vergil. But Milton's relationship to Diodati was of far greater intensity than his acquaintance with King: the two young men were very close friends, and in addition to this natural and affectionate relationship there is a good deal in this and other poems addressed to Diodati to indicate that their intellectual conception of what friendship was and how it was practised was based on the ideals Plato expresses in the *Symposium*. We – and we are the poorer for it – have lost the Renaissance understanding that friendship between members of the same sex may be of high emotional intensity without any whiff of homosexuality, and that it is not just dependent on emotion but is an art which can be consciously practised and developed. There are many treatises on the art of friendship from antiquity, the Middle Ages and the Renaissance, and the key idea in all is that in a good friendship the friends unselfishly seek each other's ultimate good – much as Antonio seeks Bassanio's in *The Merchant of Venice*. And through intense emotional and intellectual friendship of this type, the participants may be ennobled and matured, and see through the veil of their love the lineaments of the Good, the True and the Beautiful. Diodati is missed, as King is not, as a confidant of Milton's innermost thoughts:

> Pectora cui credam? quis me lenire docebit
> Mordaces curas, quis longam fallere noctem
> Dulcibus alloquiis. . .
> (ll. 45–7)

('To whom shall I entrust my thoughts? Who will teach me to soften biting worry, to while away the long night in pleasant conversation?')

Diodati was a fellow musician, a learned physician from whom Milton learnt much, and a man who shared the same keen sense of humour:

> Quis mihi blanditiasque tuas, quis tum mihi risus
> Cecropiosque sales referet, cultosque lepores?
> (ll. 55–6)

('Who will bring back to me your delightful conversation, your jokes, your wit and Attic salt, and your cultivated humour?') Their relationship seems to have been as close as that of Horace and Vergil, whom Horace calls 'animae dimidium meae' – 'The half of my own soul' – (*Odes*, I. iii. 8).

Structurally, the poem is unlike *Lycidas*. It uses a refrain to hold most of the poem together and to mark out movements in the development of the thought, but as the poem moves into its final vision after line 202 this plangent refrain ceases to be heard. For then, after all the expressions, through the pastoral mode, of a very personal sense of loss, Diodati is imagined among the gods; it is sinful to weep for Damon in heaven. The passions of the soul have been chastened and intensified into ecstasy (ll. 218 ff.); as in *Comus*, Virtue and Chastity (as there defined) have won a heavenly Bridegroom, and the grief is burnt up in the joy of Heaven. More personal, and in some ways finer, than *Lycidas*, the poem completely refutes Dr Johnson's remark that 'passion runs not after remote allusions and obscure opinions . . . Where there is leisure for fiction there is little grief.' As a conclusion to *Poems* (1645) it restates a lot of the ideas of *Lycidas*, reasserting faith in Providence even in the face of evil and loss, and it is also a moving tribute to a man who, more even than Thomas Young and his father, had a major influence on the formation of Milton's mind. Originally an intensely personal poem, its printing in *Poems* (1645) is at once an act of piety, a public memorial to a very talented man, and a further demonstration that the voice of the new Vergil is being heard.

Notes to Chapter 4

1. He became one of the most distinguished publishers of the middle years of the seventeenth century. His stable of living authors eventually included Waller, Suckling, Cartwright, Vaughan, Cowley, Crashaw, Denham, Carew and Descartes; new editions of (among others) Bacon, Ralegh, Guarini, Beaumont and Fletcher, and Quarles also issued from his office. The quality of his work is generally very high, and his prefaces are an invaluable insight into the mind, taste and practice of a cultured businessman of his day, revealing an interesting conception of the publisher's job. It might be because he had recently published the poems of the Parliamentary general, Waller, that Milton decided to work with him.

2. For a discussion of these issues, see Chapter 1 of my *Shakespeare's History Plays*.

3. Cromwell's remark about his attitude to religion and the Church is typical: 'I can tell you, Sir, what I would not have, though I cannot, what I would.' The man who, with hindsight, we might easily suppose to have had a complete and comprehensive plan of action was a social and political traditionalist, and the most pragmatic of all the men of power of the time. He hesitated for weeks on end while seeking to discern God's will in the turn of events, and then acted ruthlessly and decisively once he thought it was God's work he was doing.

4. Provost of Eton, but before that ambassador to Venice and one-time secretary to the Earl of Essex: a connoisseur of architecture and author of some exquisite verse.

   When the volume appeared, Rous, the librarian of the University of Oxford *asked* for a copy for the library – a fair indication of Milton's reputation.

5. See K. J. Höltgen, *Aspects of the Emblem: Studies in the English Tradition and the European Context* (Kassel, 1986), Chapter 3.

6. A translation might run: 'When you look at the appearance of the original, you perhaps may say that this likeness was drawn by the hand of a novice. But, friends, since you do not recognize what is represented here, have a good laugh at this caricature by an artist who doesn't know his job.'

7. The other five muses are Thalia (comedy and pastoral), Euterpe (lyric),

Polyhymnia (sacred song and music), Terpsichore (dance), and Calliope (epic poetry).

8. The double-tailed sonnet (the device imitates an Italian variation on the form, often used for satiric purposes), 'On the new forcers of conscience under the Long Parliament', was written at about the same time as the publication of *Poems* (1645), and indicates just how (rightly) worried Milton was by the trends he observed in politics.

9. The date is probably around 1630. It was unwillingly that he turned to pastoral again for *Lycidas* (ll. 1–2)

10. Among others, the sensuousness, the almost tactile quality of his imagery, the ability to create an entire detailed world in his verse – comparing the techniques and sensibility of *Ode on a Grecian Urn* with *L'Allegro* and *Il Penseroso* is instructive – and the wealth of classical allusion as a touchstone for the values of what the poet is talking about.

11. The manuscript preserved in the library of Trinity College, Cambridge, in its revisions, gives a few clues about such an order. Other clues about dating may be found in references in the poems to events or to other poems – for example, the openings of *Lycidas* and *The Passion* refer, respectively, to *Comus* and the *Nativity Ode*.

12. The matter is of some importance, for it provides not only a source of imagery and polemical allegory – in poetry, pamphlet and print – but also, for those who accept it, a predictive and interpretative model for their understanding of the historical events in which they are caught up. Milton's use of the story of Samson is another good example, but there are many others, including the ironic use of the history of King David as a political allegory by Dryden in *Absalom and Achitophel*.

13. 'While the blind boy [Cupid] permits', he is preparing to go back to Cambridge, to 'leave the halls of the deceiver Circe'; in ll. 85 ff. he links the delights of women with Circe's deceptions, and stresses the need of the herb moly to escape them: the correspondence to motifs that appear in *Comus* (written later, of course, but in this volume appearing earlier) is striking.

14. It was usual to celebrate the fifth of November in the universities with 'epic' poems like Milton's *In Quintum Novembris* or the even more anti-papal *Locustae* and *Apolyonists* of Phinehas Fletcher. It was conventional in such poems to have a formal council of devils in hell to begin the plot against the English king: a motif that may have suggested the council of the devils in Book II of *Paradise Lost*. Satan's journey in that book and in Book IX is anticipated in his journey through the earth in this poem.

15. The two sides of the debate are best represented by George Hakewill, *An Apologie or Declaration of the Power and Providence of God* (London, 1627), and Christopher Goodman, *The Fall of Man* (London, 1616).

5 'Holy Song': The Nativity Ode and the Religious Poems

Poems (1645) has at its centre and at its end two poems which tackle the question of loss and death, and closes with a – wholly serious – vision of the delights that await those saved by God's grace (and, one might add, their own virtues – see p. 121), so far as they can be expressed even in metaphor. The book opens with a celebration of birth: the birth of the Redeemer through whom the means of grace and the hope of glory have been given to sinful men.

The seven poems Milton chose to put at the beginning of *Poems* (1645) are all religious or devotional, and the only ones in the book that can be so classed. Before we can look at the most important of them, it is necessary to stress some facts about religious poetry which in our age are easily overlooked (though they are obvious enough) and which sharply affect the way we can read individual poems. In the first place, what we loosely call 'religion' is deadly serious: Christianity and other great religions (as well as atheism) are making statements about the cosmos which must be either right or wrong, and it is intellectual dishonesty, and worse, to pretend that religion is as optional and unimportant a matter for a person as the football team he supports or the colour of tie he wears. Moreover, the great religions cannot all be right (though they could all be wrong), for the major religions of the world are making mutually exclusive statements about the nature of the universe. Thus religious poetry by convinced Christians – such as Milton – is not a serious game, as even the most serious political or love poetry can be, but a response to a unique Person and to a unique Event, in which the Creator of all of us intervened at a datable moment in a specific place by taking humanity upon Himself.

The fact of the matter is that if the claims of Christianity are right – and Milton and many since him have had no doubt they are – then we live in a world that is absolutely terrifying: a universe whose Creator is absolute master, and yet deigns to ask our love and cooperation individually; a world where there are no limited liabilities, but only the choice, on the one hand, of an open-ended acceptance of a relationship with God, more dangerous, painful and ecstatic than any love affair, which will destroy us in order to remake us, or, on the other hand, of an eternity of being, in all our need for love, unspeakably ignored. Christianity – or Judaism or Islam, for that matter – says there is no middle way, no balanced, well-mannered aloofness on the sidelines, for the universe knows nothing of manners. It is a matter literally of life and death for all of us whether the claims – and they are exclusive claims, despite what fashionable modern clerics say – of Christianity are right or wrong. If wrong, the sooner a foolish superstition is reduced to the status of a quaint historical curiosity the better: if right, then we had better soon be on our knees in fear and trembling – and love. Religion is a matter about which, in the end, no one can be neutral.

The *Nativity Ode*'s subject, once we think about it from this angle, is literally unspeakable. The saccharine sentimentality of carol and crib and card has reduced our perception of this stupendous event to the anodyne, seasonal picture of a baby in a manger; yet the Gospels make it clear that that birth was nothing so simple for the shepherds, or the Magi, or for Herod, whom it terrified. (T. S. Eliot's *Journey of the Magi* gives us a glimpse of how disturbing it must have been.) Christians believe that in that event God took humanity upon Him, actually became a man physically related, in however distant a way, to every one of us. They also believe that after a life of perfect obedience to the law of God, that God-Child died in appalling and ignominious suffering on the Cross, and, inconceivably but in hard fact, rose from the dead in a totally new mode of physical and spiritual existence. It is a central principle of Christian thought from the very earliest times that the relationship with the risen Lord, certainly and necessarily one of awe, is also one of the most intimate and abandoned love, constantly refining and being refined. Finally, they believe not only that all the shadows of the truth, the anticipations of myth, are fulfilled in that event, but also that that risen Lord is lord of all men, of whatever colour or creed, and that each one of us will be judged by Him, and given a free choice whether or not to accept Him, failed and fallen as we are. There is a sense in which we should read the best devotional poetry, like that of George Herbert or G. M. Hopkins, for example, as a special sort of love poetry: the love of the restless soul for Him who alone can give it rest and fulfilment.

Milton's religious poetry is undoubtedly serious and committed, but it is, nevertheless, sharply different from the predominant type in the period. There is never that sense that we are overhearing the 'dialogue of one' that we get in Donne or Herbert; there is none of that almost feminine longing for the Lover of the Soul that we glimpse in Donne's *Holy Sonnet XIV*, and Milton never calls God 'my dear' as George Herbert does *(Love III)*. That emotional intimacy is simply not there. But, on the other hand, neither is Milton as distanced and objective – even programmatic – as Francis Quarles or (a far inferior poet) George Wither. His religious poetry has passion, but it is a passion for the rational and almost, one might say, impersonal pursuit of Truth. God for him is not a lover, but the King of Kings and his 'great Taskmaster', the Lord of the Vineyard and the Master in the Parable of the Talents (cf. the Sonnet 'On His Blindness'). The hallmark of Milton's religious poetry is not surrender, but doing.

The *Nativity Ode*

So when we come to the *Nativity Ode*, for example, we have to recognize, as Milton clearly did, that the poem must be a failure: words and human art can never begin to comprehend the Infinite. The subject is too big to talk about, yet, ultimately, it is the only one worth talking about. We must expect Milton, knowing this, to have built into a poem on so stupendous a subject just about every possible means of conveying what he knew he could not talk about: words, metaphor, simile – for the language of religion must be the language of metaphor and simile – form, pattern, structure and number. All will, ultimately, fail; and at the heart of the poem's most triumphant passage is an acknowledgement of its failure.

Early Christian poetry had tended to concentrate far more on the events of the Passion and Resurrection than on the Nativity. But with the growing interest, theological, artistic and poetic, in the humanity of Christ in the early Middle Ages, poems on the Nativity began to be written in some number. One of the earliest known to me is the Christmas Sequence 'Laetabundus', of about the year 1100 (*Analecta Hymnica*, LIV, no. 2, p. 5), which shows features that will become standard in a multitude of later treatments of the theme: the choir of angels, the mystery of the Incarnate Word, the prophecies of both Israel and the pagans fulfilled. Later artistic handlings add the visits of the shepherds, the Magi, and the physical details of the scene in the stable, and of course some or all of these details form part of the fabric of the Europe-wide, Mystery Play treatments of the theme – as in the well-known Towneley *Secunda Pastorum* – and in the Nativity Play still acted in many British schools today. In all these the kernel of the matter is the miracle centred on the Baby.

Milton's contemporaries, then, would recognize the *Ode* as belonging to a well-worked tradition. Indeed, comparison with other Christmas poems from the same period shows both the large amount of common ground and the individuality and virtuosity of Milton's treatment.[1] Milton's *Ode* is not only far more formally and linguistically elaborate than any comparable English poem, but it also approaches its subject in an unusual way. For while Milton is clearly aware of the great motifs associated with the story, such as the angelic choir, the Cessation of the Oracles[2] and the flight of the pagan gods, the Child in the manger and the holiness of His Mother, he nevertheless says remarkably little about her actual motherhood. The poem noticeably allows no opportunity for the sentimentality to which Nativity poems are often prone, and looks at the Child in the manger from an angle that is unusual: instead of the usual concentration on the flesh which the Creating Word took upon Himself, we have a concentration on the Creating Word itself manifested through the flesh. (Milton's Platonism is once again affecting his response to his poetic subject.) The Baby is never allowed to obscure the Lord of Creation. The main focus of the poem is not the incarnation of Christ but the cosmic effects of that incarnation, and one major theme is the triumph of the infant Christ over the gods of paganism, and their banishment to darkness as the Sun of Righteousness arose.[3] Milton made it clear in *Elegy* VI that Christ's natal triumph is his area of interest:

> Paciferum canimus caelesti semine regem,
> Faustaque sacratis saecula pacta libris;
> Vagitumque Dei, & stabulantem paupere tecto
> Qui suprema suo cum patre regna colit.
> Stelliparumque polum, modulantesque aethere turmas,
> Et subito elisos ad sua fana Deos.
> Dona quidem dedimus Christi natalibus illa.

(ll. 81 ff.)

('I am writing of the peacemaking king, of Heavenly seed, of the blessed times promised in the holy scriptures; I am writing of the infant cries of God, of the stabling under a mean roof of him who with his Father rules the highest Heaven. I am writing of the star-filled sky, the hosts singing in heaven, and of the gods suddenly destroyed in their own shrines. These indeed are my gifts for the birthday of Christ' (my translation). Tasso's *Nel Giorno della Natività*, which Milton probably knew, has a similar emphasis, and some interesting parallels with Milton's treatment.

This emphasis is not the only way in which the poem is unusual. One of the climaxes of this poem on the Nativity is flanked by a vision not of the Child in the manger, but of the Man on a Cross. Moreover, the poem is, as I shall demonstrate below, a large part of its own subject. The struggle of human language and art to respond properly to an event of such magnitude cannot help failing, and Milton makes the admission of that failure one of the poem's important motifs. Human language and intelligence must in the end fall silent, like the oracles, before the greatest of all mysteries. We have looked in some detail already at Milton's view of inspiration, and his serious belief that his poetry, in some inexplicable way, was inspired by the Holy Spirit. The *Nativity Ode* was a poem Milton believed to have been 'given' to him, as he tells Diodati in line 88 of *Elegy VI*, but even such a gift can only be communicated through the fallibility of human language and art, the palest reflections of the Creating Word and the Cosmic Art of God Himself.

Form

The expression of that Christmas morning inspiration demanded from Milton a choice of form, for even Milton nowhere suggests that his 'Celestial Patroness', Urania, has any great interest in the nuances of the canzone or the Spenserian stanza. The form he uses for the 27 stanzas of the hymn has no exact precedent. The syllabic movement of the lines – 6, 6, 10, 6, 6, 10, 8, 12 – emphasized by the rhyme scheme – a a b c c b d d – allows the treatment of each stanza as a tripartite movement, where the longer, rhyming lines 3 and 6 make subsidiary climaxes before the final climax in the two lines, on a new rhyme, at the end. The final Alexandrine, which reminds us strongly of Spenser, is a peculiarly emphatic end to the stanza, and frequently seems to sum up its key motif. Milton was much interested in the grand lyric manner of the Greek Pindaric ode and how it might be transferred into English, and in the Italian Renaissance canzone he found a vernacular form that offered a possible model for a solution (see p. 148). As in the case of *Lycidas* (see pp. 146ff), the Italian canzone does influence Milton's treatment. The ode, as a genre, would be entirely germane to the seriousness of this poem's theme; moreover, the self-conscious presentation of stanzas 5–31 as a 'hymn' makes a lyric form imperative. So it seems to me that Milton's form is developed after consideration first of the type of poem – the ode – most decorous to the subject, then of the Italian canzone and the developments from it for serious occasional poetry made by Spenser in *Epithalamion* and *Prothalamion*.

The first four stanzas of the whole poem are differently constructed, as they must be since they form no part of the hymn but act as a sort of frame for it. They have to be distinguished formally and sonically from the more obviously musical stanza pattern that follows. Here Milton employs a pattern he had used before, in *On a Fair Infant dying of a Cough*. This is developed from the old rhyme royal, used by Chaucer (and many others), which is the basis of Spenser's stanza form in *The Faerie Queene*. The rhyme scheme a b a b b c c is identical to that of the regular rhyme royal; but the dignified and weighty first six decasyllabic lines are closed not with a seventh in the same form, but with the much heavier and grander alexandrine. The seriousness of what these verses are talking about could be grasped simply from their sound, even if we did not understand the words.

The poem certainly does not deserve Thomas Warton's scathing dismissal as a mere 'string of affected conceits'. Some of those conceits are part and parcel of a visual and devotional tradition Milton inherited and would not have wanted to change once given the nature of the poem he wished to write; its architectonic arrangement, moreover, is of considerable subtlety, and needs full discussion. Such a discussion is, however, best left until after a sequential reading, for when we come to the poem for the first time we cannot know what the whole structure is going to be; that can affect our reading only after it is complete – though if we are alert we may notice, and be intrigued by, a developing pattern as we read. After reading we may find that the signals conveyed by the structure reinforce, or throw into relief, what the verbal text has communicated to us and how we have received it.

The first four stanzas are more than just a prelude or introduction: they announce the theme of the Nativity, and unambiguously declare the status of the hymn that follows. The first stanza turns on the fulfilment of ancient promise in the extraordinary and paradoxical event of Christmas, a fulfilment 'then' but also 'now' – 'This is the Month, and this the happy morn'.[4]

The central lines pull the whole thing together: the unspeakable paradox of the Virgin Birth expressed in the chiasmus of 'wedded Maid, and Virgin Mother', in which language admits in contradiction its impotence in the face of miracle, and what the 'holy sages once did sing' bracket, in the central line, the 'great redemption' won by Christ's Incarnation. The second stanza moves from the 'Light unsufferable' of the Divine Majesty in its fullness of glory to the 'darksome House of mortal Clay'. The basic contrast between the glory of God and the humility of His human body is the dynamic of the stanza, which is wholly built on the idea of relinquishing light and fullness of being for darkness and time and limitedness: the 'Day' is 'everlasting', its rhyming 'clay' is 'mortal'. The two stanzas together, therefore, are no bad summary of the central doctrines of the Incarnation: the prophecy of the birth, the virgin birth, the nature of Incarnation, the birth of Him who was fully God and fully man, and, finally, what it all means for human beings. The stanzas' ideas are a distillation into remarkably brief compass of the central Pauline and Johannine doctrines of the Nativity, which have always been the basis of orthodox Christian belief.

Looking at the stanzas on the page (*Poems* [1645] prints I and II on the recto, III and IV on the verso) makes us notice that the first two begin with the same consonantal sound, with a demonstrative pronoun and a demonstrative adjective, while the next two begin with imperative verbs, again beginning with the same consonantal sound. And indeed the induction does break exactly in the middle: the first two stanzas categorize the event, the next two demand a response ('run') to it through the human sense of speech and action, through the action that the composing of the hymn represents. The muse of line 15 we have met before: reworking the Classical convention by which a poet began a serious poem by invoking the muse and thus agreeing upon an authority for it with his audience, Milton is asking Urania for the hymn that is the body of this poem. But while so doing he delicately connects its writing with the song of the angels in the darkness before the (real and symbolic) dawn, whose song we hear more fully in stanza XIII of the hymn.[5]

He goes further. The hymn not only is to be a gift like that of the Magi, whose gifts symbolized the royalty, the divinity and the sacrifice of Christ, but also is to be presented before their arrival ('prevent', l. 24, means 'get there before'). The star over the stable in ll. 240–1 when the hymn is completed shows their arrival to be imminent.) The voice of the muse – the poem – is to be joined to 'the Angel choir', and finally, the poet's voice and lips have been touched with 'hallow'd fire' just as were those of the prophet Isaiah (see p. 74). Isaiah, 'a man of unclean lips', was made the messenger of God, and it was he above all who foretold the Virgin Birth and the coming of Christ as the Suffering Servant: were one not certain that Milton thoroughly, and with odd humbleness, believed his own poetic calling to be holy, one by which God spoke through him, the identification of himself and his poetry with such a pattern would announce a pride bordering on dementia. For there is not a whisper of ambiguity: the verse plainly claims that the hymn *is* holy, inspired, an act of worship. In short, these four stanzas of induction set out the significance of the event, and the terms – they are very demanding terms – on which we should read the hymn. The poem that now follows is claimed to be as holy as the great prophecies of the greatest of the Four Major Prophets.[6]

By the merest slide over a 'once upon a time' past tense in line 29, the 'here and now' Eternal Present of the induction changes to the temporal present of the Nativity. (Most of the main verbs in succeeding verses are in the present tense.) The grammatical oddity of the first sentence of the hymn, with a present tense ('lies') where we should expect a past in the adverbial clause, underlines that we are, so to speak, no longer thinking about a past event but responding to the immediate: this is literally and metaphorically a new beginning, with the Child in the rude manger. The 'solemn strain' of the Heavenly Muse must be judged by how well it measures up to the understanding of the event in the induction.

The ideas of the first two stanzas focus on the nakedness of the earth in winter. The semantics stresses glory removed, disguise: the Child is 'meanly wrapt', Nature 'hath doff'd her gawdy trim' but hides 'her naked shame' with 'Saintly Vail of Maiden white', the 'innocent Snow' that hides 'her guilty front'. Gradually the commonplace personi-fication of Nature hardens into personality: first awed by her master, then a girl knowing when not to sport with her lover (l. 36), and then overcome with shame and guilt, she acquires motivation and complexity, an allegorical vitality which prepares us to accept the introduction of the masque-like figure of Peace (l. 46). This peace 'sliding / Down through the turning sphear . . . with Turtle wing' is both the song the angels sang (*Pax in terra*) to the shepherds and an allegorical reminder of the peace on earth that Christ's coming announces. (Indeed, it is a matter of fact that throughout the Roman world at the time of the Nativity there was 'a universall Peace through Sea and Land' for the first time for centuries: Milton is referring to this in stanza IV.) Yet the allegory works dynamically too: the Child's birth challenges all that is in Nature's domain to know itself progressively more deeply, to feel increasing shame for what it is and has been, and thus more and more painfully its separation from 'her [Nature's] Maker'. There can be no solution from Nature's side to this appalling disjunction: the resolution can only come by the gift of grace, the coming of peace from God.

That allegorical, transcendental peace is seen in detail in the cessation of wars – peace among men – and the calm that allows the halcyons to breed (l. 68) – peace in the elements. Stanza IV stresses negatives and silence: 'No War, or Battails sound', the chariot is 'Unstain'd', the 'Trumpet spake not', the kings 'sate still'. Complementarily, the semantics of stanza V stresses peace ('peacefull', 'peace', 'forgot to rave') and love ('kiss't', 'whispering new joys', 'brooding'). The notion of things suspended in awe continues through stanzas VI and VII: the stars 'will not take their flight . . . Untill their Lord . . . bid them go', and the Sun, in a fine personification that plays on the age-old pun of Sun/Son, 'himself with-held his wonted speed, / And hid his head for shame'. Yet though in this bravura conceit Milton underlines that everything in the world of Nature is recognizing the Lord of Nature, he subtly suggests that men's ceasing from war is more ambiguous. It is not to be seen as consequential upon the coming of Christ, for the kings 'sat still' only '*as if* [my italics] they surely knew their sovran Lord was by' – the mood of the verb and the structure of the clause imply they sat still for other, less admirable, reasons.[7]

In stanza VIII, just as this grand allegory and the cosmic worship could be getting all too much, there is a sudden movement to the shepherds 'simply chatting in a rustick row'. Cousins to those in Theocritus and Vergil who talked about 'their loves, or els their sheep', these shepherds decorously worship Pan, little expecting the event they are to witness.[8]

Now suddenly all the pictures of hushed stillness, of the hushed darkness before dawn, are swept aside by the first mention of sound in the hymn: the heavenly music of the angels in stanza IX. The music is really rather fashionable, the summit of the art as Milton understood it: it is a symphony of voices and a 'whole consort' of stringed instruments (ll. 96–7) which reminds us of *At a Solemn Music*; it is embellished with melismata that linger on the air and self-referentially echo each other (l. 100). But it is also music that 'as never was by mortall finger struck', the music that expresses the harmony of heaven (l. 107) towards which mortal music can only strive. This music that ravishes the shepherds (as well it might) is, literally, power: the power to hold 'all Heav'n and Earth in happier union' (see p. 120). The Nature who was overcome by shame in the opening stanzas now thinks it signifies that her job as God's vicegerent is done, that the creation of a new heaven and a new earth is at hand – and, from a Christian standpoint, so, of course, it is. The music does after all recall the mathematical music, harmony and proportion (Wisdom of Solomon XI, 21) by which Divine Wisdom made the world in the first place: stanza XII draws the parallel explicitly, and implicitly suggests the parallel between the Creation of the World and the New Creation that starts with the Incarnation of God as Man in Christ. But Nature's reaction to this music is a sort of false climax, enhancing stanza XI in which what the shepherds hear is trumped by what the shepherds see. Indeed, their *vision* of the host of heaven is suggestively bracketed by the music of stanzas X and XII – music that, perhaps, like the Penseroso's preferred type, can 'bring all Heav'n before mine eyes' (cf. l. 148; see p. 135).

Stanza XI is extraordinarily rich.[9] To begin with, 'At last' announces that we have reached a climactic point. The darkness that has dominated the poem so far is dispersed; the shepherds' sight is overwhelmed by the vision of the angels in their serried ranks, wings spread, 'terrible as an army with banners'. The war materials of men in stanza IV suddenly seem trivial and comic in comparison to this heavenly, stupendous power; the darkness that men have been in both literally and figuratively suddenly is 'shame-fac't' before this light.[10] The silence in which the hushed world attended the birth explodes into 'loud and solemn quire', which hymns the real royalty, not the provisional royalty of earthly kings, of 'Heav'ns new-born Heir'. It is as Heir of Heaven, not just as Child, that the angels worship Christ. This stanza pulls together all the major themes of the preceding ten in the remarkable concentration of ideas, but that is not the end of its importance. For, it is from the point of view of the shepherds watching it that we read this stanza. It is not described objectively, but as what they see: we watch them watching. The centrality of Man in the drama of Creation and Redemption could hardly be better stressed, for it is to the 'silly' shepherds that the news the rest of Creation knows already has to be announced. This cosmic *son et lumière* is put on for Man's benefit.

With stanza XIII, the hymn turns to a celebration of the *musica mundi*, and many of the ideas recur in *At a Solemn Music* (see p. 118). The relation between music and the physical and moral order of the universe; the power of music to enable us to glimpse the perfection of Heaven; the power of music to lift us actually to participation in that perfection and to heal the breaches caused by sin; and the idea of the joy music expresses as the serious business of heaven are all there. Admittedly, the statement that the music sung by the angels was comparable to that sung at the Creation itself is hedged by '(as 'tis said)' (l. 117); but this is less a caveat than an assertion of the authority of the comparison, for this is the music of the new creation. The question is, as line 126 emphasizes, whether the music of the spheres can be heard by mortals still clothed in this muddy vesture of decay (*Merchant of Venice*, v. i.). But if (ll. 127, 133) the music of the nine spheres (ll. 125, 131), 'consort[ed]' with the music of the Nine Orders of Angels, could be heard by people, its power would be such that it would heal Man's sin – seen, significantly, as disease in lines 136–8 – and 'Time will run back, and fetch the age of gold'.[11]

Notice again the same sort of sleight of hand with the verbs we saw in the first stanza: the conditional clause of lines 133–4 has a subjunctive verb, but the main verb, where we might expect 'would' (implying it is *not* happening), is in the future indicative: 'will run back' implies a certainty. (That 'will' is emphatically repeated three times.) Such a certainty is consequent upon the 'fancy' [imagination] being 'enwrapt' (with a play on 'enrapture') – in other words, consequent upon the power of the mind to create a new world. For the lines are not merely saying nice things about music: their complex ambiguity hints at the power of art to reveal to men truths that cannot be expressed in other ways.

In stanza XV, Truth, Justice – Astraea – and Mercy enthroned between them are visualized as if in some baroque ceiling painting, passing through the rosy clouds and honouring the ruler whose room they decorate; and the intention is as entirely serious as such a painting would be. For this vision, hypothetical for the meanwhile, is the fruit of that music sung at the Saviour's birth. Had we ears to hear the music, we would see just such a backdrop to the Child in the manger in the stable: the whole host of heaven and the allegorical figures of Virtue disposed round Him to emphasize His importance and significance. And, indeed, when His victory over death and sin is won, it is in such glory that He promised to come again (Matt. 24.30 f.).[12]

Stanza XVI, however, dismisses this euphoric vision: three times the word 'yet' stresses that this vision of glory is still in the future. At the heart of this stanza, the relative clause almost grotesquely connects the 'Babe . . . in smiling Infancy' with the Man on the Cross 'redeem[ing]' Man. Those central lines, which superimpose in our minds the Man in agony on the smiling Babe, make a bridge between the prohibition by 'wisest Fate' of the vision of glory at the beginning of the stanza with the Last Judgement at the end, when Hell, glimpsed in defeat through the power of the enraptured mind in line 140, has to be Harrowed (l. 155).[13]

The stanza as a whole is a very strange, and very bold, superimposition of ideas: Last Judgment and Harrowing over the joy and peace of Heaven, the Man crucified over the Child in the manger, a future 'then' over a present 'now' – and finally, a positive future promise which is contained within and implied by a present negative prohibition. Moreover, for the first time in the poem, the syntactical structure is not coterminous with the stanza structure: the final weighty alexandrine, which hitherto has created a massive, summarizing close at the end of each stanza, here merely pauses before hurling us on into the first three lines of stanza XVII. The effect of this is to link the vision of the promised Last Judgment with the terrifying events on Mount Sinai when the Law by which mankind was both ruled and judged was given to Moses (Exod. 19.19–20.21). The two stanzas contract the beginning of the Old Law and the fulfilment of the New in Christ in Glory at the Last Judgment into a single moment.

The terror of line 164, when 'The dreadfull Judge in middle Air shall spread his throne', is also the moment when the 'bliss' of Heaven, 'now begin[ning]' with this birth, is complete for the elect. From this moment of the incarnation the reign of Satan begins to fail (ll. 167–72), and the poem now turns, as a natural consequence and development, to the flight of the pagan gods. The ancient legend of the cessation of the oracles (see p. 122) is elaborated in some detail to include not only the Greco-Roman deities like Apollo (ll. 176 ff.) and the Lares and Lemures (ll. 191 ff.), but also the Canaanitish gods against whose devotees the ancient Israelites had to fight, as recorded in much of the Old Testament. The 'brutish gods of Nile', too, are put to flight as Osiris 'feels from *Juda's* land / The dredded Infants hand' (ll. 221–2). The whole passage, in which the enemies of the true God are being put to panic-stricken flight, is being used to balance those stanzas before the vision of the triumph of Christ in stanzas XIII–XVI, in which nature and the angels, and finally the shepherds, welcome the birth of the Child. The peace that comes to earth there is not shared by the deities here.

Similarly, in the earlier stanzas there was a stress on truth revealed, the fulfilment of the work of time, while here there is a stress on the banishing of deceit and the false worship of idols. Within the passage (stanzas XIX–XXV) itself there is a general movement from those gods that are relatively innocent, to those that are plainly devilish and monstrous: from the Greco-Roman through the Near Eastern to the Egyptian deities, ending in the dragonish Egyptian devil, Typhon. Apollo's 'pale-ey'd priest' (l. 180) may have had some vision of the truth in his 'prophetic cell', but the priests of Osiris, represented often as the bull Apis (l. 215), are 'sable-stoled Sorcerers' (l. 220). For the not unpleasant spirits of woods and streams and trees, the nymphs of stanza XX, we can feel some pity: the pathetic glimpse of their mourning is echoed in the plangent alliteration and assonance of 'With flowre-inwoven tresses torn / The Nimphs in twilight shade of tangled thickets mourn' (ll. 187–8). But for 'sullen Moloch', with his burnt sacrifices of living children, whose cries of agony were drowned by the clashing of cymbals (stanza XXXIII), there is merely horror and disgust. The service of the Lares and Lemures is 'quaint', hardly to be taken very seriously: the worship of Dagon, of the Baalim, and of Astarte is now a waste of time. Indeed, three times (ll. 204, 208, 219) Milton stresses that such worship is 'in vain'. These gods, too, inhabit a world of dimness and half-light, which is both directly descriptive of the gloom of their temples and figurative of the half-truths (and worse) their worship contained: Apollo's trance is 'nightly', the nymphs of line 187 are in 'twilight shade', and the Lares and Lemures 'moan with midnight plaint' (l. 191); the temples of the Baalim are 'dim', Ashtaroth's image is lit by 'tapers', Moloch has 'left in shadows dread' his 'blackest' idol, and the fire under it is 'blue': Osiris's priests wear 'sable' and his eyes are 'dusky'.

This gloom is in emphatic contrast to the light that burst into the poem in stanza XI with the 'Globe of circular light'. Perhaps the most extraordinarily compressed image in the whole sequence is the way 'The rays of Bethlehem blind his dusky eyn' (l. 223): this must refer not only to the infant Christ as the Sun of Righteousness rising to dispel the gloom of paganism, and to the physical light of the star piercing the gloom of midwinter night, but also to the god Osiris outfaced by the Person of Christ. Finally, the whole passage is contained within the two mentions of the dragonish devil in lines 171 and 226: Satan, the 'old Dragon under ground' (l. 168), does not need to be directly named nor the breaking of his power stressed, for the discomfiture of his ministers in these stanzas is enough. The paradoxical power of the powerless Child, which the opening of the hymn stressed, is such that 'in his swadling bands [he can] controul the damned crew' (l. 228). He fulfils in reality the legend of the infant Hercules (commonly seen as a type or foreshadowing of Christ), who strangled twin serpents in his cradle.

Stanza XXVI is composed of a strikingly elaborate simile. Milton glances at the Classical myth of the dawn goddess, Aurora, who leaves the bed of her husband Tithonus, in making the Sun 'Pillow his chin upon an Orient wave'. Just as the darkness is dispelled, the fairies cease their dancing in the moonlight on 'the quaint mazes in the wanton green' (*Midsummer Night's Dream*, II. i. 141), and, according to the legend familar from *Hamlet*, ghosts troop back to their prison in hell below (l. 234), when the sun rises, so these pagan gods are put to flight by the Son and Heir of Heaven lying in his cradle. The light shines in the darkness, and the darkness does not overwhelm it, as St John says. The main purpose of the simile is to summarize the polar opposition of light and truth and darkness and falsehood that these preceding stanzas have described in detail; it also makes the pagan gods seem, if anything, comic: how could men have been so foolish as to take them seriously? It marks, too, a further movement in the time of the poem. Beginning in the darkness, before the appearance of the angels in dead of night to the shepherds, the hymn begins its close with the first flush of dawn. For in the last stanza, we finally see not the Heir of Heaven, or a 'dredded Infant', but the human child and his mother as the new star shines above the stable (ll. 240–1). The cosmic reverberations of the Birth which have occupied the body of the hymn here, in this first glimpse of the child as human, reach their natural climax, and there is really no more that can be said. The mother lays her child to rest as the poet lays his poem aside; the whole content of the inexpressible paradoxes of the poem is summed up in the final verbal and visual oxymoron of the 'Courtly Stable' surrounded by the 'Bright-harnest' Host of Heaven.

There are several ways in which we can analyse the structure of the hymn. The basic units of that structure are the verses, and as we read it, we might notice how the final alexandrines of each verse (with the single exception of that in stanza XVI) always close off the ideas of their stanzas. Taken with the line that precedes them, they make whole sense units, and are often marked off from the rest of the verse by a strong pause, colon or semicolon, at the end of the sixth line. They act as obvious climaxes to the ideas in their stanzas, but also seem to summarize them in a single key idea. It is not wholly to overstate it to say that these alexandrines provide a conceptual scaffolding from which the progress, verse by verse, of the hymn could be inferred.

Furthermore, on a first reading the circular movement from the 'meanly wrapt' Child in the manger of the first stanza, then to the implications of that Child, and finally back to the 'sleeping Lord' in the stable is obvious enough. There is also a clear movement through time, from the last hour of pagan darkness to the shining of the Daystar and the rising of the Son/Sun at the end. A little reflection also shows that the hymn breaks into three sections which support these two complementary structural movements: stanzas I–VIII describe the setting of the nativity, stressing darkness and silence; stanzas IX–XVII flood the hymn with light and the music of the angelic choir; and stanzas XVIII–XXVI describe the flight of the pagan gods in confused noise, disorder and darkness before the final stanza returns with an evocation of light and 'serviceable' order to an acknowledged sovereign – a return, in fact, to the 'awe' of the first stanza.

The return to the notion of royalty which has just triumphed over its opponents would perhaps have suggested to the first readers of the poem the idea of a formal triumph. Descriptions of Roman triumphs had, for much of the Renaissance, been used for the detailing and sometimes the structure of public ceremonial, and this fondness for the triumph spills over into the visual arts, drama and poetry. In Renaissance reinterpretations of Roman triumphs, one of two basic strategies could be employed. In the one case, the triumphing figure, preceded first by those who herald and celebrate his coming and then by those whom he has vanquished, appears last, suitably attired or presented; in the other, he appears at the centre of the procession, preceded by his heralds and spoils, followed by those he has overcome. What had been a public political spectacle in ancient Rome was easily adapted to Renaissance needs, and the repeated representations of it as art tell us as much about how Renaissance painters saw themselves and the ceremonial of their day as they do of what ancient Rome looked like on holiday. Mantegna's *Triumph of Caesar* at Hampton Court is an admirable example of what I mean. Moreover, the structure of the triumph converted easily into a model for the structuring of art. In Petrarch's very influential *Trionfi*, which Milton certainly knew, the formal arrangement of the parts of the individual poems, and of the poems that make up the work, is organized so that each poem has a triumphal climax, and then each poem forms part of the procession (so to speak) in the work where the final climax comes at the end. In other poems, and in most paintings, the central place is the triumphant one.

Now if we bring this idea, which was very familiar to Milton's readers, to bear on the *Nativity Ode* some interesting patterns emerge: we move very rapidly away from that first brief glimpse of the Child in the manger in ll. 30–31 to a sequence that enumerates and describes in turn the harbingers of his coming. In the centre stanzas of the hymn, XI–XVII, the Music of Heaven, the expression of the Platonic Logos, or Creating Word that Christians, following St John's hints, identified with Christ, floods the poem. But after this triumph song of Heaven, the Child, who briefly appears again in stanza XVI, is followed by the long procession of those whom he has defeated and conquered: the unwilling witnesses of his triumph. If we accept this reading of the poem as 'triumphal', not only do the structures I noticed above fall into powerfully supporting place, but also some of the imagery becomes entirely decorous: the baroque visualizations of the arrival of personified Peace (ll. 46 ff.), of the Sun treated like a character in a masque (ll. 80 f.), and of Truth, Justice and Mercy (ll. 141 ff.) fit exactly with our visual expectations of triumphal pageantry. And, finally, the hymn is, after all, an act of homage to the King of Kings, and what more appropriate skeletal structure might it have than that of the triumph that, in celebrating earthly potentates, pointed men's minds beyond the man to the immortal royalty he represented?[14]

But there must be more to it than this, for analysis on such simple lines ignores completely any structural relationship of the hymn to the induction, in which we were primed to listen to the hymn in a peculiarly alert way as something 'holy', as a gift comparable to the acknowledgement of Christ's royalty by the Wise Men. The hymn is ostensibly a poem written about the coming of the Light in the darkness before the dawn, yet, taken with the four-stanza prelude, the whole is written in full knowledge of the events that flowed from that Nativity. We must expect therefore to find what we might call structural irony in the whole poem, where the self-contained structure of the hymn and its implications form part of a further independent structure based on all 31 stanzas of the whole.

I have outlined above (p. 14) how Renaissance readers expected to work hard with a text, using techniques that we would find not in the least poetic to look for subtle clues to the labyrinth of the necessarily inexact words of the poem. One such is, of course, looking at centres as we have just done. If we apply this here, the results are startling: the central stanza of the hymn, XIV, is a celebration of the power of music and poetry (a subset of the music of heaven as Milton says in *At a Solemn Music*) so to possess human sense that the ills of the world will be cured and earth be made like heaven. The central two lines of that verse, 'And speckl'd vanity / Will sicken soon and die', suggest not only a plague dying of its own disease, but also the banishment of sin itself (cf. *At a Solemn Music*, ll. 17 ff.). Within the hymn, therefore, which is defined in lines 27–8 as the joining of the poet's voice to the angelic choir that sang the Nativity, the triumph seems to be that of the harmony of the universe that man's fall disrupted. But when we look closer, this magnificent vision, expressed in the certainty of verbs in the indicative mood, is nevertheless qualified by the conditional clause with which the verse begins: 'For *if* [my italics] such holy song . . .' It is exactly the same paradoxical mixture of conditionality and certainty that provides the structural tension in *At a Solemn Music*. The hymn, therefore, both asserts its own power and the limitation man has to receive that power. Here there is a paradoxical statement of both the triumph and the failure of art, and thus of the poem.

Putting the hymn back into the whole poem suggests an equally intriguing idea. Stanza XII is now the centre: the centre lines of the whole poem look back to the act of Creation itself, God's Art, making the original Age of Gold which the Fall ruined. Thus man's art, exemplified in the hymn, art which allows glimpses only of perfection, is linked to, contrasted with, its source in God's Art. Stanzas XII–XVI, further, straddle the centre of the hymn in an interesting symmetrical structure: they start with Creation, and end with God's intervention in the act of the New Creation, where God becomes Man and manhood is taken up into Godhead (XVI). This Creation will end, in Judgment (XVI): works, even works of art of divine origin, must be redeemed by the Sacrifice on Calvary, glimpsed in XVI.

Renaissance readers were also perfectly prepared to look for the symbolic meaning that might be conveyed by number (see p. 13). It was after all common ground that God had created the world by 'number proportion and weight': Andrew Marvell wittily suggests in his lines 'On Paradise Lost' that Milton, like God, has done the same in *Paradise Lost*. One of the advantages of this number symbolism to a poet was that he could limit the ambiguity (or increase it!) of the necessarily inexact words he used, whereby no single word will mean exactly the same thing to any two people, by casting over his poem a net of numbers. The meaning of the numbers, which could be more exact than that conveyed in the continuum of a verbal sentence, could confirm, or undercut, the signals of the verbal text – and even introduce ideas that were not openly stated. A poem dealing with the literally inexpressible, as this one is, is exactly the place where one might expect to find this symbolism used.

The hymn has 27 stanzas. This can hardly be an accident, for 27 is literally a number to conjure with. For the Neoplatonics, the number 27, the cube of the number 3 that symbolizes the Trinity, is the number of the World-Soul, or Entelechy, identified with Christ.[15]

It is precisely the Incarnation of the Word that is the occasion, and subject, of these 27 stanzas. Alone, this might be mere, if unlikely, coincidence, but there are many other examples. For instance, 16 is the foursquare number associated with justice and judgment. It is in the 16th stanza that the redemption and the Last Judgment that it necessarily implies are both first mentioned. And this stanza, uniquely, as if to mark out its importance, does not stop with its final alexandrine but carries straight on into the stanza that refers us to the giving of the first Law and the First Covenant with Israel on Sinai. It is here that the judgment of the blessed to bliss and the casting out of the old gods begins. Again, the number 10, being the sum of the first four numbers and itself a return to unity (since zero is not a number), had special meaning for the Pythagoreans and Neoplatonics as a symbol at once of unity and perfection: in the tenth stanza of the hymn Nature knows that 'such harmony alone / Could hold all Heav'n and Earth in happier union'. That music is first heard in the ninth stanza, and there were supposed to be nine spheres that made the inaudible harmony, 'still quiring to the young-eyed cherubim'. The next number after 10 usually symbolizes a new beginning, which is exactly what we get in the vision of the shepherds in the 11th stanza.

The details can be much extended. When we know that the number 7 was often used to symbolize man, who was supposed to be composed of three souls – vegetable, sensible and rational – and the four elements of earth, air, fire and water, the choice of the seven-line stanza for the four opening stanzas becomes significant. Here we have human art, faced with the subject to end all subjects, invoking divine aid for the task of writing, and doing it in stanzas that symbolize the marriage of matter and spirit in man. There are four stanzas: and the number 4 frequently symbolizes the perfection of Art as distinguished from the perfection of Nature. In the Revelation of St John the Divine, the New Jerusalem, the perfect city, has four sides. Furthermore, the 28 lines of the poem's induction amount to the second 'perfect' number. (The first is 6. A perfect number is one equalling the sum of all its divisors.) The hymn, seriously claimed to be inspired, that follows is in eight-line stanzas; 8, as the eight-sided fonts in many churches symbolize, is the number symbolizing rebirth – wholly appropriate to this poem's theme and its consequences for its reader. One might even add that 12, the number of the tribes of Israel and of the Apostles, was frequently used to symbolize the New Jerusalem: it is peculiarly appropriate that every verse ends with a 12-syllabled alexandrine.[16]

As a last example, the total number of stanzas in the whole poem is 31. The orbit of Saturn, the outermost of the then known planets, was taken to be 30 years, and so in the 31st year the cycle of Saturn begins again: a new beginning, but also, with the return of Saturn to his first position in the heavens, a return of the Age of Gold, Saturn's age, for which, in stanza XIV of the hymn, time will run back.

Modern people tend to shake their heads in irritation and disbelief at all this, just as they do about seventeenth-century poems whose lines form shapes and patterns. But we have to accept the fact that our forefathers said they used number, shape and pattern in this way as an adjunct of meaning, and so we cannot ignore it in our reading of their work. It seems to me that the number symbolism actually adds something valuable to this poem. It sets up a parallel discourse to that of the words, almost as a sort of harmony to their melody: the hymn about Christ is also a hymn about judgment and new birth; but it is a hymn, however inspired, framed by the limitations of human art, and ultimately inferior to prayer. The whole poem turns on one central idea, which is the open theme of the first four verses and the basis of how we look critically at the hymn: how can man properly respond to the Incarnation? The numbers suggest that he seek the perfection of art knowing that in the end that will not be enough, for a new beginning through the gift of grace is all that will admit him to the new age of Gold.

The *Nativity Ode* has always had its detractors. Even those who admire it often classify it as 'early', almost implying that it is immature. I still find my reactions to it mixed. But I think we have to recognize that Milton could never have wanted this poem to be approached purely as a poem. It is self-declaredly moving through the art of poetry to an act of worship, and ultimately it is as an act of worship that it must stand or fall. In a real sense, this is not a self-justifying poem that stands or falls on its own internal dynamic, but is as much applied art as a design on a cereal packet. That is one of the things that makes it so very difficult to digest for, in the end, it points us beyond itself.

The Psalm Paraphrases

The *Nativity Ode* is a hymn of man's deliverance, through the act of

God, from the bondage of sin. In *Poems* (1645) it is followed by two paraphrases of psalms that celebrate Israel's deliverance from the Egyptian captivity and God's support of them in their journey to the Promised Land: these events were traditionally seen as prefiguring Christ's freeing men from the bondage of sin and His extending to us the hope of Heaven. It can hardly be accidental that they are placed where they are: they are a natural continuation of the devotional theme of liberation in the *Nativity Ode*.

Many serious and devout poets tried their hand at translating some or all of the psalms – Sir Thomas Wyatt, way back in Henry VIII's time, for example, or later Sir Philip Sidney and his sister. Milton's versions do not have a great deal of poetic interest for us, though his Psalm 136 has found a regular place in English and Scottish hymnals in an altered and shortened version. (Indeed, the metrical versions of the psalms are ideal for musical setting, and until the end of the eighteenth century, they were the only congregationally sung material allowed in Anglican churches.) In his poem *Upon the translation of the Psalmes by Sir Philip Sydney and his sister the Countess of Pembroke*, John Donne puts his finger on the devotional and poetic problem posed by this activity: how to 'the highest matter in the noblest forme'. For, if the Reformed Church really did see itself as the People of God, analogous to the Chosen People of Israel, Israel's psalms were not just part of a heritage but were a vital part of the Reformed Church's understanding of itself and God's relationship to it.

So Milton's publishing these two psalms here cannot be seen as just a courting of admiration for his skill, but must be seen as one more assertion of his understanding of poetry as a high and holy art, an art justified by criteria that are ultimately not poetic, and one intimately connected with the life of the nation. Here is 'the highest matter'; here is what a 15-year old boy could manage as 'the noblest form' – and while the son translated, the father was responsible for many of the four-part settings in Thomas Ravenscroft's *The Whole Book of Psalms* (1621). For these two psalms were done when he was very young, as *Poems* (1645) tells us – he might even be apologizing for them, for they are, patently, not terribly good; but in 1645 the movement of events has made them acquire the topicality of a battle cry. They are an integral part of that section of devotional poems that begins *Poems* (1645), not only staking out a claim for Milton as a serious sacred poet – which he did anyway in the introductory stanzas to the *Nativity Ode* – but also reminding a beleaguered New Israel of the promise extended to it.

The Passion

Milton knew *The Passion* was a failure: 'This Subject the Author finding to be aboue the yeers he had, when he wrote it, and nothing satisfi'd with what was begun, left it unfinish't.' Yet he still published it, an act only explicable if we take the view that *Poems* (1645) is both an extremely confident poetic autobiography and a deliberate demonstration of the poet's range.

It is just conceivable that at some point Milton might have intended a sequence of religious or devotional poems on the great festivals of the Church's year. *The Nativity Ode, The Circumcision* and *The Passion* would fit such a plan; but against this there is the fact that *The Circumcision* is probably to be dated to January 1632/33, whereas *The Passion* was written only some three months after the *Nativity Ode*, and clearly looks back to the writing of that poem (ll. 1–7).[17]

It could be that the *Nativity Ode* gave Milton the confidence to tackle the subject of the Passion, either as a devotional exercise for late Lent or as simply the sort of occasional poem a religious poet ought to be able to write. There is clearly a preparation, in the appeal for inspiration (stanzas V–VI), for an attempt to 'realize' the Gospel narrative of the passion in terms as vivid as if the reader were present at it – the sort of focusing of the mind that the discipline of meditation, practised by Catholics and Anglicans in surprising numbers, depended on. But Urania did not deliver the goods here.

The verse form of the unfinished poem is that of the first four stanzas of the *Nativity Ode*, but with that form any comparison stops. The crackle and excitement of the *Nativity Ode*'s verse is quite absent. The movement of the verse is wooden and ponderous in its metrical regularity and encrusting of virtually every noun with an adjective. The rhymes merely chime, rather than enhance and point the movement of the thought. The 'I' of the poem is hopelessly stagey, even sentimental: his hands are 'feeble', his verse 'plaining', his fancy 'flattered'; he is 'tuning his song', 'setting his harp' – and the final preposterous image is mind-boggling: 'th' infection of my sorrows loud / Had got a race of mourners on som pregnant cloud'. Reference to the myth of Ixion's begetting of the Centaurs on a cloud does not help that last line at all. The problem is, I think, that the choice of mode and register is quite wrong: the poem is far too self-conscious and its imagery is visually incoherent; the last stanza particularly shows not only a mis-handling of pastoral setting but also the inappropriateness of choosing that setting in the first place.

There is little good one can say about the poem. Yet it is not without one area of interest: here Milton is attempting for the first time in

English something like a grand and 'heroic' style, and through the shadows of the failure one can begin to guess at the richness of the unrhymed, weighty verse of *Paradise Lost*. It might even be that the failure to deal with a subject of such cosmic importance in stanzaic form encouraged Milton in his growing conviction of the suitability of blank verse for matters of high seriousness. It is, after all, entirely appropriate that the poem for the Nativity should look and sound like a song, for it is joined to the angelic music that celebrated that birth; but it is difficult to see how *any* song-like form could properly do justice to the topic of the Passion.

The Circumcision

The Circumcision, the occasion of the first shedding of the blood of the infant Christ, is traditionally a foreshadowing of the great sacrifice on Calvary. The poem is a very small-scale canzone: Milton makes no attempt at multiple extended repetition of the complex stanza form that was usual: he contents himself with giving the two verses he does write a reciprocating relationship. The first 14 lines focus the mind on the first suffering of the Christ Child; the second 14 lines widen out to consider the significance of that event, the justice and love for sinful men it shows as part of the divine nature. To my mind, it is a far more successful poem than *The Passion* – perhaps because it is much less ambitious in tone and less portentous in the way it introduces itself. Its two-stanza structure fits its argument very neatly, and the climax of each complex verse in the utter simplicity of its last three short lines of meditation, first on the pitifulness of the pain the child suffers, and then on the agony of the man, is very powerful.

Each verse of the poem is built of seven lines of ten syllables, then two of seven or six, then two of ten, and a final three lines of (in the first half) five, four and six syllables, and (in the second) six, four and five. The rhyme scheme of each 14-line stanza – a b c b a c c d d c e f f e – (which resembles closely Petrarch's canzone, 'Vergine bella', to the Blessed Virgin), with the closer rhymes towards the end, becomes stronger and more noticeable as the line lengths, mirroring the pain of the event, become shorter and more irregular. The form supports very well what is, in effect, a disciplined little meditation on the event, the 'composition' occupying the first half, where we consider the pathos of the human pain, and the response to that 'composition' occupying the second half.

On Time

On Time, like *At a Solemn Music*, is in the less demanding form of the madrigal – a single, unrepeated, canzone-type stanza. One manuscript heads it, '. . . set on a clock-case', but this has been deleted and 'On Time' substituted as a title. Attempts to explain the highly irregular line-length pattern by seeing the poem as one of the fashionable 'shape' poems, like George Herbert's *The Altar* and *Easter Wings,* do not really work – the only clock case of a shape this might fit would be one of those hideously curvilinear, rococo bracket clocks that were still at least a century in the future. The 22 mainly couplet-rhymed lines[18] are more important sonically than visually: the regular pulse of the initial five decasyllabics echoes the tick-tock of the clock, and this pattern is then, progressively, more confidently disrupted as the attention turns away from the appetite of greedy Time (a cliché as old as Ovid) to the vision of the bliss of Eternity, closing in the final triumphant Alexandrine where Time is defeated. The central lines of the poem are occupied by the vision of eternity and the assertion of personal immortality, marked by an 'individual kiss'.[19] It would be perfectly possible to design an allegorical painting of the Triumph of the Risen Soul from the last ten lines: the vision of Heaven is once again full of the same baroque personifications – Joy, Truth, Peace, Love – that populated Milton's visual imagination in the *Nativity Ode*. They cluster round the throne of God, the souls sit in triumph 'attired with stars' – an echo of the Book of Revelation – while beneath their feet are the defeated personifications of Time, Chance and Death – all utterly commonplace personifications in the visual arts of the period.

No-one could claim this to be a great poem. It is a good one, but is not in the same league as Donne's sonnet 'Death bee not proude'. It has more than a little interest, however, for the way it looks back to the visual manner of the *Nativity Ode*, and parallels the sort of vision of eternal bliss the Attendant Spirit describes at the end of *Comus*.

At a Solemn Music

Though at Cambridge one of Milton's academic exercises had been on *De Sphaerarum Concentu*, the Platonic myth expounded in the *Timaeus* and the end of *The Republic* of the sirens of the stars, there is no clue about the occasion of this poem – if indeed there was one. It dates probably from about 1633, close to the dates of *Arcades* and *Comus*, and the ideas about music that we have seen to underlie the central section of the *Nativity Ode* are here stated much more fully; they also relate very closely to the understanding of music in *Comus*.

The poem is itself in what can often be a rather lightweight musical form, the madrigal, and it could very easily have been set to music. But by the use of a large number of decasyllabic lines (over half) Milton has given it a weight and dignity that indicate the seriousness of his subject. The complex, extended sentence-structure and the elevated language point forward to the grand manner of *Paradise Lost*. It is built of just two sentences: first, the injunction to the 'Blest pair of *Sirens*' in ll. 3–5 is hugely elaborated by enriching and qualifying subordinate clauses until we reach the big pause at the end of line 16, before the point of this musical extravaganza is described in the purpose clause that follows. Then the second sentence, governed by the optative subjunctive verb 'may we renew' brings the poem to a close in a prayer that man's faltering voice may soon take part in this celestial harmony. The elaborate structure of this first grand sentence, piling idea on idea and seeking to reach Heaven, seems to be a deliberate attempt to mirror in words the development of a musical theme, while the much quieter, more plangent tone of the second hints at the awestruck reaction to what has just been glimpsed.

It is not surprising that when, in 1741, Newburgh Hamilton was preparing a libretto for Handel's *Samson* and needed a grand climax for the oratorio he drew not only on *Samson Agonistes* for the main plot, but also on *At a Solemn Music* for the elaborately magnificent final air, 'Let the Bright Seraphim', and the chorus, 'Let their celestial Concerts all unite'. In Milton's poem, 'Voice and Verse' do 'wed [their] divine sounds . . . and to our high-rais'd phantasie present / That undisturbèd Song of pure concent.' The poem is 'about' music, but it must also be considered a serious devotional poem. It is, in fact, difficult to distinguish the two in Milton's case. Even if one were tempted to dismiss the extreme position stated in *At a Solemn Music* as resulting from an occasion or a commission, one could not ignore Milton's remarks in *Ad Patrem* ll. 21 ff., when he speaks with urgent sincerity to his own father through the mythological discourse they both understood:

> Carmen amant superi, tremebunda Tartara carmen
> Ima ciere valet, divosque ligare profundos,
> Et triplici duros Manes adamante coercet.

('The gods love poetry and song: it has the power to call up the fearful, frightful deeps of Tartarus, to bind the gods of the underworld, and to control with threefold adamant the unforgiving Shades of the dead.')

Milton's view of music, in this poem as elsewhere, had solid Neoplatonic foundations. In Plato's *Republic*, 616–17, which Milton paraphrases in *Arcades* lines, 63 ff., Necessity has a distaff on which are threaded the eight concentric whorls of the universe. On the rim of each stands a siren who utters everlastingly a single note, these notes together producing a harmony. This harmony, according to the Pythagorean idea behind Plato, was audible only to men of pure heart: Milton explains this in the *Second Prolusion.*[20] This *musica mundana* harmonized with the music, equally inaudible to sinful, mortal men, of the angels around the throne of God. (Milton in line 64 of *Arcades* makes Plato's eight spheres nine, following Dante – *Paradiso*, XXVIII. 25–78 – who relates the nine spheres to the Nine Orders of Angels.) It is the glimpse of that song sung by the two highest of the Nine Orders, the Cherubim and the Seraphim, that the 'blest pair of Sirens, Voice and Verse' gives to human 'phantasie' – the faculty we might call imagination, intermediate between human sense and reason (cf. *Paradise Lost*, V. 100–13). The idea that music could produce such ecstasy as to separate soul and body was common – indeed, the Academies of Poetry and Music of the sixteenth century (see p. 63) depended on just this idea, which descends from such Fathers of the Church as SS. Basil and John Chrysostom, and from the Neoplatonists Iamblichus, Porphyry and Plotinus.

But, according to Renaissance Neoplatonists, the *musica humana*, the music of men, does not harmonize with that of heaven: it marks a break in Creation caused by the Fall. None the less, even human music and art is a 'pledge [or assurance] of Heav'ns joy' (l. 1) since it reminds men of the divine music. Thus the sounds that Voice and Verse, the 'Sirens' carried in this earthly sphere, can make are 'divine' in some sense; and when taken to its height, as in the case of Orpheus, such mortal music can fill 'dead things' like trees, or rocks or streams with 'inbreath'd sense' – an idea that Milton returns to in *Lycidas*. Milton's choice of the word 'inbreath'd' is important: it means 'inspired', but alludes fleetingly to the way God made man of the dust of the ground and 'breathed into his nostrils the breath of life' (Gen. 2.7) – the ultimate act of creation.

The enlivening illusion of music and poetry, Milton continues, can present to the mind properly prepared (or 'high-rais'd') for it the vision of the bliss of heaven that expresses itself in perfectly harmonious music: the same idea captivates the Penseroso. In lines 7–16 Ezekiel's vision of the Lord on his sapphire throne (1.26) is fused with St John's vision of the musical concert of the redeemed singing with the angels in Revelation 14.3–4. The peculiar joy of the angels around the throne of God lies in music: this is why angels are so often represented in art with instruments of various kinds. (The medieval Angel Gallery in Exeter Cathedral has its angels playing a virtually complete collection of available musical instruments.) This song that man glimpses through art is 'everlasting' (l. 16), as his art is not; but through that glimpse man may learn how 'rightly [to] answer' with 'undiscording voice' the song of Heaven. That man's fall, and the discord ('disproportion') of sin broke the harmony of the universe and affected all those parts of creation below him in the Ladder of Being is a cliché (ll. 19–21); but Milton's suggestion that that damage might be repaired by art and music, a suggestion which is the clear implication of his first sentence and of his wish in the second sentence, is not a conventional one. It is a bold statement that salvation is not an act wholly of grace[21] but of grace consequent upon works of art – an interesting contrast with what seems to be his position in the *Nativity Ode*. The restoration of the 'perfect Diapason' – the word means both the concord of the octave and, as Robert Burton puts it in *The Anatomy of Melancholy*, 'a true correspondence, perfect amity' – is to be partly the result of man's glimpsing through art the music and the Creating Word of Heaven, of his tuning his own string to harmonious pitch.

The theological ideas that grow out of this rhapsody on the power of music and poetry seem to have been thought out with some seriousness. Milton's view, like those of many Platonists, of the culture and wisdom of the past was that the sages of Greece, Rome and Egypt had had some substantial notions of the truth, and that those notions were fulfilled in the Christian revelation (see p. 69). It is on this position that the medieval and Renaissance respect for Plato and Pythagoras, for Orpheus and Aristotle, depended. *At a Solemn Music*, a poem about harmony, is also an attempt to bring into the unity of the poem the separate but related visions of God given to the pagans, the Jews and the Christians. For, in the first five or six lines of the poem, the terminology and references send us to Plato, to Pythagoras and to the myth of Orpheus – to the wisdom of the ancients, in fact. Next, but still in the same sentence, the Jewish angelology is directly referred to, as well as the great visions of Isaiah and Ezekiel of the Ancient of Days on his sapphire throne. Finally, from line 14 the Christian hope of glorious resurrection, building on the vision of St John, completes the sentence. The three great families of theological insight are here kept distinct, yet are unified into a single sentence cast in the form of what is ultimately prayer. This triad of reference points is ultimately unified, syntactically, into a trinity: and the consequence of that sentence is the prayer for the healing of the discord of the world. Moreover, the three follow each other in the sentence as they were thought to do in point of time: the poem brings together in its 28 lines – a perfect number (see p. 113) – all human times in a single artistic instant.

At a Solemn Music is crucial to our understanding of how much importance the younger Milton attached to music and its sister art of poetry. There is no pulling of punches here, just a plain and very powerful statement of the supreme moral importance he attached to both. *The Ode on the Morning of Christ's Nativity*, which is both poetry and music in itself, and also a poem about the song the angels sang which at last broke for sinful men the silence of heaven, is a paradigm of exactly that music and verse *At a Solemn Music* discusses. The 'unexpressive nuptial song' *Lycidas* eventually hears is that glimpsed in this poem. And we may be sure that Henry Lawes, attired as the Attendant Spirit in *Comus*, would have agreed that such strains might create a soul under the ribs of death.

Notes to Chapter 5

1. E.g. (in English) The Jesuit Robert Southwell's *The Burning Babe* (which shows how much common devotional ground there is between Catholic and Protestant), Henry Vaughan's *Christ's Nativity*, Richard Crashaw's *In the Holy Nativity of Our Lord God*, Robert Herrick's *An Ode of the Birth of Our Saviour*, and Thomas Traherne's *On Christmas Day*. The subject is a common one in Neo-Latin as well as in the other vernaculars of Europe.

2. See C. A. Patrides, *Premises and Motifs in Renaissance Thought and Literature* (Princeton, 1982), Chapter 7. There was a tradition, going back to Plutarch, that at the time of Christ's birth all the oracles of the pagan gods fell silent. Milton might well have used in this poem a passage in Prudentius' *Apotheosis* (ll. 402–502), or in Mantuan's *Parthenicae* (III. i) which draws on Prudentius' poem. The silence of Apollo's priest at Delphi, the fear of the god as he leaves his shrine, the interruption of the heathen sacrifice, and the departure of the lamenting gods are all there.

3. The subject was one many humanists, Catholic or Protestant, discussed. It clearly relates to the understanding of Classical religion as a foreshadowing of Christian truth – as, for example, in Boccaccio's *De Genealogia Deorum* – and was lectured upon at Cambridge during Milton's residence by Joseph Mead, the lecturer in Greek. Stanzas XVI–XXV are an interesting stage on the road to Milton's view of the pagan gods as devils in *Paradise Lost*, I. 392–540.

4. Milton is not, I think, thinking of Christmas as merely an anniversary, but as an event that takes place both in and out of time. If God's existence is eternal, then (as Boethius pointed out in the *Consolation of Philosophy*, V), all times are present with Him in an eternal Now. If Christ was God Incarnate, then He experienced time both sequentially as a Man and instantaneously as God: so the Incarnation and the Crucifixion are literally happening 'now'.

5. 'The spangled host' is the stars shining symbolically in the darkness – cf. *Comus*, p. 189 – but also the angels, whom Spenser, too, draws up in 'bright Squadrons' *Faerie Queene*, II. viii. 2).

6. Isaiah, Ezekiel, Daniel and Jeremiah. The recognition of the work of three authors in the Book of Isaiah is much later than Milton's time.

7. It is a common enough idea, in Milton's as in other times, that man, who ought to know better, ignores the evidence of God that the world he inhabits so amply shows.

8. Their surprise is not insignificant: the unpredictability of God's coming is

axiomatic – 'The day of the Lord cometh as a thief in the night' (1 Thess. 5.2, 2 Peter 3.10; cf. Acts 1.7). Pan, according to E.K.'s gloss to Maye in Spenser's *Shepheardes Calendar*, is 'the greate and good shepherd . . . Pan signifieth all, or omnipotent, which is onely the Lord Jesus'.

9. Its full force depends on recognizing that 'unexpressive' is used, as in line 176 of *Lycidas*, in the sense of 'inexpressible, and that 'surrounds' and 'globe' are used in their Latin senses: 'overwhelmed (with water)' and 'troop' (cf. *Paradise Lost*, IV. 581).

10. Cf. 'The people that walked in darkness have seen a great light' (Isaiah 9.2).

11. Milton here is remembering not only the biblical Paradise, but also the Golden Age described by Hesiod and Ovid, and anticipated in Vergil's *Eclogue IV*. *Eclogue IV*, which, in fact, celebrates the promise of the young Marcellus, heir of Augustus, claiming that with him the golden rule of Saturn will return and the virgin goddess of justice, Astraea, will return to the earth, was often interpreted during the Middle Ages and Renaissance as a prophecy of the Virgin Birth and the coming of Christ. (Milton uses the myth of the departure of Astraea elsewhere: *Elegy IV*, l. 81.)

12. Readers who are familiar with, for example, Rubens's painting on the ceiling of the Banqueting House in Whitehall or Mantegna's ceiling paintings in the palace at Mantua will easily grasp my point that the scene represented with all the resources of illusion and art has as its focus, as its completion, the human figure of the potentate below it, who – like James I in state at Whitehall – not only becomes a mobile part of the static design but also has his regal nature expressed by it.

The basic ideas, as distinct from their treatment, in this passage probably depend on the beautiful lines of Psalm 85.10: 'Mercy and truth are met together, righteousness and peace have kissed each other.' Psalm 85 was often interpreted as an allegory of the effects of the Atonement.

13. The tradition of the Harrowing of Hell, when Christ during the three days in the sepulchre descended there, destroyed its power, and released those imprisoned unjustly, begins with the apocryphal Gospel of Nicodemus. It was a favourite subject for religious paintings in the Middle Ages, and figures as one of the episodes in the Mystery Play cycles.

14. This is the idea of 'The King's two Bodies', the one the fallible mortal man, the other the immortal kingliness of which he was the temporary embodiment: see my *Shakespeares's History Plays*, pp. 59 ff.; see also E. R. Kantorowicz, *The King's Two Bodies: A Study in Mediaeval Political Theology* (Princeton, 1957); and M. Axton, *The Queen's Two Bodies: Drama and the Elizabethan Succession* (Royal Historical Society, London, 1977).

15. The reasons for this are far too complex to go into here. Those interested might look at the texts I refer to on p. 19.

16. The number of the Blessed in the New Jerusalem is given in Revelation as 144 000, which factorizes as (12×12) $(10 \times 10 \times 10)$.

17. Such sequences do exist; for example, a sequence of sonnets, *La Corona*, by John Donne, whose sermons, at least, Milton must have known when he was a boy at St Paul's School. Donne's sequence runs 'Annunciation', 'Nativitie', 'Temple', 'Crucifying', 'Resurrection', 'Ascension'. There are traces of a similar structural scaffolding in George Herbert's far more complex *The Temple*.

18. What in most modern editions appear as the last two lines are printed as

an alexandrine in *Poems* (1645).

19. 'Individual' (l. 12) usually means 'unable to be separated' – that would mean the kiss is everlasting. But in *De Doctrina Christiana*, I. 33, Milton argues that each man will have in Heaven the same identity as he had in life, and that seems to be the meaning here.

20. Cf. *Comus*, ll. 1020–1; *Ad Patrem*, ll. 33–4; Shakespeare, *Merchant of Venice*, v. i. 60–87: like Shakespeare's Lorenzo, Milton says we cannot hear it unless 'our hearts should grow to snowy purity'.

21. The orthodox Calvinist and Lutheran position declares, in the famous phrase, that 'even the robes of righteousness are to be counted as filthy rags': man even at his best is utterly sinful, and Heaven cannot be won by works.

6 'Deluding Joys': The Double Vision of *L'Allegro* and *Il Penseroso*

With the possible exception of one or two of the sonnets, *L'Allegro* and *Il Penseroso* have long been the best known of Milton's poems. There is hardly a conventional *Anthology of English Verse* which does not include one or both. There is no doubt they established this position in the canon firstly because of what were perceived to be extraordinary merits, and secondly because they gave great pleasure – as they still do. Here is the comment of Dr Johnson, for example, in his *Life of Milton*: 'Opinion is uniform; every man that reads them reads them with pleasure . . . they are two noble efforts of imagination.' Such repeated exposure, however, has had the paradoxical effect, for a large number of readers, of making them seem 'easy' poems: most of us read them when young, and then go on to something that appears more meaty, like *Lycidas* or, ultimately, *Paradise Lost*. I think the two poems deserve better than this: they are not only written with a felicity of expression and acuteness of vision remarkable in themselves, but they also raise issues of great interest about the nature and operation of the poetic mind and its moral function. They should occupy an important place in any study of Milton's developing idea of his own poetic vocation; and, like all good poetry, they present a challenge to our own assumptions, ultimately escaping the nets in which criticism attempts to contain them.

Most people date the poems to the last year or two of Milton's time at Cambridge, though there have been attempts to link them to his residence at Horton. The year 1631 or 1632 seems the most probable date – the period when Milton had been greatly affected by the reading of Plato and was beginning that course of intensive reading in authors ancient and modern the thought of which makes even his critics wilt. A common academic exercise, with deep roots in the Middle Ages, in the universities was the setting of topics for discussion and dispute –

such as are represented by Milton's *First* and *Seventh Prolusions* (respectively, 'Whether Day or Night is more excellent' and 'Learning makes men happier than does Ignorance'). These subjects were often highly artificial, their chief purpose being to develop dialectical skills in the presentation of a case and the marshalling of evidence in an argument. (That did not preclude their often being the occasion for a good deal of wit and humour.)

There is a clear connection between this practice and the companion poems *L'Allegro* ('The Happy Man') and *Il Penseroso* ('The Thoughtful or Melancholy Man'), in which each poem states the extreme case and dismisses the alternative; some critics, indeed, have seen them as parodies of hackneyed themes in undergraduate courses, and their contrasted introductory exorcisms do remind us a little of the certainly comic mythological description of the den of murder (the Vatican!) in lines 139 ff. of *In Quintum Novembris*. Yet to see them too myopically in this way would be to ignore the importance of the established convention in Renaissance art and poetry of the 'paired' or, to borrow a term from painting, 'diptychal' set of paintings or poems, in which each side is complete in itself, but the meaning of the whole is contained in neither alone, but in the dynamic contrast between them. Such dialectical opposition was a common technique of Renaissance philosophical and moral thought as it had been of medieval. In a much-used subject for emblem pictures, for example, Hercules is shown standing between two women, one of whom, by a series of visual clues, is to be seen as offering him Pleasure, the other, Virtue. The picture represents his moment of choice between equally balanced claims, and part of the legend of Hercules, found first in Xenophon's *Cyropaedia*, concerns how he found a way to reconcile two things mutually so strongly opposed.[1] In Renaissance drama we are becoming more accustomed to recognizing the importance of scenes being constructed in detailed structural parallel to each other in order to explore a contrast, and the same holds good for poetry. Andrew Marvell uses just this technique in *A Dialogue between Soul and Body* and *A Dialogue between The Resolved Soul and Created Pleasure*. The irony in the first of those poems is that since man to be man is both soul *and* body, neither of the extreme positions stated can be right: the reader sees much more of the game than the passionate speeches openly reveal.

So, too, with Milton. Neither *L'Allegro* nor *Il Penseroso* 'wins' the argument outright, for each is put in an ironic light by the other, and each begins as a rejection of a *perversion* of the other's theme. Milton's audience, used to the form, would expect to have to work fairly hard to get at Milton's real area of interest, and, of course, they would themselves be drawn into the dispute: part of the meaning of such paired poems lies in how the reader is made to react and in what he brings to their reading. It therefore makes excellent sense to see *L'Allegro* and *Il Penseroso* not as two poems but as one, the ultimate area of discussion lying between the two statements. Indeed, so extreme are the statements here that neither can be wholly right, since each excludes an element essential to the balanced temperament (see p. 140); the ideal temperament lies in something like the Aristotelian Golden Mean, 'Nothing in excess', in a balanced self-knowledge, and the arguments of each half should be examined for the lines of convergence underneath their apparent detailed contrast. Nevertheless, *Il Penseroso* is the longer by 24 lines, and, it being the second of the two as well, this might perhaps suggest where Milton's personal bias lies. *Il Penseroso* also rises to an intensity of religious expression that is not paralleled in *L'Allegro* – itself a significant oddity, since the structural organization and formal argumentation of each poem almost exactly overlap those of the other except for this one section.

It might be as well at this point briefly to outline just how exact this 'diptychal structure' of the two poems is. The first ten lines of each aggressively banish the parodic version of the other's dominant humour: the form in both cases is an alternating pattern of six- and ten-syllabled lines (with some feminine endings), rhyming a b b a c d d c e e c – a pattern which in line-length echoes the Italian canzone, and in rhyme the sonnet. At line 11, the form then changes to what are basically iambic octosyllabic couplets, but with frequent trochaic heptasyllabic lines – twice as many in *L'Allegro* as in *Il Penseroso*, as befits the much lighter movement of the verse in the first poem.

The main body of the poems begins with a welcome to the respective goddess, and a description of her ancestry (*L'Allegro*, ll. 11–24; *Il Penseroso*, ll. 11–30). Milton continues with a repetition of the invitation for her to be present (*L'Allegro*, l. 25; *Il Penseroso*, l. 30), and then gives a list of her companions (*L'Allegro*, ll. 35 ff.; *Il Penseroso*, ll. 45 ff.). What happens next is best set out in tabular form, as shown overleaf.

Here (l. 109) Penseroso (so I shall call the speaker in the poem) enlarges on the private reading and study by which he will seek wisdom. Retirement is a prelude to contemplation, which, in turn, leads to worship whose end is the Beatific Vision of God glimpsed in the act of worship (ll. 160 ff.); the man so touched (with the hallowed fire of the *Nativity Ode?*) will have true wisdom and the capacity to write in the 'Prophetic strain'. Both begin their welcome to their respective patron goddesses with a reference to Heaven and saintliness; Allegro seems to be seeking the delights of the refined sense, and ultimately the power to free and heal that was nearly won by Orpheus, while Penseroso is

L'Allegro	*Il Penseroso*
l. 40: The lark and day	l. 56: The nightingale and night
l. 60: Sun rises; day and its activities	l. 59: Moon rises; night, evening and quiet
l. 69: Vision of the landscape by day	l. 66: Vision of night scenes
l. 83: Inside the cottage (day-evening)	l. 77: Inside the room at night
l. 105: Country spirits like Puck	l. 90: Spirits and daemons
l. 131: Comedy performed	l. 97: Tragedy read
l. 137: Poetry and music that relaxes and heals: wish for Orphic power	l. 104: Poetry that exalts and redeems; wish for Orphic power

seeking knowledge and wisdom and the power to understand and communicate 'things unattempted yet in Prose or Rhyme' (*Paradise Lost*, I. 16).

Clearly, we are presented with a very evenly balanced display of the two temperaments, each moving from its visual and sensuous pleasures towards its artistic ones and ultimately to its understanding of the power that, among other things, makes the poet. But in neither is the 'I' Milton. Each poem is a self-description of the make-up and pleasures of a particular temperament taken to a quasi-Platonic fulfilment, and the voices, as the titles indicate, are those of the 'happy man' and the 'melancholy or pensive man' in whom predominate, respectively, the sanguine humour and the melancholy humour of black bile (see p. 140). We are therefore expected to read them with a good deal of objectivity; not, as it were, to look outward through the speakers' eyes (though, up to a point, we must do so) but inward through them: what each speaker sees reflexively shows his tastes and values, his individual vision.

Establishing the ambivalence of the two-poems-in-one gets us only, as it were, to base camp. There are many ways in which a contemporary reader might have been expected to read the poems, and one thing Milton would have taken for granted is some knowledge of the psychological theory lying behind them. Each poem, in beginning with a representation of the psychological dangers of the extreme of the temperament expressed favourably in the other, draws on a long tradition of understanding of the mind's make-up. It is hardly to be doubted that Milton had a pretty good idea of the psychological theories of his time, as well as of the psychiatric practice; for us, these are most accessible through *The Anatomy of Melancholy* by Robert Burton (1621).

This is, at least in origin, a medical work (though, with surpassing interest, it turns into a great deal else), written as self-therapy as well as self-examination by a man we might class as a depressive. Burton's introduction starts from the premise that melancholy is an 'inbred malady' in every man, and the first part of the book deals with the definition, causes, symptoms and properties of the humour. Burton then goes on to discuss its cure, and the special sorts of melancholic illness associated with love and religion. The entertainments Allegro enjoys fit very well Burton's theory that pleasure and certain types of distraction can be a cure for the dangerous melancholy which ends in an insanity very vividly sketched in the first ten lines of *L'Allegro* – a phantasmagoria of horror, fear and ugliness. In contrast to this, *L'Allegro* shows a man of Jovial temperament, dominated by the hot and moist sanguine humour: such people are energetic, good-tempered, out-going, and enjoy life and its pleasures.[2]

Il Penseroso's opening lines, on the other hand, scorn the flibbertigibbet folly of overexcited grasshopper minds, for whom life is ever such fun, and the poem praises instead a life of quiet contemplation and study, of the seeking of wisdom and the contemplation of the sciences that lead both to the mastery of nature, and, in the Neoplatonic thought of people like Marsilio Ficino or Paracelsus especially, to the vision of God. Yet what *L'Allegro*'s opening rejects is as much a parody of the nobly Saturnine temperament as *Il Penseroso*'s is of the Jovial; the body of each poem leads ultimately alike to a seeking of wisdom and understanding.

The noble seriousness of Melancholy may be grasped better if we glance at the nowadays well-known engraving by Albrecht Dürer which elucidates very well the sort of philosophic tradition on which Milton's noble melancholy draws. The immensely detailed engraving *Melencolias I* of 1514 shows a winged female figure – the wings suggest her power to 'soar / Above the Aonian Mount' *(Paradise Lost,* I. 14–15) – sitting in an attitude of deep contemplation, as suggested by her head's resting on her left hand. Her right hand holds a pair of compasses that symbolizes both constancy and the architect's skill; above her head are the scales of justice, the hourglass of the astronomer, a Pythagorean square figure made up of 16 (4^2) numbers symbolizing the mystery of number by which all Creation was built (see pp. 15,113); and at her feet are the tools of the carpenter, and the sphere that symbolizes perfection. A dog, symbol of natural appetite, lies asleep at her right side, while also to her right are a half-hewn polyhedron of stone (the mastery of matter by mind), a seven-runged ladder of contemplation (the mystical ladder that leads the mind to the vision of God), and a little Cupid (Desire) doing what looks like his sums. In the background the sun flames in the heavens over the sea, surrounded by the rainbow of God's Promise after the Flood. The whole engraving is a picture essay on the qualities of the humour at its most noble and on its characteristic interests and activities.

All this is already beginning to make the 'two poems in one' seem much more philosophically serious than our usual experience with them might at first suggest. As we have seen, Renaissance readers were quite accustomed to complicated moral and philosophic dialogues of values being presented in symbolic terms, and to being asked to bring to their analysis a good deal of prior knowledge,

Take, for example, the well-known painting by Titian usually (and misleadingly) called *Sacred and Profane Love*, in the Galleria Borghese in Rome. It can be responded to merely as a very well-designed and finely executed painting of two beautiful women, one clothed and one naked, and it is greatly enjoyable on that level – just as *L'Allegro* and *Il Penseroso* are on a superficial level. Yet it has to be 'read' as well, to get at what Titian was exploring. At the centre of the picture is a fountain: it is clearly a fountain of Love, for Cupid (Amor or Desire, neutral in itself) bends over the water. But the surround of the fountain is decorated in an odd way: in bas-relief we see a man being scourged, a woman being dragged by the hair, and an unbridled horse being led away by the mane. Now, the horse is a standard Platonic symbol of sensuous passion which must be bridled. The man and woman are being chastised to symbolize that sensuous passion must be put away, and love in each of us refined from mere sense. All this acts as a sort of commentary on the main figures in the painting, the women who sit at each end of the fountain. The gorgeously clothed woman who sits on the left of the picture gazes calmly into the viewer's eyes, demanding his attention, and in her hair is a sprig of myrtle, the plant of marriage; behind her is a castle. The naked woman on the right is much more active, looking across the picture to her companion and pointing towards heaven. A church is behind her. The picture, therefore, seems to be discussing in Platonic terms the interrelationship and the distinction between two types of love, noble human love and love divine, the latter's truth and innocence emphasized by the convention of its nakedness. Desire mediates between the two, stirring the water of the fountain from which both drink; each is different, yet each relates to the other and poses a serious issue to the viewer.[3]

Titian's two figures, like Milton's two poems, are separate yet complementary, presenting in the tension between them the terms for a discussion of matters of high philosophical, moral and religious concern. The two poems demand a similar familiarity with the terms of philosophical and moral discussion, and with the symbolism extracted from

Classical mythology, and they also demand a reflective caution about our own first response to them.

I find it hard to take the opening 'exorcism' of *L'Allegro* seriously. How it is said is passionate and vigorous enough, but the mishmash of echoes from Vergil (*Aeneid*, VI. 418, 426-7) and the topography of nightmare seem to be consciously overstated. The concentration on ideas of blackness and darkness is certainly powerful, but the anthropomorphized 'low-brow'd Rocks' and the birth of Melancholy from the dog of Hell and 'blackest midnight' in a '*Stygian* cave forlorn / 'Mongst horrid shapes, and shrieks, and sights unholy' is – well, inconceivable; even the resounding alliteration of line 4 serves only to draw attention to the conceptual clashes of the words and the pompous passion of their utterance. It seems to me that, as with the corresponding opening of *Il Penseroso*, we are meant to look at these ten lines very obliquely indeed: their target can in no way correspond to the Melancholy addressed in the next poem (and vice versa); they demonstrate an hysterical rejection of what is not understood, and, by distancing us from the narratorial voice, encourage a critically objective reading of the remainder of the poem.

This stridency and lack of focus, duplicated in the opening of the other poem, is highlighted by the opening of the next section in each. In *L'Allegro*, the verse loses its clangour and sluggishness, and becomes mellifluous and light, bouncing along from rhyme word to rhyme word. And just as in *Il Penseroso*, Milton fully exploits mythological reference as a means of setting parameters for the poem's ensuing discussion. The first section, to line 35, concentrates on the ancestry of Mirth: Euphrosyne is one of the same Three Graces (her sisters were Aglaia and Thalia) who are locked in eternal dance in Botticelli's *La Primavera*, and they have a distinguished Stoic and Neoplatonic ancestry. Milton first follows one common tradition in making them the children of Venus and Bacchus – children of Love and the god of the wine that maketh glad the heart of man – but then omits their interpretation as symbols of the fruitfulness of the earth we find in some mythographers (for example, in Natalis Comes, IV. xv). By identifying Euphrosyne as Joy, or 'heart-easing Mirth', he seems to be alluding to the Neoplatonic interpretation of the Graces as representing the unceasing circle of *emanatio, raptio, remeatio*: the Creator giving in love to his creatures, the joy of those creatures in accepting, and their giving it back in love to the Creator. (See Marsilio Ficino, *In Plotinum*, I. iii; *De Amore*, I. i–ii.) But he makes this parentage only conjectural. It is rejected in favour of what 'som Sager sing', which, in fact, is Milton's own invention:

a descent from the West Wind and Aurora, the dawn, both of whom are, unlike Midnight, standard personifications regularly presented in art. The blunt physicality of lines 20–4, Zephyr and Aurora making fruitful love on beds of the springtime flowers of love and youth, is oddly lovely; and the effect of the two genealogies is to suggest that, on the one hand, Mirth is a transcendental quality that gives us a glimpse of Heaven; on the other, a natural gift in the texture of the world. This is the Joy that determines the progress of the rest of the poem, the Absolute glimpsed through all the little local examples that the poem goes on to describe. It also establishes a respectable authority for being happy.

The handling of Euphrosyne's companions anticipates a similar feature in *Comus* – indeed, this passage is echoed there (see p. 187). The personification technique is of the simplest: they are merely capitalized common nouns, mainly without any qualification; it is only the vigour and bounce of the lines, and the splendid climax in the little picture of 'Laughter holding both his sides' that makes them feel real. The companions are engaged in a dance, a symbol of order and harmony as well as joy, a dance that might just allude to the ecstatic dancing of the maenads, the priestesses who followed Bacchus across the mountains celebrating his godhead. The train concludes with Liberty – another personified absolute, but immediately qualified by the line (40) that ends the section: the unrestrained pleasures will be 'unreproved', free of guilt. Through joy, Milton suggests, we get a glimpse of that Golden Age when men knew not the doctrine of ill-doing.[4] Moreover, if we read these discrete figures allegorically as a group, they add up to a quite detailed picture of the behaviour, attitude and expression of the 'happy' man who is blessed with Euphrosyne's company.

Examples of specific pleasures now follow – all, as far as line 116, appropriately in the pastoral mode (see p. 10ff) and therefore, by implication, all capable of being read in terms of the poet and his job. If we accept this view, it becomes clear that the two poems (for *Il Penseroso* picks up this idea, too) do, in fact, look in some depth at the experience, attitude, and reading of the Poet before homing in on Orpheus, the great archetype of the sacred poet, whose art, immortal where he was mortal, was of such power as to move not only the trees, stones and animals into ecstasy, but also the gods.

This section of the poem begins at dawn in spring or summer – the time and season of Euphrosyne's conjectured parents.[5] The lark ascends as the first flush of dawn lightens the sky: unlike the corresponding section in *Il Penseroso*, the section covers the daylight hours and the activities from early morning, through the midday meal of the peasants, to the evening dancing and telling of stories over the ale. Notice how the visual focus alters: it closes in from the high lark, the distant dawn on the hills, to the flowers around the 'country cottage' window – a cliché then as now; then, in the barnyard, we see movement, the cock 'stoutly strut[ting]' (the line captures his self-important movement beautifully); and then, again, the sounds are distant and the eye seeks out the hunt on the far side of the valley, still not in full light.

There seems to be a real attempt to catch, in the manipulation of the effect of words on our minds, something of the actual chiaroscuro of the growing light of the day, the play of light and shade on the landscape; yet it is odd that what many find so effective and naturalistic should be so full of personifications of the times of day – morning, night and so on – a trait we notice again in *Il Penseroso*, and in *Comus* and *Lycidas*. The night is capable of being 'startled', and has a 'watch-towre'; the military image is continued in 'scatters the rear'. The morn is 'slumb'ring' and needs rousing from the hill where it is asleep – just as, in *Il Penseroso*, Night has a 'rugged brow' suggestive of worry that is 'smoothed' by the nightingale's song (ll. 57–8). The Sun is a great monarch beginning a royal progress (Biblical echo here, of course); the clouds are his liveried servants. It is as if Milton's imagination instinctively attached personality to everything it conceived – and this personification is rarely done by simile, a figure of speech which underlines the artifice and states the non-identity while it states the likeness. For example, the metaphor of the 'great Sun begins his state, / Rob'd in flames' comes so quickly, and is so woven into the texture of the lines that it catches one's mind unawares, and one has accepted the appositeness of the image and its attached *feelings* (awe, grandeur, majesty) before the rationalizing mind stops and questions whether such images do in fact describe the natural happening, or the suggestive *effect* of the natural happening on an imagination both peculiarly visual and peculiarly prone to think in terms of allegorical personification.

The six lines after line 63 are full of the human sounds of an early summer day – the ploughman whistling as he ploughs the fallows, the milkmaid singing, the mower sharpening his scythe and the shepherd counting his sheep; but then, in a series of self-contained couplets, the eye again rapidly sweeps from the distant hills to the sheep that have broken into the fallow common field; the view shifts from looking down at the meadow and brook to looking at the distant 'romantic' castle. The impression of a three-dimensional landscape is strong; but it is a landscape strongly tinged with literature. The bucolic poetry of Vergil seems to be echoed in the lines about the nibbling sheep, and the simple fare offered in the cottage is eaten by people with names straight out of Theocritus, while the castle sheltering its mysterious beauty is straight out of medieval romance. One could claim that the eye is running over the various types of poetry in which the 'I' of the poem delights. And the same with the picture of the pastoral celebration in lines 91 ff.: Milton knew perfectly well that real peasant life was hard, demanding and on the edge of survival for most of the time; but what he has given us is a literary and artificial picture of unalloyed pleasure, the literary would of pastoral. Even the reference to the drudging Goblin (l. 105) seems to send us to *A Midsummer Night's Dream* rather than to an everyday story of countryfolk.

At line 116 night has fallen; and we leave the pastoral to move to the pleasures of the town. Again it is no real town, but a town conceived in romance terms – 'Knights and Barons bold', holding 'high triumphs' while the regard of the sort of ladies one meets in chivalric romance is sought in tournaments. (There are a lot of echoes of the world of Spenser here.) When she 'whom all commend' is won, the marriage is an elaborate literary one – indeed, both the personification of Hymen and the other Classical paraphernalia sound very like an echo of Jonson's *Masque of Hymen*. But just as it is all getting too much, too arty, Milton cleverly turns it into a neat and ironic self-reference through the aposiopoesis of lines 127–8: – 'Such sights as youthfull Poets dream/ On Summer eeves by haunted stream'. Our literary Allegro therefore, having run through most of his library, now turns to the theatre – and, in contrast to *Il Penseroso*, it is clearly the real theatre. As we know from *Elegy I*, Milton took a lively interest in the theatre while he was near London, and he admired Jonson and Shakespeare (see p. 37).

The image of Shakespeare 'warbling his native Wood-notes wild' makes a subtle link between the pleasures first of vision and then of words and fiction, and the pleasures of music. The music with which Allegro seeks to drive away 'eating Cares' (an echo of Horace, *Odes*, II. xi. 18; cf. *Epitaphium Damonis*, l. 46) is in the Lydian mode: the mode which, though thought enervating and effeminate in contrast to the austerity of the Dorian or the nobility of the Ionian, was recommended in medical practice, on the authority of Cassiodorus in the sixth century, to treat depression and worry. But there is a good deal more to it than a bit of sound medico-psychological theory on keeping happy when the distraction of the play is over, for the poem is now reaching a wholly serious climax dominated by ideas of music and its power, in comparison with which its own medium, words, can only be inadequate.

The music Allegro desires is clearly, as in many surviving Renaissance songs, a setting for fine poetry in a mutually enhancing partnership of sister arts (cf. *Ad Patrem* and *At a Solemn Music*). He has passed, as Penseroso will pass, well beyond the enjoyment of what Renaissance men called the 'wild music' of the birds, heard first in the lark of lines 41–2, and echoed in the hidden comparison of Shakespeare to a bird singing with – in Shelley's phrase – 'unpremeditated art'. The uncertainty whether 'Such' (l. 138) refers to the verse or the music is surely deliberate; and in a minor *tour de force* of wit, Milton captures in the rhythm and structure of lines 139–42 the impression of a sweet voice moving, now slowly, now rapidly, through a series of melismata – the 'mazes' of sound of line 142. (We even get the vibrant low tones in the 'm' alliteration in line 142.) But this sensuous pleasure goes deeper: it 'pierces' 'the meeting soul' with its music, for serious music for those who understand it is a direct link to the musical harmony and proportion lying at the heart of the universe. As in *At a Solemn Music*, it is through music and poetry that men may again glimpse that harmony when 'they stood/In first obedience and their state of good.' In Heaven, man will again, redeemed, be united to 'his celestial consort' and 'sing in endles morn of light'.

This mystical and moral musical insight is, however, governed by the imperative 'lap' (l. 136): it has not yet happened, any more than any of the events and experiences of the poem have, for they are all grammatically putative consequences of whether or not Euphrosyne *does* 'admit' Allegro 'of her crew' (l. 138). But *if* such blessing as being admitted to the company of the Graces does happen, then the consequence will be a music that even Orpheus, the *ne plus ultra* of the poet-musician (see p. 69), will envy in Heaven, a music that 'would have' completely, and not momentarily, won back his 'half-regain'd Eurydice', who is still lost in Hades. When we recall that a common Renaissance interpretation of the Orpheus story (see p. 70), which stemmed from Nicholas Trivet's influential commentary on Boethius's *Consolation of Philosophy*, was to see Orpheus as the intellective part of man, as Eurydice as the appetitive, and the story as a myth of the redeeming of sense and desire by reason and wisdom – a redemption which *failed* – the poem takes on a much deeper seriousness. The appeal to Euphrosyne with which it opens and which is syntactically its structural anchor is an appeal not just for cheerfulness, but for a healing of man's fallen nature so that he may indeed live in 'unreproved pleasures free'. But we never know, even in the fiction of the poem, whether the appeal is successful. The argument is conditional, and the last couplet's ironic echo of Marlowe's *The Passionate Shepherd to his Love* stresses the open condition of the promise – the clause 'if thou canst give' says neither that she can give them, nor that she cannot, and it indicates, moreover, reserve before commitment on the part of Allegro himself.

The introductory ten lines to *Il Penseroso* have an emphatic semantic stress on illusion, on a divorce from reality: 'deluding', 'toyes', 'idle', 'fond', 'dreams', 'fickle'. The joys they reject are deceitful, meaningless as dust in a sunbeam, the bastards of mere folly (l. 2) – a manic cheerfulness that is akin to madness. Just as the Melancholy rejected in the first poem bears no relation, except that of a common name to the serious, philosophical, uplifting melancholy that is explored in the second, so these joys show no inkling of the serious and healing joy we have just glimpsed.

The invitation to Melancholy, in the same form as the invitation to Euphrosyne but moving with much slower and more dignified pace, is also longer: we do not reach the mention of her ancestry until line 22, as against the mention of Euphrosyne's in line 14 of *L'Allegro*. This invitation is also more serious: Melancholy is not only 'fair and free' but also 'sage and holy'; her visage is so chasteningly 'Saintly' that human beings cannot look at it directly. The black colour associated with her is a black that would suit the evening (personified as Himera, sister of Memnon), or the stellified Cassiopeia. This seriousness prepares us for the clues Milton gives us, in the account of her descent (ll. 22 ff.), about how to understand the Melancholy he is talking about. The descent is not said to be conjectural like Euphrosyne's: she *is* the daughter of the god Saturn who ruled in the Golden Age and of Vesta, virgin daughter of Saturn, goddess of flocks and herds, and of the household and hearth. The 'unreproved pleasures free' of the Golden Age, to which Allegro fleetingly alludes, are commonly represented by Classical and Renaissance authors as including innocent sexual freedom (see note 4), and incest between father and daughter is, explicitly, 'not held a stain' here.

Melancholy is the result of those unreproved pleasures free. Saturn, besides being the ruler of the cosmos in the Golden Age, is also the planet whose influence engenders melancholy in human beings, and, for Neoplatonists, symbolizes the collective angelic mind. Vesta's motherhood is Milton's invention, and it suggests that by Melancholy he means to signify the linking in the wise man of the contemplative intelligence and the world of action and physical existence. Their quiet, repeated ('Oft') lovemaking takes place in a world unfallen, before the revolt of Jove against his father that ended the Golden Age (l. 30); and it takes place in monochrome half-light, in shade and privacy. In contrast, Zephyr and Aurora's lovemaking is full of colour, openness and vigour, and happened only 'once', on impulse (*L'Allegro*, l. 20). The suggestion is there that joy steals on us (as it does) unawares, whereas the joys of 'divinest Melancholy' are more enduring, more rational.

The repeated invitation (ll. 31 ff.) to the goddess stresses again the link with the religious life we might guess at in lines 11–13: the three adjectives of line 31 qualify the word 'Nun', and suggest a life of self-control and self-denial, as implied in the three adjectives of the next line, which contrast strongly with the extrovert impression of the three adjectives of line 24 in *L'Allegro*. Melancholy is to arrive like a queen, deep in a contemplation of high matters (ll. 38–40) that moves her to the ecstasy of religious insight (l. 41) – an anticipation of the mystical experience Penseroso anticipates in lines 165–6.[6]

Her companions are personified common nouns like Euphrosyne's, but they do not add up, as hers do, to a visual picture of a man enjoying a particular mood. Rather, they refer to qualities of attitude and the result of that attitude: thin Fast, in a clever pun, not only does without food, but also holds council ('diet') with the gods and hears the heavenly music of the muses in the intellectual pleasures the arts give. Leisure enjoys the formal and mathematical pattern of 'trim gardens'.[7] And, climactically, in a clear reminiscence of Ezekiel's vision of God (l. 4–6), Contemplation is summoned; he is a cherub, of the highest of the Nine Orders of Angels, who are on fire with the love of God and whose faces are always turned towards Him. The subtext of this whole passage, therefore, suggests something plainly devotional about the melancholy attitude.

L'Allegro's catalogue of pleasures began with the lark at dawn: *Il Penseroso*'s begins with the 'wild music' of the nightingale and the evening. Again the description is structured by the seeing eye: the moon over the oak, the moon 'riding near her highest noon', the moon 'stooping through a fleecy cloud'. The moon can be the planet of lunacy, and it can also be that of poets (Natalis Comes, III. xvii); its half-light dominates the nightscape, as the Sun does *L'Allegro*'s description of the countryside at the same point in that poem. Then we get sound: the curfew, the roar of the sea, the cricket on the hearth and the watchman calling the hours. But there is no extended description of a landscape as in the earlier poem, for Penseroso retires to the lonely tower – might it, ironically, be the one Allegro saw through the trees? – to study the stars; to spend all night in reading Hermetic philosophy and the works of Plato; and to study the operation of the Aristotelian Four Elements of Fire, Air, Earth and Water (l. 94). These are books that attempt to provide an understanding of the universe itself, and are far removed from Allegro's romances and pastorals. Then Penseroso turns to Tragedy, in a personification that reminds us of Melancholy herself (l. 98). In contrast to Allegro's, this is not drama for the stage: despite the passing allusion to modern tragedy – probably Jonson's (l. 102) – this is Greek and Latin tragedy read in the quietness of the study, by authors 'unequall'd yet by any'.[8]

Yet reading the great works of the past merely whets the appetite for deeper and deeper artistic and intellectual experience. First, Penseroso wishes that Melancholy had the power to raise from the dead Musaeus, the great poet encountered in Elysium in *Aeneid*, VI. 66–8, who 'before all' is asked to reveal where the soul of a loved one dwells. Then, raising the stakes, he wishes she could command the dead Orpheus to sing a song such as once won Eurydice from Hades. There is, however, a subtle irony in these lines, with their echo, in the Classical myth, of the Christian doctrine of redemption and the Christian myth of the Harrowing of Hell, for the syntax makes it certain that it is not that song itself that can ever be heard, but one like it. Penseroso recognizes the limitations of art; that it is a similitude rather than the real thing. (Allegro, on the other hand, in lines 148–50, implies simply that Orpheus' art did not go far enough.)

It is at this point that the detailed structural mirroring of *L'Allegro* ceases (though there is a further echo of Allegro's pastoral walkabout in lines 122–50). Where *L'Allegro*'s final, climactic image was that of Orpheus hearing what he *should have* sung, *Il Penseroso*'s recognition that we can never hear exactly what he *did* sing is much more open-ended. The search for wisdom and knowledge is never over. So, Penseroso wishes first to hear the poetry of the mythical Musaeus whom Vergil made Aeneas, led by the Sybil, meet in Hades (*Aeneid*, VI. 665 ff.); then he wishes to hear Orpheus, some of whose inspired writing had survived, it was believed; and, as a climax, at much greater length, he wishes to hear the spirit of Chaucer, whom Milton, in *Mansus*, sees as his own illustrious predecessor. The tale referred to is the unfinished *Squire's Tale*, which we do not admire as much as some of his other work. Yet, in it, Spenser found something of surpassing interest, and, greatly lamenting its lack of completion (*Faerie Queene*, IV. ii. ss. 32 ff.), used it as a starting point for one of his own highly symbolic and moral narratives. Milton seems to have reacted similarly, and it may be that he saw the magical ring, glass and brass horse in Chaucer's original tale as symbols of the intellectual power and capacity for understanding the world to which Penseroso aspires in the closing lines of this poem. It is a nice point, too, that the chivalric romance that delights Allegro and affects his vision of the landscape and the town is here looked at *as narrative* 'where more is meant than meets the ear' (l. 120): serious poetry – and there is a clear self-reference – is never simple and never reveals all its meaning on the surface.

Penseroso has been engaged in these literary pursuits and intellectual imaginings all through the night, until 'civil-suited Morn appear' (l. 122) – a very different Aurora from Allegro's, both as personification, as literary memory, and as weather. Penseroso's personified dawn is cloudy, showery and a bit blowy: the eye moves from the sky to the drips from the thatch eaves. Then, as the sun breaks through, Penseroso moves into the shade of the woods, into a Horatian retirement from

the busy-ness of the world. There the sound of the bees and the
murmur of water – naturally musical – lull him to sleep and visionary
dream, whence he is woken, by magical music like that in *The Tempest*,
to a new and beneficial understanding (l. 153). But the climax of this
movement lies not in the experience of art, however Orphically exalted,
but in religious mysticism. The emotional response to the majesty of
the church building and the light cast by the stained glass culminates
in the response to the combined words and music (cf. *L'Allegro*, ll.
136–7) of the service which 'Dissolve me into extasies / And bring all
Heav'n before my eyes'. What Penseroso is seeking is nothing less than
the mystic's vision of God, after which the only life possible is that of
the hermit, the life of penance and study. That study of both the highest
and lowest; of the stars and the plants and their connection to each
other may lead to the attainment of understanding and the 'prophetic
strain' of utterance. The final lines are far less ambiguous than those
of *L'Allegro*, despite the echo: here there is no question whether
Melancholy *can* give these pleasures, only whether she *will*.

All this is very well, but the ending of *Il Penseroso* should leave us
uneasy. Penseroso's experience of the church building is one that is
emotional to the point of sentimentality, and the stained glass that
affects him would have been regarded by many of Milton's contemporaries
as uncomfortably near the idolatrous. His picture of his old age as a
hermit seems to owe more to literary fiction than to a sound Protestant
understanding of the nature of the religious life: there were no hermits
in hairy gowns in seventeenth-century England. The hermit is as much
a gnome in the literary garden as was Coleridge's hermit in *The Rime
of the Ancient Mariner*.

As with Allegro, whose characteristic optimism is undercut by the
syntactical conditionality of his vision of joy, Milton seems to have
surrounded Penseroso's voice with an irony dependent on our perceiving
how his committed, almost lustful course of serious reading has led
him to reduce the world of action and moral struggle to literary terms.
We should certainly not take cynically the desire of the one for the
power to free and heal, or of the other for the ecstatic vision and
understanding that leads to prophetic power: both are entirely noble
desires. But the overlap between the poems surely suggests that there
is a world between them that neither persona sees whole and clear,
any more than the world we live in is ever wholly in daylight or wholly
in moonlight. Milton is not undercutting the Platonic Idea of Joy or
Melancholy that either poem invokes, but he is indicating the fallibility
and the myopia of their transference of the Idea to the world they
create through their language. Penseroso and Allegro, the voices of men
dominated by a single humour, have no proper complexion, no proper

balance or moderation. While each has some substantial part of a truth, neither has it whole or recognizes the need for balanced cooperation between absolutes; and the weaknesses of each are revealed both by the contrasting poem and by the internal discourse of each.

In the end, the way for the moral man lies in the seeking of the quality that neither poem mentions – what the Greeks called *sophrosyne* and the Romans *temperantia* or *modestia* – modesty, prudence, self-control. This is an issue that Milton felt to be crucial to the man who would be a serious poet, as he says of himself on many occasions (see p. 59). As both Allegro and Penseroso are literati who aspire to high poetic power, it does make rather good sense to see the two-poems-in-one as exploring the qualities that, held in proper balance, the wise poet needs. On the moral side, of course, *sophrosyne* is an issue we meet again, head on, in *Comus*.

Notes to Chapter 6

1. The importance of the emblem in Renaissance art, thought and literature is hard to overestimate, though many still ignore it. See my *A Century of Emblems, An Introductory Anthology*, pp. 1–28; for Hercules, see pp. 4, 13, 28.

2. The idea of the four humours – blood, choler, phlegm and melancholy or black bile – was still a usual way of explaining the psychological and physical make-up of individuals; in words like 'complexion', 'temperament', 'humour' and so on, it is still powerful in our everyday language well after the theory, which goes back to the ancient Greeks, has been exploded. The four humours and their mixture or complexion in any individual were affected, too, by the planetary sign that dominated that person's horoscope. People born under Venus, for example, would have a great propensity to Love; those under Jupiter or Jove, supposedly the best of all planets to have as dominant, would be fortunate, well-balanced and generous; they would be natural leaders and rulers. Those born under Saturn – the planet of *Il Penseroso* – would, at their best, be slow, thoughtful, wise, intellectual people, long-lived and of deep intellect; at their worst they would be chronic melancholics, often tipping over into depressive madness.

3. For a fuller discussion of this painting, see Edgar Wind, *Pagan Mysteries in the Renaissance* (Oxford repr., 1980), Fig. 37 and pp. 143 ff.

4. The idea is very important, and is referred to again in the opening to the companion poem. See Ovid, *Metamorphoses*, I ; Propertius, III. xiii. 25–46; Tibullus, II. iii. 69–74; and Harry Levin, *The Myth of the Golden Age in the Renaissance* (London, 1970).

5. Though westerly winds in Britain are far from uncommon at any time of the year, in the Mediterranean they are the spring and summer winds. Pastoral, in poetry or painting, preserves this convention.

6. The 'sad [i.e. serious] Leaden downward cast' of line 43 is an allusion not only to Saturn's metal but also to the conventions of contemporary acting.

7. In the Renaissance, even in the odd form it took in England, gardens are highly symbolic places, and the art of gardening is an analogue of man's general relationship to Nature and to the world in which he is God's steward. Compare Milton's description of Paradise and of Eve's symbolic gardening in *Paradise Lost*, IV. 689 ff.; IX. 205 ff., 425 ff.; see also R. Strong, *The Renaissance Garden in England* (Thames and Hudson, London, 1979).

8. When he published *Samson Agonistes*, Milton prefaced it with a short essay 'Of that sort of dramatic performance which is call'd tragedy', from which these words are taken. He stresses there the spiritual value of tragedy, and his dissatisfaction with modern tragedy as it was presented on the stage.

7 'Forc'd Fingers Rude': An Approach to *Lycidas*

> One of the poems on which much praise has been bestowed is *Lycidas;* of which the diction is harsh, the rhymes uncertain, and the numbers [rhythmic structure] unpleasing. What beauty there is, we must therefore seek in the sentiments and images. It is not to be considered as the effusion of real passion; for passion runs not after remote allusions and obscure opinions. Passion plucks no berries from the myrtle and ivy, nor calls upon Arethuse and Mincius, nor tells of rough satyrs and fauns with cloven heel. Where there is leisure for fiction there is little grief.
>
> In this poem there is no nature, for there is no truth; there is no art, for there is nothing new. Its form is that of a pastoral, easy, vulgar and therefore disgusting.

Samuel Johnson clearly felt *Lycidas* to be less than satisfactory. The praise he admits it had received must have been based on an understanding of it quite different from his own, and it is my business now to try to see why it might have been so praised. But in one particular Johnson was perfectly right: the supposed mourning for Lycidas is not the grief of a genuinely sorrowing friend. If the poem has merits, they cannot be based on that.

The circumstances of the poem's composition are quickly stated. In 1637 Milton was asked to contribute a poem to a volume marking the death by drowning of Edward King, his contemporary at Christ's. King was a good scholar, a fair poet and apparently an honest enough clergyman to justify a conventional portrait of him as a 'good shepherd' of the sheep whose neglect by a corrupt clergy Milton condemns both in the poem and elsewhere. So far as we know, Milton and he were never close; and, anyway, a memorial volume of this common type was no place for deeply personal expressions of grief, any more than conventional 'obituary' poems (p. 52) were expected to be. But the parallel, almost openly stated, between the narratorial voice of the poem[1] and King allows King's death to open up issues of deep concern to himself. Milton was about to travel abroad – a dangerous business, and one necessarily raising fears about his own mortality. What if Milton himself were to die, having achieved nothing and with the gifts God gave him unused? [2]

Moreover, the apparently meaningless death of an admirable young man always raises questions about the nature of Providence and about God's justice: the stress on the untimeliness of this death – Milton's own potential death – dominates the first three-quarters of the poem, from the 'forc'd fingers' plucking the unripe berries out of season, before the 'mellowing year',[3] to the imaginary bier strewn with spring flowers in lines 139 ff. When that young man was also a poet sincerely committed to the Christian faith, examining his death leads naturally to an examination of Milton's understanding of God's purpose for himself at a time, apparently, of some spiritual and poetic drought. Lycidas becomes a symbol of Milton's own past, present, and possible future.

The poem's first audience, in 1637, could not but have noticed that *Lycidas* stuck out like a sore thumb. The collection, *Iusta Edovardo King Naufrago*, has 19 Latin and 3 Greek poems in its first half, followed by 13 'Obsequies to the Memory of Mr Edward King'. Some of them are – unintentionally, one hopes – hilarious: a Latin poem by one Coke has dumb fishes swallowing King's tongue, which had dripped with the sweetness of honeyed words! Most of the English offerings strain after fashionably paradoxical wit: Isaac Olivier of King's College, for example, perpetrates lines like the following:

> Or else (like Peter) trod the waves: but he
> Then most stood upright when he bent the knee.

Milton alone went to a much older tradition, reaching back, via Spenser, to Theocritus and Vergil: the Classical and Christian tradition of the pastoral elegy, a mode at once insincerely arty and potentially genuinely moving. Many poets wrote them, and Milton's own *Epitaphium Damonis* was to remind us how powerfully the genre could be used for real personal grief. The basic structure of the pastoral elegy was fairly standard, and had been set in its essentials by Theocritus' *Idyll I*, the lament of Thyrsis for Daphnis: these included the invocation to the muse, expressions of grief, enquiry into the causes of death, the sorrowing of nature, a description of the bier, a lament, and a concluding consolation. Milton follows this pattern in both his elegies. The fact that there was this familiar tradition means that we, who see Lycidas/King in close focus only as a symbol of Milton himself, tend to miss an important set of unstated assumptions that lie behind all pastoral elegy, and these need teasing out. Those assumptions do not destroy the Milton/King parallel, but enhance it greatly by putting it in a much wider context.

In Classical pastoral elegy – for example, Theocritus' *Idyll I* – the subject of the elegy is not an individual so much as a representative of the cycle of dying and rebirth we perceive in nature. We are, in fact, talking about the Dying God: and it should not surprise us that our forebears were as familiar with this concept as any modern who has skimmed through Sir James Frazer's *The Golden Bough*, for they read the same texts as Frazer did and were perfectly capable of making similar inferences. (They were, after all, greatly interested in the meaning of myth.) The archetypal myth behind all pastoral elegy is that of Adonis – the beautiful youth beloved of Venus, cut off by accident in his prime, who on Venus' prayers was allowed for a part of the year to return to life. Milton was familiar with the story, and identifies Adonis with 'Thammuz yearly wounded' (*Paradise Lost*, I. 452), whom the 'Syrian Damsels' lamented 'all a Summer's day'.[4]

Adonis, by death, achieves immortality. This motif is common in Classical pastoral elegy: Vergil, for example, says of Daphnis in *Eclogue V*, 'Deus, deus ille, Menalca' – 'He is a god, a god indeed, Menalcas'. On one level, therefore, the poem moves through well-trodden paths when its focus swings from the grief at the untimely destruction of the budding flowers of Lycidas' youth to the vision of him in immortal glory and bliss. The first readers would have been perfectly happy to accept the use of Lycidas as a symbol to look at the perennial problem of the relationship between earthly suffering and heavenly bliss.

For Christians, however, there is a further dimension. It was axiomatic among such Church Fathers as Augustine that pagan myth contained, veiled indeed, truths about God's world. The Dying God myths foreshadowed and were preparations for the reality: the Incarnation of God in Christ Jesus and His suffering, death, resurrection and ascension to glory. The concluding vision of *Lycidas* is not a pagan but a Christian one, of the bliss of the Lamb's high feast; and behind the poem's examination of God's purpose and the validity of human grief lies the paradigm of the death and Resurrection of Jesus.

Calling the elegy *Lycidas* was not just to pluck a nice name out of the air. There is no modesty, false or otherwise, in such an act. Lycidas is a character – a poet and shepherd – in Vergil's *Eclogue IX*, and such a title demands that its learned audience explicitly measure the new poem against the old. It suggests a huge claim for the poem's quality and importance. The name immediately signals, too, the use of pastoral: the mode that above all others in antiquity (especially in Vergil) and in the high Renaissance deliberately develops the pretty fiction of singing shepherds to discuss important moral and political matters (see p. 10ff). The pastoral necessarily implies a distance between the narratorial voice in the poem and the creating poet: Johnson spotted this, but drew the wrong conclusion, when he saw the picture of the King and Milton together 'Batt'ning their flocks' as merely ludicrous. Milton, as poet, is wholly controlling the apparently impulsive response of the narratorial voice to death within the pastoral allegory, just as Vergil knew that a literal identification of Julius Caesar with the beautiful youth Daphnis was not even good fiction. The artifice forces a look beneath the surface.[5]

I have already drawn attention to the importance of the quotation from Vergil on the title page of *Poems* (1645), and the need to put that quotation back in context. In this poem the claims and ideas of the quotation are taken much further. The reminiscences of Vergil's *Eclogues* are substantial, deliberate and part of the means whereby Milton controls our reading of this poem. For example, what seems like a merely trivial passing reference to Neaera is much more significant: she is the lover of Aegon, the shepherd who has abandoned his sheep to the care of Damoetas (cf. *Lycidas*, l. 36) in *Eclogue III*. That irresponsible shepherd, therefore, is the defining type behind Milton's attack in lines 64 ff on those who misuse their sacred gifts. Amaryllis, too, is called on to plait a magical love charm in *Eclogue VIII* – and the reference thus becomes a precise allusion to the plaited, witty poetry of, for example, some of the so-called 'Metaphysical' poets. The 'smooth-sliding Mincius' of line 86 is Vergil's river, flowing with the smoothness of his verse; it is mentioned as 'reedy' (cf. l. 86) in *Eclogue VII*. Arethusa (l. 85) is mentioned in *Eclogue X*; this well of poetry is in Sicily, where Theocritus virtually invented the pastoral mode, and where dwell those muses of high seriousness Vergil invoked in *Eclogue IV*: 'Sicelides Musae, paulo maiora canamus' – 'Sicilian Muses, let us sing of things a little more serious'.

At the end of *Lycidas* (ll. 190 ff.) we seem to be under the stretched-out shadows of the mountains with Vergil's Tityrus and Meliboeus at the end of *Eclogue I*; and there is substantial imitation, profoundly creative in the way it builds on the older poem and at the same time uses it as a backdrop for the new, of *Eclogue X*, in which Gallus laments the loss of Lycoris. In *Eclogue V*, under the guise of a lament for Daphnis, Vergil deals with Julius Caesar's death and apotheosis – the pagan immortality that anticipates the resurrection given to Lycidas at the end of Milton's poem. That poem, too, like Milton's, examines the idea of the poet and his job and the relation of his songs to the songs of heavenly Apollo, god of wisdom and poetry.

The obvious Vergilian echoes and parallels in *Lycidas* automatically imply a distinction between the serious pastoral of antiquity and the more frivolous pastoral of the late Renaissance – the pastoral of charming but lightweight Elizabethan songs to Phyllis and Amaryllis which are still sung, and the pastoral, too, of Guarini's *Il Pastor Fido* and Tasso's *Aminta.*[6]

If Milton was to use the pastoral mode for a serious subject, he had to signal hard to his audience that he was working in – or, better, re-creating for modern times – the Vergilian mode rather than the recent Italian. He gives such clues in his use of mythological allusion, heavily affected by Renaissance explanations of the significance of Classical myth. For example, Milton's invocation, a venerable convention of all poetry apart from lyric, is to *all* the

> . . . Sisters of the sacred well,
> That from beneath the seat of Jove doth spring,
>
> (ll. 15–16)

– that is, all the Nine Muses, with a stress on the divine descent of poetry. The invocations to Alpheus and Arethusa look simple enough, but much of their significance is hidden from us, who, if we pick up the names' references at all, pick them up without the Renaissance and medieval understanding of their myth. Alpheus, the river god of Arcadia, pursued the nymph Arethusa under the sea to Sicily, where she escaped him by being transformed into a fountain. Finally, their waters were mingled. According to Natalis Comes' dictionary of mythology, which Milton probably knew, 'Alpheus' means 'imperfection' and 'Arethusa', 'virtue' – the story thus becomes an allegory of the search of the imperfect for the perfect. (A parallel interpretation is given by the fifth-century theologian and mythographer, Fulgentius of Ruspe: the love of truth for justice.) That these two invocations frame the attacks on the poets and clergy who have betrayed the truth of their calling seems to hint at Milton's faith in the ultimate triumph of truth and justice, just as his use later of the Orpheus myth recalls how the song of the sacred poet could not be silenced even by death. It is only when we have taken the functional nature of all these references into account that we can begin to recapture something of what it might have been like to read the poem when it first appeared.

Form

In every way *Lycidas* is quite unusual. It is one of the very few examples in English of what the Greeks would have understood as an ode – that is, a serious complex lyrical poem on a theme of great importance – and it has not only virtually no English ancestors but also very few descendants.[7] I have already stressed the Italian influence on Milton's thinking about poetry and on the practical business of writing it. In verse and rhythmic pattern *Lycidas* has no single Italian model; rather its versification is the result of a thorough grasp and brilliant adaptation of the principles of a discussion and practice reaching back to Dante. A comparison of the verse with that of some of the choral odes of *Samson Agonistes* will show, too, that the lessons first brought to fruition in this poem were not forgotten – in the foreword to *Samson* Milton again acknowledges his Italian debt: 'In the modelling therefore of this poem . . . the ancients and Italians are rather followed . . .'

Lycidas, written unwillingly (ll. 1–4), before the fruits of poetry were ripe to be gathered, is openly occasional; and it is peculiarly pleasing that the form should be designed to give the impression of a mind thinking and feeling impulsively as a result of that occasion. The irregularity of the form, line length, rhyme scheme, and so on helps to achieve this effect – just as we have the impression of the same sort of disciplined improvisation in *On Time*, and *At a Solemn Music*. A unique event should have a unique poem in a unique shape: even the fact that it has 193 lines signals this uniqueness, for 193 is a prime number.

Let us look first at its formal pattern. There is some evidence that Milton was concerned that this should be noticeable, for when he revised the poem that had appeared in 1638 in *Iusta Edovardo King Naufrago* for publication in 1645, he altered the paragraphing so that the divisions and developments that were already present in the argument of the poem should be strongly stressed by visual means. Originally, the poem had six paragraphs (ll. 1–14, 15–36, 37–132, 133–65, 166–85, 186–end); all of these except the first (which has its own complex repeated rhymes) close with a couplet. In the 1645 volume, Milton first split the second paragraph up at the natural break, marked by a couplet, before he talks about the education of Lycidas and his persona – a semicolon in 1638 becomes a full stop and a paragraph break. Then the massive original third paragraph breaks into paragraphs 4, 5, 6 and 7 of the later version: the new layout of 11 paragraphs makes much clearer the structure of the thought of the poem. Paragraphs 6 and 7 both close with a couplet (ll. 83–4 and 101–2), while 4 and 5 (ll. 37–49 and 50–63) close with a rhyme on the last and the pre-penultimate lines.

The poem is closely but irregularly rhymed; there are ten lines (1, 13, 15, 22, 39, 51, 82, 91, 92, 161) that do not rhyme at all. The 2nd, 3rd, 6th, 8th, 9th, 10th and 11th paragraphs close with a couplet (ll. 23–4, 35–6, 83–4, 139–40, 163–4, 184–5, 192–3), and the last verse paragraph of 8 lines rhyming a b a b a b c c has the rhyme pattern of the Italian *ottava rima*. The line lengths are noticeably irregular, varying from 6 to 11 syllables. The 6-syllabled lines (ll. 4, 19, 21, 33, 41, 43, 48, 56, 79, 88, 90, 108, 145) are irregularly disposed, but they always rhyme, and rhyme with a preceding 10-syllabled line, usually immediately before them, or separated by no more than 2 other lines. One immediately noticeable effect of these lines is that, with their rhymes, they stress a pause or shift in the thought of the poem.

The major influence on the form was probably the Italian canzone as it had been adapted in the sixteenth century: we shall have to glance at *why* Milton looked to that model. It is worth spending a moment on this, since we can thereby estimate the originality and resource which Milton employed in writing what is, by any standards, up to that date his most serious and important poem – a poem that not only airs the whole issue of the nature and purpose of the poet's craft but is also a serious attempt to create in English a style and verse form that could approach the grace, dignity and flexibility of Vergil's *Eclogues*.

The canzone was one of the most exalted and serious forms for vernacular poetry. The complex structure of a normal canzone was explained by Dante in detail in *De Vulgari Eloquentia*, and had also been discussed in Tasso's dialogue *La Cavaletta*. Normally it consisted of a complex stanza, fully rhymed, of some length, repeated several times, the poem then concluding in a shorter stanza, the *commiato*. The stanza of a canzone was built of two sections, linked by a key line or *chiave* (such a stanza is also called a *stanza divisa*). One or other of the two parts might divide, too: if the first part was undivided, it was called the *fronte*; if divided, the divisions were called *piedi*. An undivided second part was called the *sirima* or *coda*; if divided, the subdivisions were called *versi*. The first part of a *stanza divisa* must be linked to the second by a line rhyming with the last line of the first – the *chiave*; the two *versi*, if they exist, must be linked, too, by a *chiave*. Dante had also recommended the counterpointing of hende-casyllabic and heptasyllabic lines as peculiarly pleasing; and in making the longer lines in *Lycidas* dominate, Milton was following Dante's prescription for a 'Tragic' canzone.[8]

The reverence for Dante and Petrarch in Italian poets of the sixteenth century did not prevent their forms from being adapted to accord with the growing fashion for irregular lyrical verse, freed from the rigidity of stanzaic verse without losing wholly the discipline it offered. The forms used in Tasso's pastoral, *Aminta*, and in Guarini's *Il Pastor Fido*, showed the possibilities for dramatic and lyrical verse in a pattern reminiscent of the formal canzone but allowing greater freedom to respond to the movement of thought – not, that is, demanding the exact concurrence of the periods of the pattern of thought with the rhyme and structural pattern.

This development was connected with the search for *latinità in volgare* (see p. 49). The problem facing all the languages of Europe, and faced first by the Italian Humanists, who, like everyone else, regarded the excellence of Latin poetry as a standard that must be at least equalled if their language was truly to be the cement of their society, was how to construct a vernacular metre and form which could be made the equivalent of Vergil's hexameters in his pastorals, moving from dialogue to song and back again without any change of structure or awkwardness. The second problem, on the structural and formal level, was how to marry an adaptation of the serious canzone, the most elaborate form developed in Italian, to the rhetorical mode of the Classical eclogue. Both of these developments lie behind *Lycidas*.

Thus, in the sixteenth-century Italian pastoral lyric, there is a tendency to make verbal patterns (including rhythm) take over the main function of providing the structural underpinning of the verse (as a Latin), with the result that less structural importance is given to rhyme. One result is what one might call a 'hidden' stanza and 'submerged rhyme' – that is, a rhyme pattern that has little obvious correspondence with the flow of the sense in long passages of verse. It may even go so far as to do away with rhyme altogether.[9]

Milton's own attitude to rhyme developed considerably: he uses rhyme, of course, in *Lycidas*, but his *Note on the versification of 'Paradise Lost'* (1667) merely makes explicit some of the tendencies that are already to be discerned in the earlier poem – specifically, the tendency to make the stress of thought rather than the pattern of rhyme the major articulative determinant:

> Rime [is] no necessary Adjunct or true Ornament of Poem or good Verse . . . but the Invention of a barbarous Age to set off wretched matter and lame Meter . . . Not without cause, therefore, some both *Italian* and *Spanish* poets of prime note have rejected Rime both in longer and shorter Works, as have also long since our best *English* tragedies . . . *true musical delight . . . consists only in apt Numbers, fit quantity of Syllables, and the sense variously drawn out from one Verse into another, not in the jingling sound of like endings* . . . [my italics at end].

The discipline of the canzone is clearly behind *Lycidas*, but it is the canzone as it had been adapted in the sixteenth century rather than the Dantesque model – the canzone developed to provide an equivalent to the high seriousness of Classical eclogue. The influence of Dante is still there, of course: Milton accepts from Dante (*De Vulgari Eloquentia*) the principle – which he observes in nearly all cases – of a couplet to end his paragraphs, and the last verse paragraph corresponds exactly in function to the *commiato*: it 'frames' the poem. The passionate voice we have listened to in the preceding lines suddenly becomes a voice we *over*heard: we now see the therapeutic effect of the poem on the singer as he 'twitches his Mantle blew', as the poem is self-referentially distanced into being considered not as a mind sequentially thinking and feeling but as a *poem*, and a poem that admits the imperfections of the singer: '*Thus* sang the *uncouth* swain . . .'

Furthermore, the counterpoint between rhyme pattern and diction that Milton learnt from the Italians allows him to give lines (including those that stand out because they do not rhyme) a differing weight and emphasis according to their position and function. His sentences do not correspond to the pattern of rhymes; the ebb and flow of the statements and the feelings they express seem to depend only on their own internal associative necessity. Look, for example, at lines 103–9:

> Next *Camus*, reverend Sire, went footing slow,
> His Mantle hairy, and his Bonnet sedge,
> Inwrought with figures dim, and on the edge
> Like to that sanguine flower inscrib'd with woe.
> Ah! who hath reft, quoth he, my dearest pledge?
> Last came, and last did go,
> The Pilot of the *Galilean* lake.

At line 107 there is a strong pause, but the next line, starting off a new series of rhymes, takes its own rhyme from those of the completed statement. In lines 165–72, the first strong pause comes at line 171, when a new rhyme is introduced:

> Weep no more, woful Shepherds, weep no more,
> For *Lycidas* your sorrow is not dead,
> Sunk through he be beneath the watry floar,
> So sinks the day-star in the Ocean bed,
> And yet anon repairs his drooping head,
> And tricks his beams, and with new spangled Ore,
> Flames in the forehead of the morning sky:
> So *Lycidas*, sunk low, but mounted high.

The principle behind this invaluable instrument of a rhyme which looks both backwards and forwards is the one in the *stanza divisa* of the canzone: that each new group or series of rhymes must be linked to it predecessor by a key (*chiave*) line. Yet Milton does not allow this basic articulative principle of the canzone to drag with it the rigidity of repeated *piedi* or *versi*, but instead makes the paragraphs, working almost like the strophes of Greek lyric, the major structural unit. The principle of the *chiave* is therefore free to affect any part of his paragraphs, not just certain transitions at fixed points.

The benefits of this freedom are very clear, too, when we look at the six-syllabled lines. Particularly when they rhyme with the ones immediately preceding, the musical effect is arresting: we are aware that a change in direction, or a point of emphasis has been reached, and they give a great sense of expectation. In their rhyme they look back to a previous longer line, giving a sense of a contracted or interrupted movement which dams up, as it were, a momentum which must be discharged by the next line, which is always full length. It is worth recalling that Tasso had said that broken or short lines, 'entering the one into the other . . . make the language magnificent and sublime, because the 'breaking of the lines holds back the course of the oration, and causes tardiness, and tardiness is a proper quality of poetry' (quoted by Mario Praz, *On Neoclassicism* (Thames and Hudson, London, 1969), pp. 16–18).

Thus, clearly, the form of *Lycidas* is intimately related to the occasional nature of its subject, the seriousness of the issues to be discussed through it, and the problem of creating an impression of a thinking and feeling mind progressing through a crisis of ideas: that, as we shall see, is the real interest in the poem. We must now look at its structure, in the light of what I said above (pp. 13,110) about the fondness for building spatial and numerical patterns into Renaissance art to control our reading of it.

There seems to be a complex, three-fold, climactic pattern which is controlled from the centre paragraphs. The sixth – the central, 'triumphal' one (see pp. 100-1) – begins with the attack on those poets who betray their high calling and resolves itself into the discussion of what fame is, with a growing confidence that God knows what he is doing; here is the first mention in the poem of any hope of future life or resurrection – a hope which looks forward to the tenth paragraph, where Lycidas is perfected in 'the blest Kingdoms meek of joy and love'. It thus looks forward to a perfection, of which the number 6 may be a symbol, from a state of imperfection. Similarly, the eighth paragraph, which deals with St Peter's denunciation of the clergy, closes with a clear promise of a divine cleansing of man's sin: again it looks forward to a future hope with a confidence that has grown out of perplexity. The number 8 may symbolize eternity after mutability, a Day of Judgment and a new beginning.

The sixth and eighth paragraphs bracket the one in which the winds and waves are made to declare their innocence of the death of Lycidas: the two long passages, that misleadingly have been called digressions, enclose a return to the initial topic of the poem, the drowning. And that paragraph contains the numerical centre of the poem: Lycidas' death is in the 'triumphal' position. Finally, the first and last paragraphs of the poem balance each other: in the first, without intermediary, we are brought sharply up against the problem of writing the poem and the pain of the occasion; in the last, we return to the singer we heard in the first lines, but this time we see him objectively, having sung his song, moving away to fresh woods and pastures new, after the day spent in the singing of the poem.

The poem can be summarized in tabular form in order to make Milton's design clearer.

Paragraph   Theme(s)

1   Milton's reluctance to write – an unseasonable poem for the unseasonable death of Lycidas

2   The Invocation: if he laments for Lycidas, someone in time may lament for him:

3   Their youth: a happy pastoral (links with Milton developed in paragraphs 1–3)

4   The loss of Lycidas: unseasonable disruption in nature

5   Why did not the nymphs save him? But not even Orpheus could be saved; parallel between watery death of Lycidas and that watery end of Orpheus

6   'Digression' I: On the right and wrong sort of poet, then on the importance of the true sort of fame: voice of Phoebus

(central paragraph)

7   Inexplicable death of Lycidas *(middle lines of poem)*

8   'Digression' 2: The shepherd's calling – the Church; voice of St Peter: the certainty of divine justice

(6–8 Reciprocally look at meanings and values of 'Pastor')

9   Funeral rites for Lycidas – all nature mourns; linked with Arion, another poet with a watery grave

10   Lycidas' resurrection in Heaven – paradigm of the holy poet

11   Distancing coda, return to the locale of the beginning – poem emphasizes itself as art

The overall principles of the structure can be seen clearly in this table, particularly the way in which the motif of the death of Lycidas is interwoven with the general and public issues that it raises. The structure is built around the two sections at the centre: before them, the stress is on grief; after, on hope. We can observe a similar bipolar pattern in all but one of the individual paragraphs, built often around their centres, and it seems to be a structural principle that Milton has deliberately employed to mirror the antitheses in the ideas of the poem – death against life, true shepherding against betrayal, spring against death, and grief and protest against acceptance and joy. Let us now look in detail at the paragraphs in order.

Paragraph 1

Milton did not want to write this poem for two reasons: first, obviously, no one would rejoice at the death of a promising young man; and second, aware of the weaknesses of the first version of *Comus* (as he wrote to Lawes), he was unwilling to publish anything until he felt his powers to be ripe. The first lines of the poem are dominated by this double idea of unripeness and unreadiness: the fruits of pastoral and lyric poetry (myrtle) and of epic (laurel) are not yet ready to be picked, just as Lycidas was not apparently ripe for death, his promise being still only in the bud. The setting of the poem in spring is thus doubly significant: it is the spring of a poet's life before the ripe fruit can be expected, and it is a spring disfigured by death. At the end of the poem we are reminded that the poem is 'uncouth': here we are warned that the fingers are 'forc'd' and 'rude' and the berries/poem will be 'harsh and crude'.

The centre of the paragraph is occupied by the two lines that sum up its whole thrust: the compulsion to write out of due season, and Lycidas' death 'ere his prime'. The anadiplosis, stressed by the caesura, of

> For *Lycidas* is dead, dead ere his prime

throws great weight onto the three key words: 'Lycidas' (repeated in the next two lines), to establish the reference point I discussed above; 'death', which not even poets can escape; and 'prime' which is unfulfilled. But while the ostensible subject of the poem is the death of Lycidas, this paragraph indicates that the real subject is the writing of that poem. Lycidas occupies the important centre of the paragraph, but that centre is flanked by the narratorial voice's reluctance to write, and then by the necessity to shed some 'melodious tear' – the extraordinary collocation of that adjective with that noun demanding our attention to and judgement (whether or not it is melodious) of the poem that follows. The paragraph begins, therefore, with 'Milton', swings out to the dead Lycidas, and then returns to its first subject.

Paragraph 2

Like Theocritus in his lament for Daphnis, 'Milton' begins by invoking the muses, whose power is ultimately from God (cf. *Il Penseroso*,

l. 47). But the ideas swing back to his own predicament: the central
lines of the paragraph turn to the thought of his own death (throwing
a heavy stress in line 20 on 'my'), and the poem that might be written
for his own 'destined urn'. (*Mansus* has the same idea.) The ideas of
Fame in lines 76 ff. are thus neatly anticipated; but their later development
casts an ironic light on this wish for the regard of fellow poets.

Paragraph 3

This purports to describe the pastoral intimacy between the two swains,
but, in fact, sketches more serious parallels between Lycidas and Milton.
They studied together, and studied hard – from morn until night; they
both wrote poetry. There is a subtle distancing of Lycidas and 'Milton'
from the pastimes of other students, whom Milton did not always
respect: it is not *our* 'rural ditties' that were 'not mute', but 'the' – the
other undergraduates are the rough satyrs and fauns with cloven heel.
Damoetas, traditionally a clown, may not have shown a very discriminating
appreciation of what he heard either. There is a delicate, complex
movement in the two sentences of the paragraph around its central
image of the chariot of the evening star setting in the west: from the
darkness before dawn we move to that of late evening, before ('mean-
while') recapitulating the day's events in terms of the practice of pastoral
poetry – the training-ground of the great poet (see p. 54). There is a
skilfully constructed impression of serenity – look at the softness of
their sounds, the slowness of their rhythm (except in the appropriate
onomatopoeia of 'Rough *satyrs* danc'd') – which contrasts sharply with
the plangency of the first two lines of the next paragraph.

Paragraph 4

The major stress, supported by the caesura, in the first line falls on
'change': the rhyme has suddenly become, and remains, much more
urgent and emphatic. The repetitions of 'now thou art gon' and 'Thee,
shepherd, thee the Woods' suggest a passionate protest, a devastating
loss; and the run 'now' . . . 'now' . . . 'never' offers a bleak finality.
We glimpse the beauty of the landscape, neatly sketched by glancing
down, close focus, at the tiny thyme, and then up at the climbing
tendrils of the vine, and then further away to the hazels and willows:
a beauty that is now painful because it seems so out of key with the
fact of death. It is a landscape alive with almost human feeling: the
vine is 'gadding', the echoes 'mourn', the leaves were 'joyous'; the
leaves are not moved passively by the divine afflatus of poems, but
actively 'fan' their leaves in applause. (The passage looks forward to

the catalogue of flowers the landscape *actively* throws on Lycidas' bier in lines 140 ff.)

The centre line of this paragraph, however, undercuts this beauty:

> Shall now no more be seen,
> Fanning their joyous Leaves to thy soft lays.

With that, the paragraph turns to stock images of the fragility of youth and beauty – the canker in the rose, the frost on the buds in May just when everything is looking full of the promise of future harvest. But this latter group of images is not used quite so simply as their stock nature might make us expect. In the first half of the paragraph, it is, by a pretty fiction, the landscape that will miss Lycidas' song; now the frosted landscape, the flocks riddled with destructive parasites, and the rose bud that rots on the stem have themselves become images, symbols of the 'loss to Shepherd's ear'. The movement of the paragraph is thus quite complex. It starts with the response to loss, moves at the centre to the loss itself in a picture of a happy time before that loss occurred, when the leaves *were* joyous; then it turns again to how the loss of Lycidas' poetry is perceived by fellow poets.

Paragraph 5

The first lines recall Thyrsis' reproach to the nymphs in Theocritus' *Lament for Daphnis*, suitably altered to fit the actual place – off Anglesey – where King was drowned. Here, according to William Camden, the father of British antiquarian scholarship, the ancient poets and priests of the Britons were buried. It seems as if Milton is counting on his readers picking up the echo from Theocritus, for he immediately throws it away as a 'fond [foolish] dream': loss and death cannot be neutralized in a merely pretty fiction, but must be tackled in a much more serious way. The aposiopesis in line 57 – 'Had ye bin there – for what could that have don?' – just after the central short line stresses this rejection, and sends the paragraph off to its climactic assertion that even the divine Orpheus 'Whom Universal nature did lament' – not just the various vegetables of lines 40 ff. – was not proof against death (see p. 67ff). Yet in this allusion, and the horrid picture called into our minds in lines 61–3 of the body dismembered by the 'rout that made the hideous roar', we are given the starting points of two new movements in the poem: the 'rout' who refuse to listen to holy poetry and destroy the pastor are not only those who deny their true rational nature, like Comus' monsters, under the power of sense, but also are, or can be seen as, the bad poets and bad pastors of the two digressions. Orpheus, the type of the poet, and sometimes seen (as by Boethius, whom Milton certainly read) as a symbol of the divine, rational part of man's soul, is the one who suffers, but is one whose words are never silenced. There is a subtle mingling here of pain and triumph, failure and vindication, which determines the ending of the whole poem.

Paragraph 6

Grasping this ambivalence, we can follow the elliptical thought movement that takes us from Orpheus to the false poets who do not 'tend the homely slighted Shepherds tradȩ'. These fellows neglect their sheep (see p. 165), and are usually taken to represent the Cavalier poets and what Milton saw as the frivolity of their verse. I consider this probably too narrow an interpretation; rather it should be widened to include, as Milton says in *Of Education* (cf. p. 31), virtually the whole literary scene in his day – writers who were failing to face up to the challenge of creating a national voice by which England might know itself.[10] By implication, those who do 'meditate the thankless muse' are doing just that – Milton is making it plain how he sees his own poetic importance, implying precisely the same view of his mission that he publicly stated a few years earlier (see p. 56). Therefore, this passage is not just an easy opposition of sacred against secular poetry, but is concerned with the *poet* as a creator of a language by which men perceive, describe and understand reality. The 'homely slighted shepherd's trade' is exactly what the narratorial voice of the poem is practising; the self-reference indicates the public importance of this elegy.

All temptations, if they are to be temptations, must be attractive. Milton makes us realize that the temptation not to live laborious days is powerful by suggestively linking it with sexual delight. Sporting with Amaryllis leads on to the greater intimacy of '[sporting] with the tangles of Neaera's hair'. Men may avoid this easy pleasure by a life of self-denial and self-discipline, but those admirable qualities have to be in the service of an absolute ideal and not involve the further temptation and greater sin than any laziness or lust, of pride: the pride that demands public esteem or fame, and always putting oneself first. This is, indeed, the 'last infirmity of noble mind', and I think Milton is here glancing back to Petrarch's *Trionfi*, and beyond that to the Stoic philosophers' recognition that the passion for glory is the last from which wise men free themselves. In Petrarch's sequence of poems, fame – basically, the admiration and approval of one's fellows – is shown to be an ideal to which many sacrifice much, and a not ignoble one at that; but just as fame triumphs over other things, so, too, Time triumphs over fame: who feels men's praise in the grave, and how long does it last after death? What use would the 'lucky words favor[ing] my destin'd Urn' be to a dead Milton? Mere public repute is no ideal a true poet should pursue, even though its pursuit lead to self-denial and hard work. For no sooner does the goal appear within man's grasp, than death supervenes (l. 75).[11]

Line 76 is itself cut off sharply by the caesura. Here Milton rejects views of the poet's calling and of poetry which, on the one hand, see it as pleasure merely and, on the other, see it as a means of self-aggrandisement: the real value a poet should seek is the approval of his 'great Taskmaster's eye'. So Phoebus, god of wisdom and poetry, reminds the poet in lines 76 ff. that the real fame to be won is the doing of God's will, the fulfilment of His purpose, and being welcomed into the bliss of Heaven. (When Phoebus 'touch'd [his] trembling ears', we are reminded of Vergil, warned off too much ambition in *Eclogue VI*, lines 3–4, by the same method.) The practice of poetry, therefore, is a moral imperative.

The verbal texture of this central paragraph of the poem enhances this movement from confusion, temptation and near despair to affirmation and confidence. We move from a series of questions in the first quarter to a series of statements, emphasized by being the direct speech of Phoebus, in the last half. We move, too, from the shade where Amaryllis and presumably also Neaera entertain their admirers, to the anticipated but denied 'sudden blaze' – a blaze that cannot last because it *is* sudden – and then to the reflection of light off glistening metal foil, highlighting a jewel, and finally, to the *sight*, the clear eyes, of God Himself. (And fame is now no inanimate jewel, but a living 'plant' that 'lives and spreads'.) This movement from shadow to light is obviously symbolic: a movement from the shadows of the Platonic Cave to the light of the divine. It points up the concomitant movement from anger and pain to confidence and trust; from ideas of mortality to assertions of immortal reward. The paragraph is pivoted around the central two lines that stress the irony of man's ambition when confronted with the blind Fury who has cut off Lycidas' life, and who might cut off Milton's, too. This throws an ironic light over the fact that this poem is an elegy for a dead poet by a poet who hopes someone might write an elegy for him: the later parts of the poem make us look askance at values and attitudes we accepted in the earlier.

Paragraph 7

After this interim resolution of the stresses and perplexities that lie at the heart of the poem the poem draws back in a sort of *reculer pour mieux sauter*. The sudden irruption of seriousness in the clangorous lines of Phoebus has momentarily lifted us beyond pastoral; and for the poem to be able to finish, we have to return to that mode.[12] These lines focus on the occasion of the poem, the drowning of Lycidas, and the central lines of the entire poem stress the totally unforeseen cutting off of his life by the blind Fury: the sea was calm, there was no wind: 'not a blast was from his dungeon stray'd'. Again, the paragraph changes direction at its centre: the answers to the questions of the first half occupy the latter half.

Paragraph 8

In paragraph 7, the poem has imperceptibly moved from the voice of one man lamenting a death to several voices coming together to speak, as it were, at a funeral. Hence, after Triton, the herald of the sea, has responded to the implied question 'How did Lycidas die?', we can accept two new figures on the scene, Camus and St Peter. Camus, the river Cam personified after pastoral convention, obviously stands for the University of Cambridge, which is mourning one of its promising members: he wears academical dress wittily expressed in terms of the reeds and sedges that bounded that river before it was embanked and deepened by the building of Jesus Lock.[13] On his mantle are embroidered the cabbalistic signs ('figures dim') of the higher mathematics and philosophy, and it is bordered, as the doctoral gown still is on formal occasions, with scarlet. The 'sanguine flower' is the hyacinth – a delicate and entirely appropriate allusion once again to the death and metamorphosis of a young, promising and beloved man.[14]

But then, his entry stressed by an extraordinary hexasyllabic line of two strong stresses – a spondee – followed by two iambic feet, comes St Peter, the rock on which the Church was built, who himself had sailed the sea of Galilee and in a moment of extreme faith had walked on the water, dominating the element that destroyed Lycidas. The solemnity of his appearance is measured by the weight of the lines, the emphasis on the power of binding and loosing given to him by Christ (ll. 110–11), and his shaking of his 'Miter'd locks', like Jove himself in Classical epic. We know from these preliminaries we are in for something very important, and Milton gives authority to his devastating attack on the clergy of his day by putting it in St Peter's mouth in direct speech – just as the assertion of what true poetic fame is was put in the direct speech of the god of poetry in paragraph 6.

I have outlined above (p. 24ff) Milton's attitude to the clergy of the established church, and his reasons for not being ordained himself. This attack, however, is broader: it is against all false pastors who use the Church for their own advantage and ignore the demands of the people under their care, allowing them to feed on false doctrine ('wind, and rank mist') and thus 'rot inwardly' and spread the contagion of false religion. The attack is directed as much against the fringe Puritan movements as against unworthy Anglican incumbents. The language is pungent, colloquial and blistering: note how the contemptuous low register verbs 'Creep', 'intrude', 'Climb', 'scramble', 'shove' suggest not only a type of action but also the sort of person who does it, and how the verbs in line 115 are linked by the coordinating 'and' to suggest the false pastors' busy-ness in looking after their own interests. This astonishingly bold personification in the lines, 'Blind mouthes! that scarce themselves know how to hold / A Sheep-hook', literally meaningless, rings entirely true as a passionately elliptical condemnation of their ignorant gluttony in snatching the temporal goods of the church for their own consumption and leaving the other guests at the wedding feast (cf. Matthew, chapter 22) to starve. And the worst is that they do not care: they have got exactly what they want, and their discourse in liturgy, in sermon and in poetry shows their emptiness: 'lean and flashy songs / Grat[ing] on their scrannel Pipes of wretched straw'. But suddenly we see the pathos of the lost sheep, unfed and uncared for, some devoured by the wolf (the Church of Rome): it is not just a matter of condemnation, but of acceptance of responsibility. Yet the condemnation closes with the assertion, once more, that the ungodly shall not thrive: the 'two-handed engine', the glaive used for executions, is the two-edged sword that in the Book of Revelation comes from the mouth of the Son of Man at the Last Judgment. Like the first digression, this one, too, closes with an assertion of future certainty: justice, like fame, is final, God-given.

This is a complex passage, full of difficult and compressed ideas. One of the most efficient ways of getting such complexity across to a reader is by transposing our minds, as it were, from a verbal to a visual register. In the central lines of this passage, lines 116–17, just such a technique is used: for it is in these lines that we glimpse the parody of the Wedding Feast at which Lycidas is now present, the parody of the Communion that Christ instituted:

> Of other care they little reck'ning make,   ·
> Then how to scramble at the shearers feast,
> And shove away the worthy bidden guest.

These lines contain in an icon the whole gist of the passage, including the assertion that God knows what he is doing; for in the parable in Matthew, chapter 22, the lord of the feast cast into outer darkness the unworthy guest.

The two so-called digressions are closely related. They parallel each other in the movement from despair to hope and confidence, in the intervention of the direct speech of a figure of high authority, and they are concerned with issues that in Milton's mind were closely related, the pastor as poet and the pastor as priest. Indeed, the economy of the pastoral and its vocabulary forces the two issues together: within the terms of the mode, they cannot be separated. Disposed as they are around the central passage in which we glimpse the inexplicable death of Lycidas, I think we have to see here something like the two panels of a diptych, which can swing on their central hinge, each reciprocating and reflecting the other's concerns via the medium of the centre. This seems to be a central structural principle in this poem as a whole, for just as the individual paragraphs Milton elaborated in the poem's second version seem to pivot on their centres, to highlight visually what was always there in the words, so the whole poem moves into a new direction after its central section of these three paragraphs. I do not think this is mere form for form's sake, for it seems to reflect that bipolarity with which the poem starts – this death is meaningless, yet we have to believe it to be meaningful. We notice, too, the movement of the poem from despair and unwillingness to acceptance and hope: again, the latter depends on and grows out of the former.

Paragraph 9

Paragraph 9 begins by calling back the sources of pastoral poetry, Alpheus and Arethusa, which dried up – as in line 85 – as the poem lifted momentarily to a different level of utterance. This passage is often cited as an exquisite bit of nature poetry (whatever that is) and, indeed, the catalogue of spring flowers can evoke pleasant associations; there is a delicacy, too, in some of the phrasing and detailing that is wholly charming. But there is something very odd about the passage: it is chaotic. For a start, the paragraph structure seems to have broken down here for the first time in the poem; secondly, look at the verbs. They are all active, nearly all impossible to imagine – even if we make allowances for a perfectly reasonable anthropomorphism in the 'cowslips wan that hang the pensive head'. How are daffodils, supposedly still growing, supposed to 'fill their cups with tears' (not have them filled, which would be much more credible) and then 'To strew the Laureat Herse where *Lycid* lies' – strew what? themselves or the tears? Secondly, look at the injunction to the Sicilian Muse: she is to 'call the Vales' – a literal impossibility; and when this energetic landscape arrives it is to be told to throw the flowers that grow in it onto the bier of Lycidas. Short of postulating that the world of pastoral can produce efflorescent earthquakes to order, this is meaningless as soon as we do more than glance at it. This sort of writing cannot be explained and accepted on the same terms as the extraordinary ellipsis of the blind mouths holding sheep-hooks we have already looked at: there was passion, here is a flower stall. The passage is the more extraordinary in that the picture of Lycidas' body being washed about in the tide is utterly believable and concludes with a neat suggestion of distance in space and depth in time, where Lycidas has become part of the fables of the British. Some answer to this conundrum there must be.

The clue, I think, lies in lines 152 ff. The passage is intentionally pretty on the surface and meaningless beneath, for it is the 'false surmise' of 'frail thought'. It is consciously bad writing – and therefore, of course, paradoxically very good. There is not only no bier – as the body is lost – but also, momentarily, the facing of the issues raised by Lycidas' death has been allowed to slip, and be replaced by a meaningless sentimentality. (I wonder if the verb 'dally' (l. 153) is deliberately chosen to remind us of other poetry that was equally false and useless, the dallying with those friendly girls in the pastoral shade?) Milton is demonstrating how easily the mind that glimpses truth, as in the two digressions, can slip back from that demanding sight, and its last state be worse than its first. Even the poet who has heard holy tones can make a fool of himself.

But, as I have said, Milton at the end of the paragraph has put the poem back on its rails. The concluding lines contain two references that are more important that their brevity would suggest. The angel is, of course, the Archangel Michael, weigher of souls before the judgment seat of God: Lycidas, too, has to be judged, and so will Milton. (Lycidas' body 'hurld' about in the tide, seems an image of 'Milton's' disordered, directionless life.) The dolphins remind us of two relevant stories: that of Arion, whose music and song caused the dolphins to carry him safely to shore when he was cast overboard from ship – he is, thus, yet another symbol of the poet's power; and that of Palaemon, drowned at sea, whose body was carried ashore by dolphins. And in the world-view that attached a symbolic significance to every living creature in the world (and some not living), the dolphin is a symbol of Christ. Lycidas is now 'asleep in the Lord'.

Paragraph 10

With paragraph 10, perhaps symbolizing the return to unity, the poem turns away from grief: 'Lycidas your sorrow is not dead'. Just as his death had been stressed by the repeated phrase in lines 8 and 37–8, so, too, is the consolation: 'Weep no more, woful Shepherds, weep no more'. Now the imagery of water, threatening so far, becomes beneficent: the daystar sinks in the ocean, yet soon 'Flames in the forehead of the morning sky'. The water is cleansing, and through the 'dear might of him that walk'd the waves', Lycidas has gone through a second baptism into new life in the spirit. At the centre of the paragraph we see him apotheosized, wet now with nectar, not water, at the Wedding Feast of the Lamb, when, in inexpressible harmony, the Lamb is married to his Bride, the Church. Milton has here transposed the poem from the conventionally classical register of pastoral into the mystical visionary writing of the Revelation of St John the Divine, the vision of the Kingdom of God. It is noticeable how in these last two paragraphs there are no hexasyllabic lines, and how much more increasingly regular the rhyme scheme becomes: the perfection of heaven dimly perceived is affecting the imperfection of human art. (Similarly, in the *Epitaphium Damonis*, the refrain serving a purpose structurally comparable to the heptasyllabic lines here is abandoned towards the end as confidence and understanding grow.)

With this paragraph the climactic structure of the poem is complete. Looking back over its sequence, we can see how the poem built up to its first climax in the words of Phoebus in the first digression, a climax emphasized by the pause at its end and the need to reinvoke the pastoral mode. The poem there reaches, as it were, a semicolon. But that climax, the promise of God's love, is trumped in the second digression: the conventional fiction of Phoebus Apollo is replaced by the historical figure of St Peter, and the personal worry about 'Milton's' values yields to the far more general and public assertion of God's imminent judgment and punishment of the wicked. As we have seen, these two are reciprocally related; and after the second digression, another semicolon in the thought, the poem drops its level drastically to highlight the final climax that subsumes both the earlier ones: the vision of heaven, where Lycidas, now no longer just Edward King, but The True Poet – both the true poet of the past and proleptically the True Poet Milton will attempt to be – is judged, not found wanting, and given in heaven his meed of fame. Further, the poem moves from the vocabulary and convention of pastoral elegy to the high religious seriousness of Christian doctrine: shadow gives way to light, the allegorical curtain that goes with pastoral is drawn back to see the reality behind it.

But this high point is too high a strain on which to end the poem: its intensity needs damping down if the poem is not to leave us uncomfortable, not knowing where the narratorial voice that we have heard throughout has disappeared to. So, finally, we return, circling back to the locale of the beginning, to the pastoral landscape in the *commiato* – a regular *ottava rima* stanza. I have already suggested how this distances the poem, pushes it away, and invites us to look as much at the singing of the poem, to examine the narratorial voice in it, as at the poem itself. The unreadiness for the high task of which the first lines complained is echoed in the word 'uncouth': the poet has not yet reached his full power. But we have, we realize, watched a mind coming to terms with and understanding the purpose behind suffering and injustice: it is that that is the real subject of the poem. The mantle that is twitched is 'blew' – Hope's colour, worn by Speranza in *The Faerie Queene*. Now a whole day has passed, and the night cometh when no man may work: Lycidas' sun has set, and the sun for this swain will set one day, too. But for the time being, grief observed has been purged, transmuted into a new confidence. The pastures new wait.

We cannot leave *Lycidas* without a brief glance at its language and especially at its imagery. The question of language is one I have already aired, and it is quite plain that Milton was fully conversant with the debates about its relation to truth that were occupying much of the attention of his contemporaries. It is also plain that Milton was eventually to take the view that the redemption of man entailed as a necessary consequence the redemption of his language, but that redemption does not wipe out the effects of the Fall: those will be there – and one of them is redemption, *O felix culpa! O felix peccatum Adae!* – until the end of Time. Language can never return to the perfection of the tongue of Adam, when it expressed reality without distortion (see pp. 14–57).

This partly explains the Renaissance attempt to create new languages, either from scratch or, as we have seen, from the cross-fertilization of the best that antiquity could offer with the vernaculars of Europe. (Other factors are, of course, the sheer ambition at least to equal the excellence of the past, and the political – in a broad sense – insight that language is power, the cement of a culture whose stability and progress depends on language.[15] This insight partly explains Milton's resourceful and original wedding of an adaptation of the canzone form to equally heavily adapted conventions of Vergilian pastoral in *Lycidas*: for form is, obviously, an integral part of meaning.

Generally, the vocabulary of Lycidas is dignified, even exalted, as befits the occasion and mode. It can rise higher: in the description of St Peter, in St Peter's speech, and in the brief description of Heaven we seem to glimpse the high, exalted style that Milton developed for *Paradise Lost*. But it does not exclude vigorous colloquial and even ugly words when these are appropriate to the immediate subject. The picture of the bad priests in the second 'digression' is energetically ugly; the lines rush together monosyllabic verbs in a metrical imitation of their greed and rapacity; the feeling of anger spills over into the abrupt questions and exclamations of lines 122 ff. Milton is here following exactly Dante's conception of *il bello* – 'the beautiful' – in style: the exact matching of style to subject. If the subject is ugly, so should be the sound, vocabulary, ideas and rhyme that describe it. That matching is a principle of the poem: the onomatopoeic imitation of the corpse in the calm sea in

> flote upon his watry bear
> Unwept, and welter to the parching wind

or of the thunder of the breakers and the swash and backwash tossing the corpse about in

> . . . Whilst thee the shores, and sounding Seas
> Wash far away, where ere thy bones are hurl'd,

show how successfully Milton can manage this. (It is worth noticing, too, the use of alliteration as an *imitative* sound pattern, so that it expresses some of the details of the subject described.)

Yet this makes us notice one of the curious things about the poem: it is not short on this sort of immediate visual impression, often supported by sound imitative of the thing we visualize, yet these impressions are rarely more than momentary. If we glimpse a scene, it is one where we get only the odd detail – like the stretched out shadow at the end of the poem – before we pass on to the next in an almost kaleidoscopic series of mental impressions. It might be objected that the flower passage is an exception to this: but I have demonstrated above that this is impossible to visualize consistently, and the immediate impression of beauty is not being given by any particular handling of the words but simply by the naming of flowers that are all entirely familiar to us from a English spring landscape – in other words, we are doing the most of the work, and if we do not know what these flowers look like, there is little in the poem to tell us. What, for example, does a 'well-attir'd Woodbine' look like?[16]

This problem – and it is a problem, for it makes it apparently impossible to read the poem with anything approaching the visual precision of, for example, Spenser's *Prothalamion* or Jonson's *To Penshurst* – is, I think, closely related to and a consequence of the image-pattern of the poem. But before we pass to looking at the apparent lack of development, the imprecision, of the visual images, it is worth noticing that apart from the speeches and the onomatopoeia, the poem is one that describes very little sound: even in the vision of heaven, we are *told* only that Lycidas hears a nuptial song which is 'unexpressive' – that is, by definition, it cannot be described – it defeats even poets; at the other end of the poem, the 'gray-fly wind[ing] her sultry horn' would surely have been drowned out by the lowing of herds and the bleating of flocks in any serious attempt to describe a pastoral landscape. Yet the poem is extremely musical: its sound patterns are wholly beautiful, frequently capturing the grief and stress of the speaking voice with a plangency that is genuinely moving; long, echoing syllables are built into alliterative or assonantal patterns counterpointed by the cross rhythms of rhyme against sentence structure. Thus, I would say, the song itself becomes the real subject of the poem, and a man singing, its major controlling image.[17]

The explanation for these curious features seems, to me, to lie in Milton's counting on his audience's recognition that this poem is fundamentally literary. He knows that they know he is not describing any real landscape; he hopes that they recognize that he is attempting the creation of Vergilian pastoral in English, declaring himself the heir of that great tradition, the New Poet. This would explain why the obvious imagery is, in one sense, so unfocused, and why the poem depends so heavily on allusion. The real image economy of the poem is generated *through the remembrance of books*: the purpose of imagery, to provide a correlative so that we may thereby grasp the inner nature of the thing in question, is served by relying on or recognizing all the allusions. The fleeting reference to Orpheus, for example, sends us back to our memories of the whole story, and how it was interpreted; the dolphins send us to the accounts of Arion and Palaemon; the references to Mona and Deva rely on our having read, or at least knowing about, the ancient stories of the Druids and their religion described by Caesar and Tacitus. The reference to Lycidas himself draws with it the memory of the *Eclogues*. Thus the allusion in which the poem is so rich is doing the job we expect to be done by open imagery – the correlatives are remembered, literary ones, the landscape and context are associated with pastoral and fully described there but do not need to be described here. They are the materials from which this poem grew and which it is openly emulating. Thus, the real imagery of the poem is, as it were, submerged, capable only of releasing its full charge to a mind on all fours with Milton's understanding of the relation of ancient to modern literature.

Sometimes these pregnant allusions are merely names, calling up a host of memories and associations – exactly as Milton was later to use what we might call 'nominal' imagery in *Paradise Lost* – Namancos, Bayona, Bellera are examples of this type. More often those allusions catch at the significant moment or action whose original context we ought to remember. For example, the lines,

> Comes the blind *Fury* with th'abhorred shears,
> And slits the thin-spun life. . . .

work in two ways. First, the onomatopoeia describes both the suddenness of the action in the decisiveness of the syntax and the sound of the shears in the thin weak sounds on 'slits' and 'thin'; second, the imagery relates to a fully developed visual context in ancient literature, sculpture and decoration, by which we can fully visualize Atropos and her two sisters.

The allusions, too, may be not just to descriptions elsewhere, but to descriptions interpreted. For example, take the much-quoted phrase, 'Fame is the spur'. We all know what spurs look like, and if we have read Chaucer's *Hous of Fame* or Petrarch's *Trionfo della Fama* we might have an idea of what the allegorical personification of Fame looked like; but the two ideas will not come together in our mind. A female figure holding a trumpet is nothing like a spur. But in the emblem books which so influenced the culture and imagination of the Renaissance, Fame is a frequent subject; and in Jean Boissard's *Emblematum Liber* (1593), one emblem is devoted to Fame as the spur of Virtue. We might not recognize this – or the emblematic significance of wolves, with privy paws or not – but Milton's readers did. The importance for Renaissance readers of the emblem books in forming the visual memory, and in conceptualizing abstractions in personal and concrete terms can hardly be overstated (see p. 18), and we have to reckon with 'grim wolves' from the emblem books (and from allegorical painting) – figures of violence and avarice – being automatically transferred back to the sheepfolds of Jesus' parables and the flocks of Arcady.

There is, finally, the issue of the personification images, often nearly hidden: note the *forehead* of the morning sky, the *opening eyelids* of the morn, and that the 'still morn went out with *Sandals gray*' (my italics). These images seem to me to relate not directly to Classical myth – though their roots may be there – but to Mannerist sculpture and painting. When he wrote this poem Milton had not yet been to Florence, and could not have seen the remarkable statues in the Medici Chapel in which Michelanglo hypostatized these abstract concepts of the passing of time: but Milton's personifications are a similar visual hypostatizing of the divisions of the day, demanding for its full significance to be released a readiness to think of abstract ideas in physical terms. We are not asked to imagine the dawn or the evening; we are asked to imagine how they might be expressed in art. Once again, the ultimate reference point of the imagery is art: and thus the poem, finally, is a discussion of itself.

Notes to Chapter 7

1. And that of Milton himself, of course. But I use this ugly expression in order to distinguish between the Milton who wrote the poem and knew

exactly where it was going, and the speaking voice in the poem which we watch wrestling with grief and gradually coming to terms with it.

2. Not using his gifts is a constant worry, whether in *Sonnet VII*, or in the *Sonnet 'On his Blindness'*, in which he painfully reaches a new faith in God's plan despite being unable to use the talent 'lodged with me useless'.

3. The plucked berries relate, clearly, both to the immature fruit that was Lycidas, and to the poem itself, written unwillingly.

4. Thammuz and Adonis are similarly identified in St Jerome's commentary on Ezekiel 8.13–14, and the Syrian legend is recounted not only in Sir Walter Ralegh's *History of the World*, but also in travel books that Milton quite probably knew. His friend John Selden (*De Dis Syris*, II. x) accepted the regular identification of Thammuz-Adonis with another dying god figure, Osiris, and treated his worship as a myth of the cycle of the seasons.

5. The choice of pastoral is more than happy here: for 'pastor' means both a shepherd (in Latin) and the shepherd of God's people, an image from Psalm 23 that from the earliest Christian times had allowed the pagan tradition of pastoral to be used in a Christian context. King was the one and can decorously be pretended to be the other; Milton decided not to seek ordination, but still saw himself, as a poet, as a shepherd of the people.

6. In English, before Milton, it is only Spenser who (in his *Shepheardes Calendar*) shows that he believed pastoral to be capable of high seriousness. General Elizabethan and Jacobean notions of it were too popular and superficial to be much use.

7. In *The Reason of Church Government* Milton says he was long uncertain whether to choose the epic form or tragic drama on the Greek model for his great work, or 'to imitate those magnific odes and hymns wherein Pindarus and Callimachus are in most things worthy.' One earlier poem that bears some relation to the ode and to *Lycidas* is Spenser's *Epithalamion*.

8. The formal structure of the sonnet, a smaller form, though one capable of being extended into a long sequence, descends like that of the canzone from the troubadour *grande chanson courtoise*. There is a similar taste for making things difficult in the German master song: see p. 13).

9. A sort of blank verse, as in some of Berardino Rota's poems. Milton's own blank verse owed a lot not only to the experimental work of the Elizabethan and Jacobean dramatists – particularly Shakespeare – but also to the Italian example.

10. One might compare Bembo's attack in the *Prose* on the triviality of much Italian Petrarchan verse – more fooling around with Neaera – when there was a need to create a new high style, a *national* voice.

11. Milton's blind Fury is a common confusion: the Furies, or Eumenides, pursue the guilty, while it is the three Fates, or Parcae – Clotho, Lachesis and Atropos – who weave the web of men's lives, Atropos being the one who cuts them off.

12. 'Mood' in line 87 may be variously interpreted. It would then have sounded like 'mode' – that is, it would have suggested a more elevated musical strain. Cf. Quarles's Invocation to his *Emblemes* (1635).

13. The wit of this personification is often missed. The poem did, after all, first appear in Cambridge in a collection by members of the university doing exactly what Camus is doing.

14. Hyacinthus (Ovid, *Metamorphoses*, X. 162 ff.) was beloved by Phoebus

Apollo and accidentally killed by him in a game of quoits. From his blood a flower sprang up that bore the sign of Apollo's grief, 'AIAI' (x. 217; xiii. 396). Hyacinths are, again, spring flowers, pushing through the soil when everything seems dead.

15. This insight, so common in the Renaissance, is one our unhappy century's crop of demagogues, and its perversion of the language of politics to the point where truth ceases to matter in the face of public reaction, should have made us take very seriously. The tabloid press, as a matter of policy, limits the range of vocabulary that it uses to a few hundred words: it is *impossible* to dissect the complexities of political or moral issues with tools so blunt, yet millions of people take their information from such sources, and have ceased to worry about it. The result is that their view of the world bears no relation to the reality – yet they have to act, work, and make moral choices in that reality.

16. When we do know the flowers, though, we recognize the dominance of bright colours, and that the phrase 'purple all the ground' must refer not so much to colour as to one sense of *purpureus* in Latin – 'dazzlingly bright'. The ancients seem to have seen colour more as gradation of tone from dark to brilliant than as we do. The 'myrtles brown' at the beginning of the poem suggest that Milton is thinking of colour in this tonal – and for him, basically literary – way, too.

17. Mario Praz pointed out years ago that in the *Ode on the Morning of Christ's Nativity* Milton has a tendency to convey feeling in sound rather than in visual imagery – for example, in line 188,

> The Nimphs in twilight shade of tangled thicket mourn,

the really important thing is not the fleeting visual impression – which is acute enough – but the plangency of the tone which exemplifies the concept in the last word in the line: the tone transcends the meaning. I think something similar is going on in this poem.

8 'The Unpolluted Temple of the Mind': *Comus* and *Arcades*

Human beings, particularly the young, do not seem to like the idea of chastity. This may be why over the years many readers seem to have been very wary of *Comus*: they have to admit its importance and merits, but, in my experience at least, they tend to shy away from what they see as its central message: the dour, killjoy insistence on dull philosophy, poor food and chastity.

It is not part of my purpose now to recommend the practice of chastity or the virtues of a high-fibre diet to those not so inclined – though they might be the better for both. Rather, I am concerned to try to clear away some of the preconceptions about this poem so that it can be seen for what it is. Sexual chastity was something Milton felt strongly about (see p. 59), but mere negative self-denial is very far from the major issue in *Comus*. The poem is concerned much more with the seeking of a true moderation, a true wisdom, where all man's confused and warring impulses will be brought into a harmonious order so that his nature may reach its true fulfilment. The poem is as much about the proper use of our strongest instinct, our sexuality, as about its not being used at all:[1] it is noticeable that the most powerful and sensuous imagery in the whole poem is in the Attendant Spirit's last speech, which describes, in terms of a perfect marriage, the bliss of the heaven from which he comes and to which the pilgrims on earth are making their way through the dark wood. The fundamental issues of the poem are ones that are as relevant (to use a vogue word) today as they ever were: the need for honesty, truth and self-knowledge; the need to recognize when one is being misled; the courage to hope when all seems lost; and, ultimately, the absolute freedom of the mind despite what is done to the body. These are exactly the issues that Solzhenitsyn, for example, handled so movingly – and comically – in *One Day in the Life of Ivan Denisovitch*; they are exactly the issues that, though we may duck them, confront us all. To ignore a discussion as complex as this merely to dismiss the poem as 'against people having a good time' is to commit a worse perversion of language and truth than the appalling Comus ever did.

Comus had been in existence in some form since 1634, and the fact that Milton himself made no attempt to publish it before 1645 suggests two things. First, his conception of his high destiny as a poet may have made him very unwilling to make public in the peculiarly final form of print anything which he felt not to measure up to the demands he made of himself and to the importance of his poetry (the same unease appears in the opening of *Lycidas*). Second, when he did change his mind and publish it, he must have had very good reasons for doing so. I have already said that the composition of *Poems* (1645) seems to have as a central theme the social and pastoral importance of the poet, and also to have clear political topicality. It is at least arguable that the deepening political crisis had so changed circumstances that Milton felt that what had started life as a one-off entertainment for a specific group of people had now acquired, by the accident of time, a general relevance and urgency. For, it is the biggest mistake we can possibly make to see *Comus* as merely a pretty entertainment advocating in the abstract the virtues of faith, hope, charity and the assurance that God's providence watches over those who earnestly seek their Father's house. It is all of that, but it is also deeply engaged with controversies that in 1634 were the matter of private discussion among the powerful, but, by 1645, had taken their place among the central issues of the war.

The first recorded manuscript of *Comus* is that in Trinity College, Cambridge, but this is not the original draft. In its uncorrected state it seems to have been the parent of the manuscript prepared by a professional scrivener (not, as was once thought, by Henry Lawes) known as the Bridgewater manuscript. Milton continued to tinker with the Trinity manuscript, which at an early stage of correction was probably the parent of Lawes's printing (without attribution to Milton) of the work in 1637.[2]

Milton's practice in revision, as C. S. Lewis demonstrated, was to delete technical terms and colloquialisms, and, even at the expense of the dramatic element, to enrich the verbal discourse by altering a simple word for one suggestive and powerful – to use Keats's phrase, loading every rift with ore. There are some significant expansions and additions, too: from the alterations and expansions to the speeches of Comus and the Lady at lines 658 ff., we can see that Milton regarded this passage as crucial. The Lady has to be given a furious independence, and an assertion of her mental freedom whatever happens to her body, by the addition of lines 661–4; the 34 lines after line 670 greatly deepen the understanding of the respective positions of Comus and herself. Milton tinkered a good deal with punctuation, too: the care he took over this shows how seriously he took the exact rhythm, pauses and balance of the lines when a solitary reader was to hear them in his or her own head.

If Milton was coming to think of *Comus* less as a masque and more as a poem to be read, the enriching of the language, even at the expense of occasional obscurity, and the elaboration of arguments and positions make a good deal of sense. The fact that there was this constant returning to the text shows that while Milton seems never to have been wholly happy with *Comus*, he never lost interest in the ideas it discusses.

Milton wrote the work, in the first place, as a sort of housewarming entertainment. But when the house is Ludlow Castle and the new occupier the Earl of Bridgewater, who is moving into his official residence as Lord President of Wales (in effect, a sort of provincial governor), it is no usual housewarming and no usual entertainment. There was an amount of formality and ceremonial we should find extraordinary in the everyday life of even quite humble families; when a family occupied a high political and social position – the two are not easily separated – the amount of ceremony and formal public reference to its members' roles is correspondingly greater. The Earl of Bridgewater's housewarming was not, therefore, just a pleasant frivolity, but a public statement of some of the important principles of his provincial jurisdiction. And as a ruler, even a minor one, he shared some of the obligations and duties of all rulers; like all rulers, his authority was ultimately from God Himself. So what is undeniably well-wishing compliment to him in the 'Mask presented at Ludlow Castle'[3] refers also to the duties of rulers in general to encourage virtue and punish vice, to maintain purity of religion and doctrine, and to foster virtue and wisdom in the young. Its first audience might well have recognized that underneath the compliment, celebration and entrancing spectacle lay a serious discussion of the nature of virtue, and that the Lady and her Brothers' coming home to their father's new house figured the coming home of the virtuous soul to the mansion of its Heavenly Father. They might also have recognized that, quite properly, it had a specific political application, and they could hardly have not seen its relevance to some extremely unpleasant events in the Earl of Bridgewater's own family history which were public knowledge.

Politics first. Some historians have called the 1630s, when for a decade and more Charles I ruled without Parliament, some of the happiest years of the century for England. Nevertheless, all was not well in Church or State, and it was universally understood that the developing crisis between the prerogative of the Crown and the authority of Parliament was merely postponed, not resolved. In matters of religion, the old division, inside and outside the Church of England, between those who wished to take reformation much further and those who favoured a more conservative form of church government was increasingly bitter, and not made easier by the policies of Archbishop Laud, who, even before his translation to Canterbury in 1632, had exercised increasing influence as Bishop of London (since 1628). A pious, energetic, reforming prelate, he sensibly wished to raise the quality and status of the parish clergy, but his lack of tact and his high-handedness encouraged the fears of those who saw his policies as about to reintroduce the 'monkish darkness' of pre-Reformation days.[4]

Theologically, Laud was an Arminian, and thus detested by Calvinists; and he consolidated the Puritan opposition to his policies by forcibly reintroducing into the worship of the Church of England vestments, paintings, and statuary – things which to many people signified an attempt to throw away the hard-won benefits of the Reformed religion and return to Rome. It ought not to be difficult for us, with the example of Northern Ireland, to grasp the fervour with which sensible men believed the Church of Rome to be the embodiment of Antichrist; to be the Whore of Babylon, offering sweet poison to unsuspecting people who, if they fell for it, thereby lost their hope of eternal glory. Though he had counted Cardinal Barberini as one of his friends, Milton wrote in his pamphlets as one of such men, and the Earl of Bridgewater's family (the Egertons) belonged to a group long recognized for their vigorous support of the Puritan cause and their feeling that the Reformation in England had not gone far enough. The family as a whole had a reputation as serious, pious and learned.

So, in *Comus*, the danger Comus poses to 'weary Traveller[s]' might have been seen in 1634, and even more so in 1645, to have a topical and political thrust. Comus could easily suggest the menace from Rome and its fellow travellers to the honest, pilgrim Christian; in 1645, when positions had hardened even further and the English Puritans were being attacked throughout Europe, the idea would have come through even more strongly. Circe is own cousin to the Whore of Babylon, and her son Comus is her agent. Devil he certainly is, as we shall see. By 1645, the political earthquake had happened, and what had once been sufficiently aired in a private and learned, if powerful, setting has accidentally acquired a new urgency and a new public relevance. Just as Spenser, in Book I of *The Faerie Queene*, makes the threatened Una figure the threat to the reformed Church of England, needing to be defended by the Red Crosse Knight, who is himself open to the temptation of vice masquerading as virtue in the false Duessa, so Milton's Lady is lost on her quest for her home (heavenly or earthly), separated from her protectors, and menaced by false rules pranked in reason's garb. The true purity of the church, as we see in *Lycidas*, or in Milton's pamphlets, is under threat, especially from the subtle beauty of Rome.

The Egerton family had also just endured one of the nastiest scandals of the century, and there are elements in *Comus* which sail very close to the wind indeed. Alice, Countess of Derby, had three daughters by her first husband. The eldest, Frances, married John, the son of her mother's second husband, Sir Thomas Egerton, and it was that young couple who became Earl and Countess of Bridgewater. Another of the Countess of Derby's daughters, Anne married Lord Chandos, by whom she had four children, and then, when widowed, Anne married Lord Audley, later Lord Castlehaven, whose son by his first marriage married Anne's daughter, Elizabeth. In 1631 the scandal broke. Lord Castlehaven, tried by his peers, was convicted of buggery with many of his household servants, of forcing his servants to rape his Countess, and of have forced one of his servants to rape the 12-year-old Elizabeth, wife of his son. He was executed in August 1631. The old Countess of Derby would not receive her degraded daughter and granddaughter into her house, though she did what she could for them in other ways, and the amount of pain this large family must have suffered is easily imagined.

With this background, what Milton – and Lawes, for he must have been consulted – chose as the plot of *Comus* is astonishing. Even without the expansions, relating specifically to sexuality, which Milton included in *Poems* (1645),[5] the temptation of the Lady and her physical vulnerability to the assaults of the bestially-accompanied Comus are very near the bone indeed – especially when the Lady is played by the 14-year-old cousin of the unfortunate Elizabeth. We should find it appallingly tasteless – and painful. How did the Elder Brother's confidence in lines 420 ff. sound to Elizabeth's sisters? Yet a case could be made that the event having happened, there was no use pretending it had not; the family had to engage in a collective act of facing up to it, ritualizing it, and recognizing that the dreadful assaults on the unwilling victims imparted no guilt to them at all. In this sense, *Comus* can be seen as a courageous plea for understanding, a plea for recognition that those who had been violated were still morally guiltless: the masque can be seen as taking, in fact, the position St Augustine takes in *The City of God* on the continuing chastity of those women who had been raped in the barbarian attacks on Rome. Those children learning their lines were, *ipso facto*, learning a good deal about their own moral freedom and, perhaps, a way of beginning a new understanding of their cousin.

The Masque form and *Comus*

All this makes the masque sound very heavy in hand, not a recipe for a jolly family party – in fact, rather the opposite – and a perfect bore for the poor Egerton children who had to act in it. Yet, I think the evidence, if only from Lawes's hint that a lot of people asked for manuscript copies of it, is quite clear that it was indeed enjoyed. Masques were, after all, a part of cultured aristocratic life, and we know the Egertons acted more than once in them.[6]

Consider *Comus* itself: it has music and singing by one of the finest musicians of the day; it has dance – though not much – and spectacle; it has some of Milton's loveliest poetry, which to an audience skilled in the hearing of complexly allusive verse would be much more immediately attractive than it is to us; and it gives the opportunity for the very basic human delight that parents take in seeing their children acting and speaking (even if they do it badly), becoming persons in their own right before their eyes, as well as the opportunity children love to dress up and play parts in a charade. And the masque's serious vindication of the freedom of the inner virtue of the mind to stand against devilish temptation, whatever happens to the body, may have offered some consolation, some way forward, to those who grieved for the victims of Castlehaven. We need feel too sorry neither for the audience nor for the young Egertons who took some of the parts.

Before we can begin to guess at the sort of pleasure *Comus* might have given, we need to glance at what the masque form was. It came to England from Italy, and there is evidence that as early as the reign of Henry VIII it was an accepted form of court entertainment. (It was never, and could never have been, a truly popular form of entertainment – it was too expensive, for one thing.) Though professional musicians and, indeed, actors did take part on occasion, it was predominantly an amateur form. At first, it was dominated by dancing, in which the actors were masked; later, the short, acted interludes which strung the dances together became more genuinely dramatic and developed into something like a plot – but a plot which was unrealistic in the extreme and in which characterization was of small importance. The action (and characters) might often be drawn from the mythology which our forefathers knew a great deal better than we do, and was often an allegorical handling of a topical issue. At one extreme, it might concern itself with the nature and duties of kingship; at the other, it might be elaborate compliment to visiting royalty, likening them to heavenly bodies or heroes from mythology.

Dancing, singing and spectacle – often of great elaborateness and expense – remained crucial to the form, and by Milton's day the court masque could be an extremely lavish entertainment. Charles I spent £20 000 in 1634 on a single production of James Shirley's *The Triumph of Peace*, and the royal court especially acquired a deserved reputation for great extravagance in the production of these curious hybrid works. In the end it was the cost of the elaborate costumes, the complex stage sets and the machinery that killed the form;[7] but before it disappeared it had been the accepted way to celebrate a great state or public occasion, to welcome a monarch or magnate, as well as the way in which private families of wealth and taste might involve their entire household on one of the great festivals of the year. (Milton's *Arcades* does just that.)

Although some elements of masque descend to opera, ballet and pantomime, we have lost completely the atmosphere and expectations that surrounded seventeenth-century masques, and it is impossible fully to recover the sensibility that fed them. Masques could be utterly trivial, but the best Renaissance ones are subtle and often highly serious. The fact that people spent so much hard cash on them suggests that they felt them to be fulfilling an important function. Some of the best minds of the English Renaissance – for example, Ben Jonson and Inigo Jones, or, indeed, Milton and Lawes – cooperated on them, exploiting music and elaborate spectacle to celebrate the one particular occasion which gives the masque its relevance.[8]

The fiction of the masque often drew into itself the real role of one of the people watching it – James I as a watching king around whom the masque focuses, for example, or Lord Bridgewater's having his children presented to him at the end of *Comus*. Classical mythology is the stock in trade of the form, and the audience (and participants, for the distinction is tenuous) were expected to have some understanding as well of music and dancing as highly intellectual ways of symbolizing and defining a relationship between man's life on earth and the harmonious regimen of the ordered heavens above him. The masque also uses that language of visual symbol which formed an accepted part of Renaissance public and political life, and which was the recognized way of making it possible to explore abstract ideas that could not be discussed in any other way – a means of saying the unsayable, in fact. In the best masques, watching it or acting in it is intended to affect the real lives men and women lead: her parents, and Milton, might well have hoped that Lady Alice Egerton, aged 14, might grow up to be a woman as formidable, and virtuous, as the Lady she plays.

Despite the great variety of form it could take, the masque, therefore, had some fairly rigid conventions and expectations attaching to them. It is fundamentally a serious form; it may be optimistic – it is certainly never in any sense 'tragic' – and it insulates the disorder that attaches to comedy away in what is known as the antimasque, where ignoble, ugly characters and monsters appear to discordant music and ugly dance. (Comus' rout of monsters is a vestigial antimasque, as is the shepherds' dance just before the end.) Its conclusion will be an expression of order, stability and harmony, and any illusion it may create, unlike the illusion of the theatre proper, will be one which does not take us in; often the last lines of the masque deliberately integrate that illusion with the watching audience. Naturalism of either plot, characterization, setting or language is neither wanted nor expected; the extreme artificiality of the form demands a comparable artificiality of discourse. Fundamentally, it is a hybrid form, where no one element should dominate the others; hence, it is essential for musician and poet and designer to cooperate creatively, each thoroughly understanding what the others wanted to do and agreeing on a common purpose.

Along with the mythology that every author could assume his audience knew – it was, after all, constantly displayed in narrative drama, painting, and even wall hangings in inns – masque frequently exploits that most useful of forms, pastoral (see p. 00). The cultural importance of pastoral drama and fiction as a tool for the isolation and examination of matters political, moral, philosophical and theological in the century after 1550 is easily underestimated: and it is with Sidney's *Arcadia* or Guarini's *Il Pastor Fido* – to say nothing of plays like *As You Like It* or poems like *Lycidas* – that *Comus* has its closest thematic relations. *Comus* is a very atypical masque in many ways and it may make more sense to consider it, especially when we *read* it, as a Platonic pastoral drama: it is stuffed to the gunwales with a thoroughly digested Platonism.

Milton had already had experience of working in the masque form: in 1632 or 1633, he had written *Arcades* for the Earl of Bridgewater on the suggestion of Henry Lawes, who was music tutor to the family. It was performed at Harefield in honour of Alice, Countess of Derby, Bridgewater's stepmother. *Arcades* is a much simpler affair than *Comus*, being chiefly an elaborate (and affectionate) compliment to her, but as it almost certainly comes after the Castlehaven affair of 1631, it also must have been seen to exemplify the vitality of the afflicted family, as a consolation and support to the old lady. It has a good deal in common with *Comus*: Lawes's music; the transposition of real, modern people into a pastoral, Arcadian, mythological world; and the motif of young folk – played in all probability by the young Egertons, Lawes's pupils – searching through a wood (for the 'rural queen' who is their grandmother). These searchers are encouraged by a protective 'Genius of the Wood' (played by Lawes), who hears the 'celestial *Sirens* harmony' / That sit upon the nine enfolded Sphears / And sing to those that hold the vital shears'.

Milton and Lawes seem to have worked very happily together. (Milton, like his father, was himself no mean musician.) Their further cooperation would only have been possible if each respected the other's art. Music and words were expected in masque generally to complement each other, but in the text of *Comus* they are implied to be interdependent; Lawes and Milton had to get the right structural balance. Lawes knew who could be given which part, and thus compose for the players according to their strengths; it has been suggested Milton took the part of Comus, who does not sing but who has to be notably handsome – as Milton was – and thoroughly understand how to get the maximum out of the verse written for him; Lawes himself took the demanding part of Thyrsis/Attendant Spirit, which entails a good deal of singing, the ability to speak powerfully and flexibly, and an accomplished and confident stage presence. The children's lines demand much less of the speakers, and could be memorized and recited, without utter disaster, with that artificiality of attitude and voice young children always seem to adopt when speaking in public. And even if Milton did not know – and it is likely he did, having worked with the family before – Lawes would have told him what would work dramatically and poetically with them, and what were the vocal capabilities of Lady Alice and the girl who played Sabrina – and also how the family stood on a goodly number of issues.

Milton clearly appreciated Lawes's originality as a musician. Six of the composer's song-settings for *Comus* survive to give us an idea of what that first performance might have sounded like, and they demonstrate the innovations that Lawes was introducing into English song-writing. For Lawes was among the most prominent and inventive musicians in an England that could seriously claim to be among the most musically literate nations of Europe. (We are talking not just of being able to sing and play at sight as a fairly general accomplishment, but of a real understanding of the complexities of composition and musical theory.) He was one of the leaders in the move away from the Elizabethan style of solo singing, which tended to assume the intimacy of one singer in a smallish room accompanied by a lute, towards something much more declamatory and powerful – something, in fact, much closer adapted to stage performance, and an ancestor of the styles of oratorio and opera. Here the dramatic effect of the words has to be given full weight, and the music has to match their style as far as possible: isosyllabic writing, where one syllable gets one note, is much kinder to the sense of the words than the elaborate use of melismata (there is a melisma at the end of Sabrina's song (l. 901), however, as a fitting climax to her rising: the water goddess flows in melody.[9]

Milton's respect for and understanding of Lawes seems to have been accompanied by affection. He makes the Elder Brother speak an elegant compliment to Lawes in line 494 ff., suggesting, albeit hyperbolically, the power of his music: he seems to have found in Lawes something similar to his own Platonic understanding of the divine origin of poetry and music:

> Thyrsis? Whose artful strains have oft delaid
> The huddling brook to hear his madrigal,
> And sweeten'd every muskrose of the dale.[10]

> (*Comus*, ll. 494–6)

In turn, Milton's verse is well adapted to the possible demands of music – for example, the dance-like couplets of Comus' address to his monsters (ll. 93–144) would fit very easily with a music prelude, perhaps as a continuo or figured bass in the newly fashionable style, to the 'measure' that they dance.[11] So, too, would the irregular couplets of the Attendant Spirit's epilogue (ll. 976 ff.) after his two songs, which though not constant in number of syllables, have a regular three stresses per line. The (mainly) octosyllabic couplets of the invocation to Sabrina (ll. 866 ff.), all one long, climactic sentence, seem to demand some sort of continuo accompaniment to this solemn conjuring of the water-spirit. These apparently obvious openings to music are, I think, important: just as the structure is much closer to musical drama and masque (see p. 174) than it is to true drama, so is its mode of writing. There is a great deal of exact, almost antiphonal balance: there is a passage of stichomythia exactly balanced between the Lady and Comus which is musical in its tightness; brother answers brother in the same sort of utterance; and the Lady answers Comus antiphonally until her tremendous climax, which finally overwhelms the Comus theme, which thereafter, to keep the musical metaphor, is only heard in a minor key. All the good characters build up to the vindication and praise of virtue which is the argument of the whole work. Comus' verse, though smooth and enticing, is out of key with all this, revealed for what it is by his noisy and unharmonious rout of monsters. And Comus never sings. All this suggests that the work was conceived in musical terms, and that Milton and Lawes were keen to exploit the symbolism of music as part of the moral definition of their masque.

The Sources of Comus

The plot (such as it is) derives elements from several sources: those sources, of course, do not explain the alchemy that transforms them into something quite new, but their nature does hint at the sort of primary assumptions Milton expected his audience to make about what they were seeing. The sources are all drawn from a non-naturalistic literary world where the supernatural and miraculous lies around every corner and enchanters are as common as blackberries – basically the sort of world that the medieval and Renaissance romance exploited as a means, often via the quest or search motif, of exploring individual ethical and moral problems.

The figure of Comus appears as a personification of Gluttony in Ben Jonson's *Pleasure Reconcil'd to Virtue* (1618),[12] and there was a Latin play called *Comus* by Hendrik van der Putten which was acted at Oxford in 1634. There Comus had been developed from the shadowy Classical genius of revelry (the meaning of his Greek name), sometimes depicted as an allegorical figure, drunk and standing with an inverted torch in his hand. The story of Sabrina Milton took from Geoffrey of Monmouth, whose account of early British History he was at this time considering quarrying for the material for his great epic on the national theme. (The use of the Sabrina legend is cleverly topical, too, since Ludlow stands on a tributary of the Severn.)

The basic motif of the girl in the power of an evil enchanter who needs rescuing by her two brothers reminds us of George Peele's *The Old Wives' Tale*; there are elements in *Comus* – like the importance of his illuminated glass and so on – which link him with Peele's enchanter, Sacrapant, and Peele also has Echo answer a calling out. But Peele, like Milton, was drawing on very ancient and infinitely flexible motifs – virtue in danger, the Babes in the Wood, the supernatural rescue – to discuss the issues that interested him specifically, and Peele's complicated comedy had no influence apart from these plot element on Milton's works.

Finally, through John Fletcher's *The Faithful Shepherdess*, revived in 1633, Milton would have come across some of the devices of the pastoral drama developed by Tasso in *Aminta* and Guarini in *Il Pastor Fido*. Fletcher's play might have suggested several motifs: the chastity of the shepherdesses Clorin and Amoret is threatened by a Sullen Shepherd who uses arguments about nature's bounty very similar to those of Comus; Clorin's certainty about the protective power of chastity (I. i) is very similar to the Elder Brother's (ll. 420–37); a friendly satyr acts as protector; and Amoret's wound is healed by a river god – who, like Sabrina, talks in heptasyllabics. The central issue in Fletcher's play, the struggle of chastity to defend itself against vice, is very close to Milton's own.

But above all in *Comus* is the memory of Spenser, with his heroes and heroines on their quests and wanderings through a magical landscape of the mind, exposed to temptation and dishonour, but ultimately to discover the Good, the True and the Beautiful. The echoes of Milton's beloved poet reverberate throughout *Comus*. Yet *The Faerie Queene* was but one of the latest in a long line of seriously moral and ethical romances going back ultimately to Homer's *Odyssey*, as Renaissance readers understood it.

The most striking visual motif of the masque derives ultimately from the *Odyssey*'s story of Circe, whom Milton makes Comus' mother. Odysseus' men transformed by her blandishments into beasts, and Odysseus himself threatened, represent the ultimate paradigm of the power of ungoverned sexuality to destroy humanity. Making Comus' father Bacchus, god of wine and intoxication, brings in the corresponding power of ungoverned appetite, and as the moralists had never tired of pointing out, indulgence in wine and food often exacerbates sexual desire. The dynamic, and the major theme, of the work lies indeed in the fundamental conflict between Reason and Appetite for control of the will and instinct in human beings. The visual symbol of men and women become partly brutish suggests that *abuse* of sexuality or appetite dehumanizes, makes men and women less capable of desiring that beauty or goodness they desired in the first place and thought they would enjoy without its affecting them.

Verbally, *Comus*, like *L'Allegro*, owes a lot to 'sweetest Shakespeare, fancy's child'. Some 32 indisputable echoes, drawn from about 14 of the plays and *The Rape of Lucrece*, have been demonstrated, and there are several words first recorded in Shakespeare which Milton uses. Spenser, too, had a considerable effect on the vocabulary, particularly in the more archaic words. There are echoes, too, of Sylvester and Jonson, and many reminiscences of Vergil as well as some of Horace. All this converges in a verse of often great density and subtlety – far more so than is usual, or even desirable, in the conventional masque. This sort of stylistic fingerprint tells us a lot about Milton's reading before and during the time he was writing *Comus*, and the choice and use of a homogeneous style composed from these elements suggests that he saw the work as standing in a tradition of pastoral drama that, on the one hand, went back to Classical pastoral and, on the other, related to some of the most adventurous work of his own day. *Comus* itself is not unadventurous either.

Faute de mieux, following Milton, we probably have to call it a masque, but comparing *Comus* with some others of the period – not all – shows how different it is. In *L'Allegro* Milton seems to associate masque particularly with the learned Ben Jonson – the appearance of Hymen in line 125 seems to be a reminiscence of Jonson's *Masque of Hymen* – and it is comparable in seriousness of thought and in its interest in moral dilemmas to Jonson's *Pleasure Reconcil'd to Virtue*. But that very philosophical seriousness of theme, with the negligible amount of comedy and clowning in it, and its considerable length, do mark *Comus* off from the typical court masque. The argument between the Lady and Comus, or the discussion between the Brothers, really does matter, and, ultimately, it is where the heart of the work lies: the Lady and Comus raise and air thoroughly issues of importance to the moral life of each of us.[13]

Nor will its dramatic structure allow *Comus* to be seen as a typical masque: it is much more like the development of the masque the Italians called *dramma per musica* (a precursor of opera), to which were adapted structural elements from the much-studied Greek drama such as the prologue-soliloquy (which is spoken by the Attendant Spirit) or the rapid stichomythic exchange in dialogue which was often used as a means of heightening tension (as in *Comus*, ll. 276–90). Yet *Comus* cannot be judged fairly as a *dramma per musica* since the amount of non-musical material, and that very important, is very large; nor can it be judged as pastoral drama, since – to say the least – there is no attempt whatsoever to create the self-contained and self-regulating illusion that is a hallmark of drama. Moreover, it would fail as strict drama since its characters speak much the same sort of verse and produce much the same kind of dramatic effect. The Lady's alarm in lines 170 ff., for example, hardly breaks the even flow of her lines, and Comus' annoyance with her after line 705 does not prevent him from developing long and elegant sentences with an undisturbed equanimity. This is a long way from Shakespeare's or Jonson's dramatic verse, where characters do have individual voices, and even from the different utterance Milton gives in *Paradise Lost* to Satan, to God and to the fallen and unfallen Adam and Eve – which shows he could write dramatically if he wanted to. In fact, there is nothing quite like *Comus*.

A cultured audience cannot have been unaware of how formally daring Milton was being when they watched *Comus* on that first Michaelmas Quarter Day performance. The publication of a text in *Poems* (1645) that had been constantly mulled over by Milton might even suggest that he was offering *Comus* to a wider public as a redefinition of the masque form and of what it might encompass. It is certainly, in its first performance, celebratory and occasional (as were they all), specific to a semi-private occasion, but it is private; but Milton is also determined to make his audience think about and remember the terms of a really important discussion by attaching to them in the memory the delights of a musical and visual spectacle. When the poem was published by Milton, it was that discussion that became of paramount importance.

Structure

Masques were frequently constructed as a series of tableaux – elaborate scenery and spectacle were, after all, part of the delights of the form – and the influence of this is discernible in the structure of *Comus*. Yet it borrows also from a feature we often meet in Renaissance drama by making the justaposition of the episodes highly significant. Shakespeare, for example, commonly balances scenes in their themes, discussion and structure: such scenes need not be, but often are, adjacent to each other.

The Attendant Spirit's prologue acts very like the usual induction to a masque, outlining what we are to see and some of the terms on which to take it. He has not yet assumed the character he will take in the action; at the end he returns to this role. Here he is alone, defined by his 'sky robes', as well as by his speech (and possibly by his entry in a *coup de théâtre*), as a supernatural being whose function is, through the grace of God, to aid mortals in their struggle. This section is immediately balanced by, and contrasted with, the appearance of Comus: another supernatural being, defined by his glass and rod and rout of monsters (who do not speak), whose nature is to mislead mortals to their harm. This immediate and quite detailed contrast is ironically underlined later by the way both beings assume the disguise of pastoral: they disguise themselves as shepherds, they disguise themselves in the pastoral mode which allows the disguised discussion of current issues. Without outside knowledge, we would not, in the situation of the plot, be able to tell them apart: indeed, the Lady has no reason not to trust Comus habited as a swain. Milton here is glancing at a quite important issue, one about which Prospero, to whom the Attendant Spirit bears some relation, warns Miranda: appearances can reveal what people are – as the sky robes or magician's props do – but they can also deceive utterly. There is, indeed, in normal situations 'no art to find the mind's construction in the face', as King Duncan in *Macbeth* found out.

The next structural block is when we see the Lady lost, alone, thinking about virtue and grace. A false counsellor, a misleading, lying guide, in disguise, whom she mistakes for something other than he is, enters and takes her off. This is immediately balanced by the episode with the two Brothers, who are looking for her in the same wood, who talk about virtue and grace at length; in their case, it is a true counsellor, an honest guide, whom they recognize, wrongly, as one of their father's *familia*, that enters and leads them off.

I do not want to push this idea of balanced structure too far, but it is necessary to try to rebut the charge of formlessness and lack of unity that has often been levelled at *Comus*. What we have seen so far is, at the very least, an intelligent control over a rather slight plot to give the maximum scope for the opening up of important issues. It could be argued that the pattern so established is continued even to the integration of the two strands, the Thyrsis strand and the Comus strand, of the action. After the scene change at line 658, an opportunity once more for the symbolic spectacle which the discourse of the piece has taught us already to evaluate, we have the formal disputation of the Lady and Comus. Her body is imprisoned in the chair, but her mind is totally active and free. There is no doubt that Milton makes her win the argument; but the awkward fact is that while she has won the mental fight, she has lost the physical one.

When the Brothers and the Attendant Spirit rush in and drive Comus away without being able to free her from the enchanted chair, several things seem to be suggested. The Brother's recourse to physical action balances her reliance on mental fight; men are neither all pure soul and mind nor all active body. The actions of each are perfectly proper, and complementary. Nevertheless, even together they cannot defeat the 'Principalities and Powers' against whom, as St Paul warns us, the Christian fights in this world. The final defeat can only come, not by man's works, but by the grace of God.[14] Therefore the Attendant Spirit has to intervene supernaturally by calling up Sabrina, a virgin whose wronged innocence won her metamorphosis into the goddess of the river Severn. River goddess and genius of the wood, the forces of the nature created by God, unite to free the mortals so that they can go to their father's house.

The last scene is that father's house: Comus' 'Stately Palace set out with all manner of deliciousness' is swept away, as the meretricious illusion it is, by the honest dignity of 'Ludlow Town and the Presidents castle'. Comus' discordant and unharmonious rout of depraved and degraded monsters is replaced by the Shepherds' dance, rustic, honest clumsiness that knows no art contrasting strongly with the art that has degraded men to ugly and monstrous figures cavorting in a dance that knows no order. (Just as in *The Tempest* Trinculo and Stephano, the corrupted men who should know better, are far more repulsive than the monstrous Caliban, who cannot.) The final movement of the piece is the Attendant Spirit's epilogue, exactly balancing his prologue, and repeating the key idea that Heaven helps in man's trial by grace.

This structure, simple as it is, is based on a series of balanced contrasts linked by the discussion of a single major theme, the whole enclosed by the presenting voice and figure of the Attendant Spirit. Lawes, as Attendant Spirit, is also Lawes as musician; it would be difficult to separate completely this double perception of him (and Milton deliberately plays on it in lines 494 ff.). It may not, therefore, be fanciful to suggest that the Attendant Spirit as prologue, epilogue and intervener carries a further, more subtle, significance: the power of art, including poetry as well as music, to teach, to guide, and to reveal things heavenly to mortal sense. We know perfectly well that this is how Milton saw his own art, a conviction that deepened with age and receives its finest statement in *Paradise Lost* – to which, in many respects, *Comus* points forward.

It will be useful to look at the progress of the masque in some detail, but, as we do, it is worth trying to keep our minds alert to how it would have been seen in its earlier existence. When 'The first Scene discovers a wilde Wood', we can be sure that in 1634 the scenery was adequate to this direction, and before the Attendant Spirit has said a word we know where we are: we are in the wood of moral perplexity conventional in romance from Chrétien de Troyes onwards. This symbol in the literal backdrop summarizes the essence of the action of the poem: a moral theme examined by acting it out in an almost allegorical, certainly symbolic way. All three settings, in fact, act symbolically and relate to each other. First, at lines 658. ff., the wild wood gives place to Comus' 'Stately palace'. This place, where 'all manner of deliciousness; soft Musick, Tables spred with all dainties' captivate the eye, is also familiar from romance: it is the Enchanter's deceptive and dangerous banquet appealing to sensual appetite and indulgence, familiar (at the least) from Spenser's Garden of Acrasia in *The Faerie Queene*, II. xii.[15] The delights of the table and the lascivious music, probably in the Lydian mode considered appropriate for this type, are preliminaries to sexual indulgence which, in Spenser as in Milton, is a turning away from pursuit of a true good to follow a partial one.[16]

Book II of *The Faerie Queene* is the story of Sir Guyon, or Temperance (that is, the *proper* use of earthly benefits and pleasures). In Canto XII Sir Verdant has given up his quest as a knight, and given in to the charms of the enchantress Acrasia, hanging his arms on a tree. Here, in the similar scene of *Comus*, the Lady is being tempted to turn aside from her quest for her (earthly or Heavenly) father's house. In this scene, enclosed and indoor as against the open wildness of the wood, the struggle of mind over sense is presented in iconic, visual terms; the setting comments on the disputation that takes place in front of it, suggesting both the attractiveness of Comus' temptation and its consequences. Both these visual settings (which the stage directions in *Poems* (1645) allow us to imagine), the wilderness of struggle and the false paradise offered by Comus, are in strong contrast to that in the last scene. The house of their father has an obvious symbolism, stressed by the Attendant Spirit's epilogue with its vision of the Garden of Heavenly Delights. It is also 'real', a place in the here and now, where rule is carried on and justice executed; it is the place where the moral victory won in the body of the masque is put into action.

These scenes, therefore, are not only suggestive, with an independent symbolism of their own, but they also help to control the audience's understanding of the action. Even in *Poems* (1645), monochrome against Technicolor, they work like this. The Attendant Spirit's appearing to speak his prologue in 'sky robes' (l. 83), whatever they may have been, is a visual reminder of a main point in his speech: that in the moral struggle which is the inevitable accompaniment of being human, God's grace still is active, and helps in temptation. As St Paul reminds us in a verse that could serve as the epigraph to this poem, 'There hath no temptation taken you but such as is common to man: but God is faithful, who will not suffer you to be tempted above that ye are able; but will with the temptation also make a way to escape, that ye may be able to bear it' (1 Cor. 10.13). Indeed, it is not fanciful to see one interest of *Comus* lying in exactly the same theological question as is dealt with in *Paradise Lost*: if God is just and good, why does he allow man to be tempted, knowing he may, through his free will, fall? 'God's high sufferance for the trial of Man' sounds like the action of a mere tyrant; yet without man's being free to turn away from the Good, his cleaving to the Good is of no value. A virtue that is never tested is no virtue at all: it proves itself only by, as St Paul says in Ephesians, Chapter 6, 'quench[ing] all the fiery darts of the wicked'. We know that is how Milton saw it, and a passage in *Areopagitica* (1644) sums up a lot of the concerns of *Comus*:

> He that can apprehend and consider vice with all her baits and seeming pleasures, and yet abstain, and yet distinguish, and yet prefer that which is truly better, he is the true wayfaring Christian. I cannot praise a fugitive and cloistered virtue, unexercised and unbreathed, that never sallies out and sees her adversary, but slinks out of the race, where that immortal garland is to be run for . . . that which purifies us is trial, and trial is by what is contrary.

Only so do we win the 'crown that Vertue gives / After this mortal change' (*Comus*, ll. 9–10).

The dignified blank verse of the prologue signals the seriousness with which the Attendant Spirit is to be taken. In lines 1–17, he says who he is, describing his errand to those who are struggling on a 'sin-worn' earth (cf. *At a Solemn Music*). He is a symbol of grace. After this, lines 18–45 concern themselves with exposition: a neat compliment to Lord Bridgewater in the audience, the pretended danger to his children coming to celebrate his installation. In lines 46–82 he launches into the description of Comus and his origin. The Circe myth, to which Milton connects Comus here, is important: it anchors our understanding of how to take Comus and the fable of the poem. In Natalis Comes' very well-known *Mythologiae* (1551, much expanded in 1581), Circe in the *Odyssey* is allegorized as *libido* or lust; the struggle between her and Odysseus as that between natural impulse and reason, the herb moly being given him as an antidote by Mercury, messenger of the gods (cf. *Comus*, ll. 636 ff.; *Elegia I*). Such a gift, as Comes says later, is a mark of the divine mercy without which we cannot stand against temptation. (The Attendant Spirit is equipped with haemony (l. 638) a plant even more powerful than moly.) As it is Circe on whom Comus models himself and whom he hopes to emulate and surpass (ll. 150–3), it is fair to deduce that Milton means us to see him as partaking of her essential nature, and using the instruments of his father Bacchus as his tools. Wine itself, invented by Bacchus, is good; but 'misused', it becomes a 'sweet poison' (l. 47) – the Attendant Spirit's oxymoron summarizes the dangers of the misused delights of sense, anticipating the sweet poison Comus offers literally in his glass and the metaphorical sweet poison of his words.

The Attendant Spirit's exposition of the danger Comus poses to 'weary Travailer[s]', many of whom fall 'through fond intemperate thirst' can be read wholly on this moral level, and such, indeed, is its enduring value. Comus, and what he represents, tempts travellers to renounce their humanity by indulging their animality: they assume fearsome shapes expressive of their inner nature (ll. 70–1), 'roul[ing] with pleasure in a sensual stie' (l. 77), forgetful of their true nature and home.This needs stressing before we meet Comus: we have to be made to feel the attractiveness of evil, of the tempter, if it is to be tempting at all, but we also have to be given quite unambiguous knowledge of what Comus really is so that we are not taken in. The monstrous vision also sets up a strong contrast for the idea comprised later in that problematic word, 'chastity'.

Yet the net result of the prologue, even while it warns us that many people do fail the test and do fall, is to set up an irony around everything Comus says and does: in the end, he cannot win against those whom God (decorously called 'high Jove', line 78) favours – or, to use the Calvinist term, 'elects'.[17] His darkness is not proof against the light of the sun and stars that are associated with the Attendant Spirit, the Lady, and the Brothers – a light ironically parodied in the 'cordial Julep' 'flam[ing], and dancing in his crystal bounds' of Comus' cup (l. 672).[18]

The prologue's definition of Comus is immediately followed by visual exemplification – the discord and ugliness of the rout of monsters. In lines 93–144 Comus speaks like the master of ceremonies of this rabble; and having seen him in this situation, after this introduction, it is very hard to sympathize with those readers who find his arguments later in the poem convincing as well as attractive. He is literally monstrous. His verse, too, contrasts strongly with the prologue: it is in lightweight couplets, predominantly heptasyllabic, usually three-stressed, but very occasionally having a 10- or even 11-syllabled line with five stresses (e.g. l. 115) for onomatopoeic congruence to its content. (We hear the slow movement and sudden dart of the fish in lines 115–16; cf. the seriousness of the invocation to Darkness and Hecate in lines 129 ff., 135). It is powerful, persuasive and detailed – exciting verse, for tempters are, by definition, plausible and attractive.

The elaborate mythological scene setting up to line 101 stresses the coming of darkness – welcomed later as a moral as well as literal darkness. The context, where we know what Comus is, makes his invitation in lines 103 ff. chilling: his discourse is a loaded one, the arresting personifications ('Advice with scrupulous head, Strict Age, and sowre Severity'), like those in *L'Allegro*, are to attach an emotional feeling – here repulsion – to an abstract idea. The rhetorical question of line 122 assumes our agreement, but it directly contradicts the wisdom of the Book of Proverbs, or even common sense, when people need to earn their living, and need to go to sleep: the shepherds have to go to bed even in a pastoral poem (l. 93). The view of morality in line 126 (the 'dun shades' echo line 17) is entirely cynical, yet it is also logically inconsistent: if there is no such thing as 'sin', why should we, or Comus, be pleased that these dun shades will never report it? This contradictory idea is repeated in '*blabbing* Eastern scout' (l. 138: my italics), and 'telltale Sun' (l. 141): the Comus who denies there is anything wrong at all is nevertheless conceding the point that there is something that we do not want revealed.

The speech concludes, from line 128, with the invocation to Cotytto. This is solemn enough, but it cuts right against the atmosphere of excitement and anticipation Comus is trying to convey. The vision of darkness is repulsive: a monstrous womb that 'spets' forth monsters – the subtext is full of ugly ideas.. The energy and confidence may carry us along almost to agreement before we know where we are, but the words tell a quite different story – and one that Comus does not want to tell.

To see animal-headed men and women – masquers whose masks had stuck to them – dancing in what, given the clue of the lightweight rhythms of the introduction to it, would be a disordered and trivial measure, a 'light fantastick round' (l. 144), far removed from serious music – would amuse, but would also be ugly. Dancing, a branch of rhetoric, as Cornelius Agrippa called it nearly a century before, an imitation in its order and pattern of the great dance of the heavens, as Sir John Davies of Hereford called it only a few years before, is grotesque when performed by such monsters; and significantly, it completes no pattern, but is abruptly broken off. Symbolically, Comus apparently does not participate: 'there is no music in him', neither does he sing in the masque at all: music is the epitome of reason and order, which he has rejected.

Breaking off the measure, Comus with a new seriousness now speaks in blank verse. He is quite clear about his motives: in pride and envy, he wants as big a 'herd' of victims as his mother, collecting them by his 'wily trains', his 'charms', his 'dazling spells' and 'false presentments' that 'cheat the eye with blear illusion' (they work on a good number of readers). What these are, exactly, Milton shows us in Comus' trickery of the Lady and his deceitful speech to her. Self-knowledge is one of the most terrible of the devil's punishments – and it is as a devil that we should see Comus. He is not served by free consent, and has only contempt for his victims. The very use of the word 'baited' (l. 162) suggests he thinks of his victim as an animal – indeed, much of the imagery is of trapping animals (e.g. 'snares', line 163). The only victims he is likely to catch, though, are those who are 'easie-hearted' (l. 163).

As he withdraws, the Lady enters. I think the change in the writing very noticeable here. The Attendant Spirit's and Comus' verse and roles demand at least reasonable maturity, if not professional skill, in the actor: hereafter, the Lady and the Brother speak much more declamatory verse with much less need for subtle change of tone and emphasis. The Egerton children's limitations are thus taken care of; but also the effect is deliberately to focus our attention not onto them as characters, for they have none to speak of (in some contrast to Comus), but onto what they have to say.

In lines 170–243, she is alone. Her blank verse befits a serious and dignified character describing her difficult situation in what she confirms to be a symbolic wood (ll. 181–2). There is thorough and detailed contrast with what Comus has just said, and not only in form, blank verse against couplets, harmonious song calling forth the natural music of the echo against Comus' interrupted discord. Her fearful dignity completely upstages Comus' self-importance. Where she has fear, Comus has none; she is alone where he is accompanied; she hates the darkness he welcomes; Comus wants to join in with the apparitions, and advises the rejection of any fear of sin, while she fears the deceitfulness (l. 205) of what were real legends, real temptations. While he invokes darkness and Cotytto, she invokes Faith and Hope, the two theological virtues some see embodied in the two Brothers.[19]

The Lady has the confidence that the 'virtuous mind' assisted by a 'strong siding champion Conscience' (l. 211), by faith, hope and the 'unblemish't form of Chastity' will prevail over all trials. Ironically, of course, a champion is at hand (l. 217); she perceives the truth that the Attendant Spirit hinted at in his prologue, that to the 'Supreme good, all things ill / Are but as slavish officers of vengeance'. Finally, she and Comus have entirely opposite views of darkness (ll. 195 ff.): she sees light and the stars Platonically, as Dante did, as images of the light of Heaven shining into the darkness of men's minds. Where she ends, appropriately, in song, he ends in mere noise. In this very first speech, in her darkness and fear, we see Faith in action. (The point, indeed, is made very explicitly: as she asserts her faith in Divine Providence, the moonlight breaks from behind a cloud, emphasized by the awkward chiming of the repeat of line 222 in line 224.)

This carefully developed contrast, the one speech coming to a climax in ideas of appetitive indulgence, the other on the theme of Chastity, brings us to the point, perhaps, where we might as well get the business of what chastity means in *Comus* out of the way. The usual triad of theological virtues is faith, hope and charity, and the apparent substitution of chastity for the last of these has shocked many critics and readers: some have seen it as a 'reduction of the highest supernatural grace to a secondary practical virtue' (M. M. Ross, *Poetry and Dogma*, p. 196). I think this shock is understandable, but mistaken, and partly the problem lies simply in the word 'chastity': today it carries (and to some extent it did then) too restricted a meaning in common use, and reminds us of cold linoleum, too much exercise, and disapproving frowns. But the Lady's chastity is not some cold abstinence from evil deeds, but rather a positive and total commitment to a transcending ideal, an exciting and demanding adventure.

It is first of all essential to grasp the effect the reading of Plato had on Milton's mind. The Lady's seeing the 'unblemish't form of Chastity' 'visibly' (ll. 215–16 – the pleonasm of 'see' and 'visibly' stresses the importance of the idea) indicates beyond any doubt that Milton wants us to see her as enjoying the contemplation of the Platonic Form or Idea (see p. 32) rather than merely thinking of dull abstinence: in other words, Milton is attempting to make chastity in the poem not negatively but entirely positively charged. A remark in Bacon's *Advancement of Learning* (1605), which Milton certainly read, is helpful here: 'virtue, if she could be seen, would move great love and affection; so seeing that she cannot be showed to the sense by corporal shape, the next degree is to show her to the imagination in lively representation' (II. xviii. 3). The Lady's vision arouses great love in her for something all-embracing, and, in *Comus*, Milton is attempting to give us a 'lively representation' of that perception which will lift the audience and the participants in the masque to something approaching that vision.

In the *Symposium*, Plato discusses and analyses the types of love. Gradually he draws the conclusion that he who loves most truly, perceiving in the beloved person the reflection of the lineaments of perfection, will think much less of physical enjoyment and satisfaction, because they can never be more than distractions (enjoyable enough, it is true) from that which the mind, running up the sunbeam to the sun, desires to contemplate – namely, the Good, the True and the Beautiful. Or, as John Donne put it in the context of love for his wife, whose Idea he had loved 'twice or thrice . . . before I knew thy face or name' [*Air and Angels*]:

> . . . by a love so much refined,
> That ourselves know not what it is,
> Inter-assured of the mind,
> [We] Care less, eyes, lips and hands to miss.
>
> (*A Valediction: Forbidding Mourning*)

Plato suggests that as we draw nearer to the Ideal, its little local reflections become irrelevant to our search to be united to that perfection in which alone we find our rest, that 'only to be guessed at desire', as Richard Hooker put it in *The Laws of Ecclesiastical Polity*. Those little reflections, indulged in, can dazzle and blear the clearing sight.

Plato's ideas were readily accepted into Christianity, and, indeed, provide a goodly part of its philosophical language from St Paul onwards. Boethius was a major purveyor of these ideas to the medieval and Renaissance West, and in his work we find stated most strongly that the world of the senses is in no way unimportant but is, nevertheless, only a prelude to that which really matters. He who commits himself to the world of the senses has lost not only his hope of the beatific vision which alone will satisfy the longing of the soul but also his very humanity (cf. Comus' symbolic monsters). None of this is in any way 'anti-life', rejecting (as Comus implies in his speech to the Lady) the bounty that nature (or God) has given her creatures in the world she made for them; it is simply a statement of order of importance. It is the difference between reading the menu and real food to a hungry man.

The doctrine of chastity in *Comus* must be seen against this background. It is not a negative chastity, anti-life, but a positive one, a search for the true good through following up the clues (which can be distractions) in the wood of sense. It is in a real sense that self-giving, self-forgetting love of 1 Corinthians, chapter 13, which strives to be united to its Author, and which is the only virtue we shall be left with in Heaven, for all the others, with their time dimension, will be irrelevant. It is, in the very highest sense, a sexual love that sees beyond sex, with its demand of individuated difference, to the unity of true marriage – the Heavenly Marriage that the Church saw foreshadowed in the marvellous poetry of the *Song of Songs*. The Sabrina episode is wholly germane to the present discussion: the persecuted virgin who has been received into a decorous analogue of Heaven, brought through the water of death to a resurrected life where she has the power only to do good, is the channel of divine grace, sprinkling symbolic water to free the soul trapped in the snare of Comus. Passive innocence becomes an active benevolence; what nature could not do – free the Lady – grace can do.

It is also extremely important that what is arguably the finest and most sensuous poetry in the entire masque is given to the Attendant Spirit in his epilogue: a ravishing vision of Heaven, compounded of the imagery of the Garden of the Hesperides, the landscape of such paintings as Botticelli's *La Primavera*, and focused on the curing of Adonis' wound by Venus, goddess of Love, harmony and plenty. Since Adonis' wound is said – in Natalis Comes, V. xvi, for example – to represent the yearly waning of the year, its cure the return of life in spring, this tableau in the garden suggests the curing of nature by love. And above all this ('farr above in spangled sheen' (l. 1003) – i.e. in the stars that light the doubt of the poem) is the lovely picture of the *wedded* harmony after their trials of Cupid and Psyche, of desire and the human soul. It shares something of the awesome beauty of the relationship between the unfallen Adam and Eve in *Paradise Lost*, each different, each with their own vision, yet each finding their fulfilment in their nature and their relationship with each other and with God. It is a picture of Heaven every bit as powerful and memorable as that at the end of *Lycidas*, conceived though it is in decorously mythological terms. It is a Heaven that is won by those who have mastered sense and learned to use it, not capitulated to it.

The Lady's song is a singularly impractical way of calling out to her brothers for help; but that is not the point. Its harmonious music summarizes and expresses the moral harmony she represents, and it has one very interesting effect: it momentarily takes away from Comus his impetus to evil, and it certainly modifies his original plan simply to trap just one more victim. He knows he is up against something very important indeed (l. 265).[20] The blank verse of lines 244–64 is somewhat irregular, with extra or deficient syllables, and conveys a sense of disturbance and wonder in Comus. He is captivated by the Lady's music as Satan in *Paradise Lost* is captivated by the innocence and beauty of Eve when he first sees her: the will to evil is momentarily stilled, and Satan 'remain[s] / Stupidly good, of enmity disarm'd, / Of guile, of hate, of envy, of revenge' (IX. 465 ff.).[21]

So Comus: his is a very interesting reaction. Milton makes him juxtapose 'mortal mixture of Earth's mold' with 'Divine enchanting ravishment', in a recognition and acknowledgement of the Platonic view of man as a hybrid, an animal with a heavenly destiny. There is irony, too, in that the enchanter through sense is enchanted by a greater magic through intellect. He himself contrasts this music which conveys a 'sober certainty of *waking* bliss' (l. 263) with the music of Circe and the Sirens, which 'in pleasing *slumber* lull'd the sense / And in sweet *madnes* robbed it of itself' (my italics); he admits that the latter de-humanized and made its listeners less than fully alive. After these admissions, it is inconceivable that Comus can seriously believe his own case either in his first speech or as he presents it later to the Lady, and I find it extraordinary that people can still take his argument seriously when its proponent has both here openly, and earlier tacitly and semantically, conceded his opponent's.

Yet, like Satan, he is a spirit, and spirits, though they may know the truth, according to theologians, cannot repent. He persists in his evil knowing it to be evil; yet the sense of wonder spills over into his address to her in line 265, drawing on Ferdinand's welcome to Miranda in *The Tempest*. And then begins his attempted deceit of her.

With the customary artificiality of pastoral, Comus does not talk like a shepherd. What he says about himself, and what he promises her, is all lies: yet, in 'such a scant allowance of Star-light' (l. 308), the Lady has no reason not to trust appearances, even though she is cautious when she has no obvious reason to be so. His apparent courtesy draws from her the unconscious irony of the conventional statement that courtesy is 'sooner found in lowly sheds . . . than in tapstry Halls / And Courts of Princes.' It is, of course, in Comus' 'tapstry hall' that we next see her, where there is only deceit and corruption in the magnificence. (Milton cannot let pass the moral, generalizing reflection in the subordinate clause, 'where it first was nam'd / And yet is most pretended.') With a final prayer that Providence will proportion her trial to her strength (see p. 185), he leads her off.

The Two Brothers, whose names we never learn nor need to learn, now enter. The movement of the blank verse they speak is dignified enough, but unnaturalistic. It is more fitted, as it must be, to the opening up of important objective issues than to the communication of individual nuances of character. It is constantly ornamented by balance of adjective against adjective, noun against noun, by assonance and alliteration. They engage in a carefully structured and argued philosophic discourse, reflecting on the situation we have seen set in motion but they have not: this part of the action is therefore almost like a commentary on the visual icon, Comus leading the Lady off, we have just seen.

In lines 331–2, there is again a prayer for that symbolic light. Again there is a semantic stress on light versus darkness – real darkness, the darkness of ignorance, the darkness of sin. The Second Brother's fear for his sister (ll. 350 ff.) draws from the Elder Brother a statement of his confidence (l. 359), recommending the virtues, practical as well as moral, of patience and fortitude. The Lady is sensible and virtuous, and, in a very close echo of Spenser, the Elder Brother asserts his faith in Virtue to aid her in her darkness (l. 373).[22] His argument makes three main points: first, mere worry is useless; second, their sister is sensible and virtuous; and, third, Wisdom can be strengthened by the contemplation that comes from solitude. Again there is an emphasis on the *inward* light:

> He that has light within his own cleer brest
> May sit i'th' center, and enjoy bright day,
> But he that hides a dark soul and foul thoughts
> Benighted walks under the mid-day Sun,
> Himself is his own dungeon.
>
>   (381 ff.)

– the prison of the self that sin makes.[23] (These lines point forward to the Lady's remark later about the freedom of the virtuous mind.)

In lines 385 ff., the Second Brother accepts the argument about virtue, but sensibly objects that his brother is forgetting that their sister is a woman, and therefore in real physical danger. In a striking image, he contrasts her with an invulnerable hermit: she becomes the Hesperian Tree (ll. 393 ff.) whose garden we glimpse again in the Attendant Spirit's concluding vision of Heaven (ll. 982 ff.), bearing not golden apples, but the fruit of virtue. This is a delicate extension of the image in 'deflowering' (cf. l. 396), and gives much power to his fear of physical attack on her, suggesting almost the idea of sacrilege and the theft of the forbidden fruit of Eden, from which came 'Death into the world, and all our Woe' (*Paradise Lost*, I. 3).

In lines 407 ff., the Elder Brother counters this with his rational inclination to Hope, one of the theological virtues – an act of will, not of mere mood. The contrast between this and his brother's attitude allows the explanation of her 'hidden strength' (l. 415), that same chastity we have just discussed. The lines that follow make it quite clear that Milton could not be talking about mere physical chastity, for then the confidence of the lines would be ridiculous, disproved on innumerable occasions. He develops the idea through the picture of the Lady, like Spenser's Britomart, 'clad in compleat steel'; and of Diana, goddess of chastity, armed as a huntress. The Lady, he says, may go through whatever moral landscape she likes, provided that her chastity is 'true' (l. 437). The thesis is developed up to line 437 and then exemplified according to the rules of rhetoric, drawing on anecdote and authority, in the following lines. They depend a good deal on common Renaissance allegorical interpretation of Classical legend: chastity was the bow of Diana, Jonson's 'Queen and Huntress, chaste and fair'; Minerva's 'snaky-headed *Gorgon* sheild' (l. 447) was the 'chast austerity / And noble grace that dash't brute violence / With sudden adoration and blank aw' – exactly as we have just seen it do momentarily to Comus, and just as we will see it rout him in argument.

The Elder Brother goes on in lines 453 ff. to contrast the spiritual enlightenment and growth to a new immortality, a fulfilment of the self, given by the grace of Heaven to those truly chaste (in the sense we have defined it), with the descent to beastliness of those who follow the demands of the senses. The two pictures are contrasted point for point, the first with its semantic insistence on sight, light and purity; the latter full of ideas of darkness, disease, a liquid curdling (l. 467), and eventually the loss of man's true nature, the 'divine property of her first being' (l. 469). The argument – even the ghosts used as examples at the end of the speech – is modelled on Plato's argument for the soul's immortality in *Phaedo*, 81: noble spirits welcome release from the passions of the body, but after death the souls of the wicked are held back on earth because of their commitment to the desires of the flesh.

The argument convinces the Second Brother – as, of course, it would. What really matters is whether it convinces us within the terms of the masque. As straight philosophy, it is unexceptionable: Plato's discussion became part of the Christian tradition; there are echoes of it in St Paul, and much fuller borrowing from it in Lactantius and Augustine. Indeed, the Second Brother is right – then, as now – to stress that, *properly understood*, 'Divine Philosophy' is anything but dull, dour and repressive, but that it is, in fact, exciting and liberating (ll. 476 ff.). Put in context, his argument acts as a structural fulcrum between Comus' exemplification, with his rout, of the effects of sensuality and his hot, excited enticement to self-indulgence, and the debate between the Lady and Comus. These thoughts have to appear in a poem that purports to examine the relationship between earthly moral action and man's heavenly destiny, but it is difficult to see how they could have been satisfactorily given to the Lady or the Attendant Spirit (though both, obviously, are fully cognisant of them). The Attendant Spirit is, after all, above the fray, and the speech from him would sound like an easy evasion; the Lady is in the thick of it and fighting in detail rather than taking the grand philosophic view.

We are, therefore, left with only the Elder Brother to enlarge on the basic philosophic underpinning of the piece; and, of course, a couple of real young men who found themselves having to learn these lines might find themselves repeating them when they were older and more prone to the temptation from which their present immaturity shielded them. Lord Bridgewater cannot have taken it ill that his two sons had to learn a digest of virtually all the Christian Platonic discussion of virtue! Here, indeed, playing a part in the masque that Michaelmas night might affect the real lives of its performers in later years. It is unfashionable to say it nowadays, but it is really not all that uncommon for real men and women in all their confusions and contradictions, backslidings and inconsistencies, to seek to live a godly, righteous and sober life. They succeed surprisingly often.

Yet the Brothers, however good they are at philosophy, cannot perform a rescue on their own, nor can the Lady fight wholly alone. Action to help them from outside each of their contexts *is* needed – people help each other, for they are God's agents, but in the end God's grace acts directly as well: the Attendant Spirit is both a *genius ex machina* symbolizing the grace that extends the saving possibility in any human situation and an enabler of other people's action. Here, at the exact centre of the work, the Attendant Spirit is given a very serious speech outlining to the Brothers the nature of the threat their sister faces.[24]

For us, this speech is a substantial restatement and reinforcement of his initial description of Comus in lines 46 ff.; for the Brothers, it is an immediate test of how well they have learnt their lesson of Faith and Hope. The Second Brother sounds a note of utter dismay (line 580 – significantly, his exclamation is in terms of 'night and shades'), but in one of the most vigorous passages in the work, full of emphatic rhythms and very precisely visualized imagery, the Elder Brother reasserts his faith in virtue's impregnability whatever its outward circumstances, in the protection of a purposive Providence ('which erring men call Chance', line 588), and in the ultimate non-entity and self-contradictoriness of evil (ll. 593 ff.; cf. *Paradise Lost*, II. 795–802; XI. 50–3). Credibly, his first impulse is to physical action, but the Attendant Spirit points out the uselessness of this to him: they need the protection of the herb

Haemony, more powerful even than moly (l. 636), by which Milton suggests not only divine mercy but also the supernatural power by which, as St Paul says, we wrestle not against 'flesh and blood' but against principalities, against powers'.[25]

When we see the Lady with Comus he has dropped his mask of benevolence. His language now is of open threat – though recalling Daphne and Apollo works in a valuing way he would not want. (Daphne fled the amorous advances of Apollo, and as he overtook her, in answer to prayer she was turned into a laurel tree. Her chastity was thus preserved.) But the Lady sees the essential stupidity of evil, destroying the thing it wants to enjoy: 'Fool, do not boast' begins her vigorous riposte that her body may be captive, but her mind is still free; and the captivity of her body is only 'while Heaven sees good' (cf. *Paradise Lost*, I. 253–5). Behind this is the idea developed most fully in St Augustine's *City of God* that those virtuous ladies, Christian or not, who are raped – like Lucretia – retain their moral chastity, integrity and the purity of their mind; it is an idea that is not unfamiliar to us from the testimony of those who have suffered under the tyrannies of this century.

Comus cannot answer this repulse, and changes his tack. His tone now become wheedling and emollient, his speech full of ideas of springtime, youth, delicious tastes, forgetfulness, and rest after toil. But the argument is also more subtle, and anticipates the line he will develop later. It is one of the chief arguments of those who justify temperance (of all kinds) that the body is a 'trust' (l. 682) 'lent' (l. 680) by nature; Comus anticipates that the Lady might deploy this argument and gets in first (ll. 680 ff.), twisting it to argue that as the body is a trust it should be cosseted and looked after. The natural conclusion of the speech is the offering of the drink to 'restore' her body after the trials of the day, but in so doing he makes a fatal mistake: his deception of her already means that nothing he offers or does can be taken at face value. He has lied to her already and she knows he is lying now (ll. 690 ff.). Everything around her shows he is not to be trusted, and an evil being cannot be expected to act out of pure benevolence, as Comus is trying to pretend to do.

So far, love: 30. Both of Comus' openings are blasted out of court, and he has no reply to her shots. So he now changes tack again, with a world-weary shake of the head, more in sorrow than anger, attacking 'budge doctors of the *Stoick* Furr'. The first few lines of his speech (ll. 705 ff.) are a clever bit of smear tactics: abstinence might be quite nice, for all we know, but it is *personified* (cf. ll. 108–10) as something ugly, unattractive and unhealthy – 'lean and sallow'[26] – and the proponents of Stoic or Cynic virtue, which taught renunciation of the world and the mastery of the senses by the mind in the pursuit of true felicity, are presented as fussy old dons in antiquated academic dress. Fussy old dons can, of course, occasionally be wise men, but Comus' line tries to make us dismiss their ideas not for what they are but because of what the lecturer is wearing. (Comus has, of course, his modern descendants in many universities.) This ridicule is a prelude to his development of his most important passage in the poem: the praise of nature's bounty and argument for self-indulgence in lines 710 ff.

The passage divides into two obvious parts, lines 710–36, and 737–55. The latter part was not in the version of the masque performed at Ludlow, and the probability is that Milton developed and included this specifically to underline the plausibility of this appeal to what is one of our strongest impulses when he was no longer constrained by its having to be spoken publicly to a 14-year-old girl. There were, after all, excellent reasons why he should not include it in the first performance. As time freed the text from the demands of that Ludlow performance, the Lady could cease to be Alice Egerton playing a role in front of her family and become a universal, representative figure. The lines are the climax of Comus' most powerful speech and the point of all his argument: it is the Lady's sexual chastity he is attacking, not her abstention from what she calls 'lickerish baits' (l. 700) – for he is unable to grasp that chastity might be something that has a dimension beyond sexuality. Milton's expansion draws heavily on a strong tradition of *carpe diem*, 'Gather ye rosebuds while ye may', a theme very popular in Latin and vernacular poetry in the sixteenth and seventeenth centuries, and going back ultimately to Ausonius and Horace. (Some of it is genuine, but a lot is ironic, like Marvell's *To his Coy Mistress*: Comus is speaking without irony, but in an ironic situation, of course.) Yet Comus' appeal – which amounts to an argument for complete promiscuity – really turns not on any logical argument but first of all on a threat – time is slipping away, her flowers will die (ll. 743–4) and so will she – and then, exactly like Satan to Eve in *Paradise Lost* (IX. 533–48, 568–612, 679–732), it appeals to her pride and vanity (ll. 748 ff.): she is made for better things than to be a good housewife (ll. 748 ff.); she is exorbitantly beautiful (ll. 752 ff.). He seeks to win her by flattering her sense of her own uniqueness, importance and power.

Comus' speech, even as delivered at that first performance, is extremely attractive: it has to be, for this is the central moral clash of the whole work. The detailed picture of nature's bounty is very powerful, and the scornful charge of ingratitude near enough to what might be true to be persuasive. But Comus even here makes slips: he refers to the 'all-giver' and the duty to 'praise' him (l. 723), thus tacitly admitting a moral sanction on conduct besides mere hedonism; the 'ore and precious gems' of line 719 are 'all-worshipt', which is the sin of avarice. Moreover, his basically syllogistic argument is grounded on a false major premise. The syllogism might run: nature gave everything to her children to be enjoyed to the utmost; nature's gifts are rejected by those children; therefore nature's purpose is defeated – the children are being unnatural. But the major premise is not certain; it demands argument itself, and it pre-empts the conclusion Comus wants to draw. Comus' argument is full of other fallacies: he implies that you should take what you can, not thinking of others (countered in lines 768 ff.), and the picture of the world sinking under the weight of uneaten food is frankly ludicrous.

Not for a second is the Lady taken in: the proof of what Comus is and where he leads is all around her. She returns his wheedling address to her as 'you' with a spate of contemptuous repetitions of 'thou'; she recognizes the attempt to present a syllogistic argument and sees that the rationality is only apparent: 'false rules pranckt in reasons garb' – the clothing image refers once again to the idea of disguise that attaches powerfully to Comus in the poem. Comus is a 'Jugler' who has deceived once and is trying to do so again by the power of rhetoric – 'dear Wit and gay Rhetorick / That hath so well been taught her dazling fence [swordplay]' (ll. 790–1). She gives in lines 760 ff. a point-for-point refutation of what Comus has argued: the selfish use of the world he counsels ignores the fact that Providence has given everything in the world a purpose entire unto itself as well as useful to man, and man has a duty not to look out just for himself but to ensure an equitable and just distribution of the world's benefits. The final, climactic picture of

> swinish gluttony
> Ne're look[ing] to Heav'n amidst his gorgeous feast,
> But with besotted base ingratitude
> Cramms, and blasphemes his feeder. . . .

glances back at Comus' monstrous following; turns his idea of ingratitude on its head; and, in its vigorous ugly verb 'crams', makes the very action physically repulsive. (It also interestingly anticipates the hireling shepherds of *Lycidas*, lines 117 ff.)

The Lady then (ll. 779–806) is given, in the later version, a response to Comus' attack on her physical chastity. Strictly speaking, it is not a reply, for it is difficult to see how a reply could be made to Comus' argument, given that his terms pre-empt any alternative conclusion to the one he reaches. Rather, it is a statement, and a powerful one, of an alternative vision. It is a vision of the 'Sun-clad power of Chastity' as an Idea that Comus could never share – 'thou art worthy that thou shouldst not know / More happiness then this thy present lot.' As he could never by his nature share it, it cannot be explained to him. Her speech rises to a magnificent and passionate climax, in which we seem to hear the voice of the Idealist Milton himself, stating at once the power of poetry to convey something of the glory that is hidden from mortal sight and its own inevitable failure to do so completely.

Comus' next lines are clearly an aside; he is admitting defeat, and in his fright he thinks of the Classical analogue of the fall of the rebel angels to Hell (ll. 803–5). Yet he continues to try, once again attempting no counter to the Lady but changing the direction of his attack. Threat has failed; apparent concern for her wellbeing has failed; argument has failed; now he seems to be beginning to try jocund bonhomie and the pressure of the argument that it would be impolite on her part not to obey the rules of the house; he also suggests she is out of sorts, and that that indisposition is affecting her thinking (l. 819). But there is no point in developing this further, for the main argument of the work has been reached and passed.

The Brothers cannot by mere physical force free the Lady from the enchantment that binds her body. The Attendant Spirit, therefore, in music invokes Sabrina, whose story was told by Meliboeus (l. 822) – probably also by Spenser, *Faerie Queene*, II. x – and who has passed from the suffering of this present time, in which the Lady and Brothers are still caught, to a new life beyond death.[27] Music, as we would expect, is the means whereby the mortal is connected to the immortal; the Attendant Spirit's song is a prayer for grace. From this point on, the masque abandons the blank verse appropriate for narrative, in favour of predominantly three-stressed heptasyllabics, usually rhymed, most often in couplets – ideal for *recitativo* setting. This more obviously song-like metre marks the lifting of the action onto a level beyond anything approaching the naturalistic; it marks an integration of the discourse of music and the discourse of words, with all the symbolism that entails.

The Attendant Spirit's solemn spell is answered by Sabrina's song and her sprinkling of water over the Lady. That water reminds us of the lustral water of Classical purificatory ceremonies, but much more obviously of the water of baptism, the washing away of Original Sin. The Lady, now freed by this solemn rite, can go directly to her 'Fathers residence' (l. 947).

The Attendant Spirit's song dismissing the dancing shepherds is really the conclusion of the human action of the masque, and it offers a useful summary of what its concerns have been. Youth has been fairly tested (l. 970) – as it must be if virtue is to have any meaning – in the three young people; specifically, they have proved their patience, their faith, and their truth, and will triumph in 'victorious dance / O'er sensual Folly, and Intemperance'. Like all summaries, it is reductive of the complexity of the experience we have had while reading; but it does offer us a line on how we should take the totality of the work. Just as in *Paradise Lost* Milton suggests that his narrative will have as one of its themes 'God's high sufferance for the trial of Man', so here he implies that the withstanding of temptation is not only a prerequisite of any moral virtue but also a mark of the divine love for mankind: if 'that which purifies us is a trial' (*Areopagitica*), it is only by going through the wood that we can reach Heaven. Without trial, there can be no raising of fallen, fallible men to the unspeakable joys of Heaven we glimpse in the Attendant Spirit's vision of the married love of Cupid and Psyche, that is, of love itself and the human soul. Tempters like Comus think they are serving their own ends when all the time they are being used by the Eternal Wisdom.

There have been many attempts to interpret *Comus* as straight allegory – that is, a form of narrative where, so to speak, one has one notation (the text) carrying two quite independent meanings. But no one reading of it as rigidly consistent allegory – there have been many ingenious ones – seems, to me, to be totally satisfactory; the work seems to work through symbolism and suggestion, and to leave a good deal to our own response to it. We have also to allow for the peculiar circumstances of the masque's first appearance, where its situation would much have affected its reception and interpretation.

Comus is clearly full of Christian Neoplatonic ideas, and interpretation as a Neoplatonic allegory has been proposed. For example, we could read it thus: Jove in line 20 could be taken as both the World Soul and the Platonic Entelechia, as well as Divine Providence – Milton's contemporaries were perfectly happy to use Classical mythology as a foreshadowing of Christian understanding of the universe, and to talk about matters concerning God himself in the disguise of Olympus. The action in the wood takes place in the realm of nature, of which both Comus and Sabrina are ministers, and describes the descent of the soul from Heaven, its struggles against the demands of the flesh, and its victorious return. The Lady might, then, represent reason, queen of the soul, and Sabrina the *mens*, a faculty of the soul that preserves the memory of its origin.[28] Haemony, necessary to the defeat of temptation and the freeing of the mind, stands for Christian philosophical knowledge; the Elder Brother, for idealism; and the second Brother, for patience. The emphasis on chastity descends from Marsilio Ficino, one of the most important Neoplatonic philosophers of the Renaissance, who argues that chastity is one of the seven ways in which may be accomplished the turning point in the soul's journey to heaven, that is, the rejection of the flesh.[29]

But it is clear that the neatness of this, and of similar readings, strains the way we *can* read it in order to fit a thesis: the allegorical view of Comus himself is odd to hold while reading, for example, and the Brothers seem to be something of a problem to reconcile with an allegorical reading. Nevertheless, such a reading cannot be dismissed out of hand: especially after the work was printed, there would be many readers with a deep knowledge of Neoplatonism who would have been happy to subject it to a rigorous exegesis on these lines.

Comus certainly has allegorical features. The externalization and hypostatizing of inner moral or emotional conflict is what allegory was invented for in the first place, and we have it here. It obviously affects the characterization, which is flat and bare, not because Milton could not cope with characterization (*Paradise Lost* or *Samson Agonistes* shows that he could very well), but because he wanted it like that. We never learn the Lady's or the Brothers' names, nor do we need to: what they represent and exemplify is far more important to the masque than what they like for supper. Together they certainly seem to symbolize the power of the three theological virtues, and it is possible to see the Lady as representing spiritual love, the Elder Brother as Hope, and the Second Brother as faith (again, though, that easy identification of individual to virtue creaks). They also indicate the limitation of the virtues without God's grace that ultimately grants salvation, while at the same time insisting on the absolute imperative for men to seek to practise those virtues.

But it would make equally excellent sense to see the Lady as (as well as everything else) the will, which, informed by virtue, transforms virtue into virtuous action – as Sir Philip Sidney insisted. The Lady and Brothers then would become parts of the ideal Christian mind, aided by grace, on its way to its fulfilment, and a different comprehensive interpretation would follow. In fact, it is actually far more satisfactory, with a work so rich and detailed as *Comus*, to avoid seeking a consistent and unvarying allegory. The characters can work in several different symbolic modes at different times or at the same time; those references will be convergent rather than overlapping; mutually enriching rather than exclusive. For, part of the pleasure of a great poem, which *Comus* undoubtedly is, is its deliberately contrived multivalency.

The complexity and richness of presentation of the masque, and the peculiar relationship of an audience to people they know acting a part, necessarily disappear in *Poems* (1645). There can be no music, no scenery save what is built in the mind, and no relationship between an audience and characters who are played by people they know. In

Poems (1645), *Comus* has become a poem, and the issues in it therefore bulk much more starkly. One could have related in something like a human way to Lady Alice speaking her lines; but the Lady has no detailed personality when those lines are read. The two Brothers might charm as children, but in the poem their symbolic and philosophical function is paramount. We can be sure Milton was aware that *Comus* (1645) was a very different thing from *Comus* (1634).

In its modified version in *Poems* (1645), *Comus* is subject to much more detailed exegesis and much deeper scrutiny than the masque ever had – for the solitary reader can go at his own pace, flick back over pages, stop and think, compare and contrast. Many seventeenth-century readers would do so, for they expected the reading of poetry to be a difficult and arduous business, not revealing anything like all its riches on a first reading. In that volume *Comus* is notable as the most open and developed statement of Milton's moral thought, and, clearly, must engage with the manifold moral arguments and theories being offered in the 1640s – Milton's own political and divorce pamphlets, for which he was already getting some notoriety, included. The masque's defence of a Neoplatonic Christianity would not have been particularly pleasing to the ears of some of the more Bible-bashing literalists on the extreme Puritan side, and some of the extreme sects like the Ranters, Griddletonians and Muggletonians deployed arguments not unlike Comus'. What may, in 1634, have been read as an attack on the policies of Laud would, by 1645, have been still more unpleasant to the ears of some of the King's party, and one more warning against the blandishments of Rome (*Lycidas*, lines 137–8, indicates Milton's worry about conversions to Rome).

Some critics have maintained that in 1634 *Comus* was a restatement of serious Neoplatonism against the fashionable, superficial Platonism of the Stuart court encouraged by the Queen, and exemplified in such plays as D'Avenant's *The Fair Favourite*, and this argument may have some truth in it; but, by 1645, *Comus* has lost this immediate topicality, but is taking its place in the developing moral controversy over what the French called 'libertinage' – a complete scepticism in religion and a consequent disregard of the normal social taboos, especially sexual – which is exemplified in Randolph's *Muse's Looking Glasse* and discussed (later) in Molière's *Don Juan*. *Comus* also gives powerful, if tacit, support to the Platonism being developed at Cambridge by Benjamin Whichcote and others (see p. 34).

Moreover, the positioning of *Comus* at the end of the English poems puts it in a naturally climactic position if only on account of its length; when looked at more closely, one can see that *Comus* is the most exhaustive and general exploration of ideas of virtue; of the relationship between human life on earth, the Providence of God, and trial and suffering that has been continually surfacing from the moment the reader first started on the *Nativity Ode*. *Comus* is also, as drama of however odd a kind, the least personal exploration of them. But most noticeable of all, perhaps, is its emphatic assertion and demonstration of the power of the poet. On the one hand, the Attendant Spirit as artist leads the audience to a vision of heaven, and guides his people home; on the other, Comus' stunning appeal to the senses through the illusion of words could lead them to hell. This is very near what I see as the central theme in this extraordinary collection of poems, this manifesto for the 'New Poet': namely, the moral and spiritual responsibility of the artist and his obligation to use properly 'that one talent which is death to hide'.

Notes to Chapter 8

1. It is well to bear in mind that there is a strong strand in Western thought – going back ultimately to Aristotle – that sees the fulfilment of our sexual nature (which, as The Book of Common Prayer insists, is God-given and therefore in itself a good) as capable of being achieved only in continence and chastity. St Thomas Aquinas gives the idea full discussion, and many will have noticed it in the poetry of the celibate priest, G. M. Hopkins.
2. Lawes gave the excuse that the demand for copies of it 'hath tired my Pen' – suggesting it was already a *succès d'estime*. Milton cannot wholly have been dissatisfied with *Comus*, for a copy of this printing was probably what Milton sent to Sir Henry Wotton. Despite the difference in their years, Wotton seems to have become something of a friend. Milton prints in *Poems* (1645) Wotton's letter of thanks, in which he says he had been unaware of the author's identity: one can see why, especially if Milton was staking out claims in that volume. Wotton would 'much commend the Tragical part, if the Lyrical did not ravish me with a certain Dorique delicacy in your Songs and Odes, whereunto I must plainly confess to have seen yet nothing parallel in our language: *Ipsa mollities.*'
3. The work was not called *Comus* until it was 'Adapted to the Stage' by Dr John Dalton in 1738. Lawes and Milton called it merely 'A Mask, presented at Ludlow Castle'.
4. Alexander Gil, the son of Milton's old headmaster at St Paul's, was fined £2000 and deprived of his degrees and holy orders by Laud in the Court of Star Chamber for speaking lightly of Charles I and of the Duke of Buckingham in the wine cellar of Trinity College, Oxford. This sort of high-handedness would hardly endear Laud to anyone, let alone Milton.
5. Some critics think they may have been part of the original, cut out by Lawes for performance.
6. They had acted in Milton's *Arcades* a couple of years earlier, and in the same year the boys took parts in Thomas Carew's *Coelum Britannicum* (for which, too, Lawes wrote the music).
7. It was commonplace for 'gods' to descend (as the Attendant Spirit does)

from 'Heaven' (on wires), or rise from the earth (like Sabrina), and for earthquakes, floods and sea-fights to be represented.

8. The masque of goddesses that Prospero puts on for the betrothal of Ferdinand and Miranda in *The Tempest*, for example, is very much a one-off thing: it will lose all point once they have married.

9. Cf the sonnet (XIII) 'To my Friend, Mr. Henry Lawes, on His Airs':

> Harry, whose tuneful and well-measured Song
> *First taught our English Music how so span*
> *Words with just note and accent, not to scan*
> *With Midas' ears, committing short and long,*
> Thy worth and skill exempts thee from the throng,
> With praise enough for Envy to look wan;
> To after age thou shalt be writ the man
> That with smooth air couldst humour best our tongue.
> *Thou honour'st Verse, and Verse must lend her wing*
> *To honour thee, the Priest of Phoebus' choir*
> That tun'st their happiest lines in Hymn, or Story.
> Dante shall give Fame leave to set thee higher
> Than his Casella, whom he woo'd to sing,
> Met in the milder shades of Purgatory.
>
> [italics mine]

10. Calling Lawes Thyrsis is also a neat compliment: Thyrsis was the name of the pastoral singer in Theocritas, *Idyll I*, who also takes part in the singing-match in Virgil's *Eclogue VII*. Lawes's art, by implication, drinks deep of ancient and poetic wells.

11. Milton's care over punctuation, which I mentioned above, indicates an extreme sensitivity to rhythm and phrasing, elements which in a musical/verbal piece are essential to clarity.

12. The title alerts us to a favourite Renaissance theme, often handled through the story of Hercules, who found how to do this apparently impossible thing. It also arises in *Antony and Cleopatra*, where Antony is often linked with Hercules. See my 'Cleopatra's Prudence: Three Notes on the Use of Emblems in *Antony and Cleopatra*', *Shakespeare Jahrbuch (West)*, 1986, pp. 119–37.

13. It is wholly just to hear in Comus' temptation of the Lady an anticipation of Satan's temptation of Eve, in Book IX of *Paradise Lost*, and of Christ in *Paradise Regained*. The clash between true wisdom and knowledge and the claims of apparent pragmatic good sense are themes Milton never abandons.

14. The central importance of the grace/works problem in Christian thought cannot be overestimated, particularly in this period when a major division between Protestants and Catholics (and between one type of Protestant and another) lay exactly in the weight given to grace in doctrine of salvation: see p. 50. (Milton, though recognizing the importance of grace, has an almost Stoic regard for the cultivation of virtue.)

15. There is a lot of common ground between the world of Comus and that of Acrasia: men turned into beasts by sensual indulgence, music, tempting food; both worlds are destroyed by an assault by men proof against such blandishment.

16. The distinction between partial or false good and true, of true felicity and

false, is one made most persuasively by Boethius in the *Consolation of Philosophy*, a book which had an enormous effect on the mind of Western man from the sixth century to the end of the eighteenth. Those who do not know the book would do well to read it: it addresses itself to the problems that confront us all, and its arguments have never been satisfactorily exploded.

17. See, for a definition of this term and a reminder of its importance in the theology of the Church of England as established by law, Articles 10, 11 and 17 of the Articles of Religion printed at the end of The Book of Common Prayer. See also p. 50.

18. Note, by the way, the importance of the imagery of light and darkness throughout the poem. Not only does the test take place at night when the only light is that of the stars, but also the language, even Comus' is full of the opposed ideas of light and darkness. All Comus' references to light are artificial, fanciful and distorted.

19. For those who do not know them, we had better list the Seven Virtues. There are the three theological, faith, hope and charity (see 1 Cor., Chapter 13), and four cardinal – justice, temperance, prudence and fortitude. It could be argued that the three children show the three theological Virtues, and also that the Lady shows fortitude and prudence in her defence of temperance. Without these virtues coming to his court, the justice is unlikely to judge justly.

20. The song is also heard by the Attendant Spirit (ll. 555 ff.). Milton makes him describe it in words very close to the description of the effect of Cleopatra's arrival at Cnidos in *Antony and Cleopatra*, words which stress its effect on the senses, and then suggest its effect is as powerful, as life-giving, as the *musica mundi*, the eternal music that creates the universe; 'creat[ing] a soul / Under the ribs of Death' (ll. 561–2). This is more than just a compliment to Lawes's music or the pretty voice of Alice Egerton: it is a definition of the sort of song we are meant to hear or imagine.

21. The supposed power of beauty and innocence to disarm malice and evil is something of a Renaissance convention. It is used, somewhat obliquely, by Shakespeare in Iachimo's response to Imogen's innocent beauty in *Cymbeline*, in Caliban's complex response to Miranda in *The Tempest*, and in the power Marina has in *Pericles* to chasten and reform the world of the brothel in which she finds herself.

22. Cf. Spenser, *Faerie Queene*, I. i. 12.: the Red Crosse Knight encourages Una in the wood of error: 'Vertue gives herself light, through darkenesse for to wade.'

23. Again, a common idea, a development from St Paul's seminal discussion in Romans, Chapter 7. Cf. Donne, *Holy Sonnet XIV*; Marvell, *Dialogue between Soul and Body*; and Quarles's emblem 'O who will deliver me from the body of this Death?' (*Emblemes*, 1635, Book V, emblem VIII, on Rom. 7.24: 'O wretched man that I am! Who shall deliver me from the body of this death?'

24. The subtlety of some of the imagery is easily missed. '"Poor hapless Nightingale"' in line 566 reminds us not only of the Lady as singer but also of the entirely apposite story of the innocent Philomel raped by Tereus.

25. These are technical terms for two of the Nine Orders of Angels identified by Pseudo-Dionysius the Areopagite; some members of each of the Orders

were believed to have revolted with Satan, and thus become devils.

26. He uses the same sort of technique in line 721, where the practice of temperance is seen as a mere 'pet', the sulky behaviour of a spoilt child. Note how the Lady in lines 766 ff. counters this by implied personifications of her own: but 'sober' (l. 766) and 'spare' (l. 767) are 'good' words, as against 'pet', 'lean' and 'sallow'.

27. Cf. St Paul, Romans 8.18: 'For I reckon that the sufferings of this present time are not worthy to be compared with the glory which shall be revealed in us.' This chapter of Romans seems to bear some fairly close relation to the moral parameters of Milton's thought in *Comus*. See especially verses 5–9, 12–14, 24–5.

28. Many will be familiar with this Neoplatonic idea from Wordsworth's *Ode on the Intimations of Immortality*.

29. See, for a fuller statement of this reading, S. Jayne, 'The Subject of Milton's Ludlow *Mask*', *Publications of the Modern Language Association of America*, LXXIV (1959), 533–43.

Further Reading

Broadbent, J., *John Milton: Introductions* (Cambridge University Press, Cambridge, 1973)

Brown, C. C., *Milton's Aristocratic Entertainments* (Cambridge University Press, Cambridge, 1985)

Bush, D., *English Literature in the Early Seventeenth Century* (Oxford University Press, 1973)

Carey, J., *Milton: Complete Shorter Poems* (Longman, London, 1968)

Chew, S. C., *The Pilgrimage of Life* (Yale University Press, New Haven, 1962)

Cohen, M., *Sensible Words: Linguistic Practice in England 1640–1785* (Johns Hopkins University Press, Baltimore, 1977)

Collinson, P., *The Religion of Protestants: The Church in English Society 1559–1625* (Clarendon Press, Oxford, 1982)

Cooper, Helen, *Pastoral: Mediaeval into Renaissance* (Boydell and Brewer, Ipswich, 1977)

Curtius, E. R., *European Literature and the Latin Middle Ages* (Routledge and Kegan Paul, repr. 1979)

Dickens, A. G., E. H. Gombrich, J. R. Hale, B. Pattison, and J. B. Trapp, *Background to the English Renaissance* (Gray-Mills, London, 1974)

Diekhoff, J. S., *Milton Upon Himself* (Cohen & West, London, 1965)

DuRocher, R. J., *Milton and Ovid* (Cornell University Press, 1985)

Empson, W., *Some Versions of Pastoral* (repr. Chatto and Windus, London, 1986)

Entzminger, R., *Divine Words: Milton and the Redemption of Language* (Duquesne University Press, Pittsburgh, 1985)

Ferguson, M. W., *Trials of Desire: Renaissance Defenses of Poetry* (Yale University Press, New Haven and London, 1983)

Fowler, A., *Triumphal Forms* (Cambridge University Press, Cambridge 1970)

Frye, N., 'Literature as Context: Milton's *Lycidas*', in D. Lodge (ed.), *Twentieth-Century Literary Criticism* (Longman, London, 1972)

Frye, N., *The Great Code: The Bible and Literature* (Longman, London, 1982)

Grant, W. Leonard, *Neo-Latin Literature and the Pastoral* (University of North Carolina Press, Chapel Hill, 1975)

Greenblatt, S., *Representing the English Renaissance* (University of California Press, Berkeley, 1988)

Grassi, E., *Rhetoric as Philosophy* (Duquesne University Press, Pittsburgh, 1980)

Helgerson, R., *Self-crowned Laureates: Spenser, Jonson, Milton and the Literary System* (University of California Press, Berkeley, 1983)

Heninger, S. K., Jr, *Touches of Sweet Harmony: Pythagorean Cosmology and Renaissance Poetics* (Huntington Library, San Marino, Calif., 1974)

Hill, C., *Milton and the English Revolution* (Faber and Faber, London, 1979)

Hill, C., *The Experience of Defeat: Milton and Some Contemporaries* (Faber and Faber, London, 1984)

Hill, J. S., *John Milton, Poet, Priest, Prophet: A Study of Divine Vocation in Milton's Poetry and Prose* (Macmillan, London, 1979)

Hollander, J., *The Untuning of the Sky* (Princeton University Press, Princeton, 1961)

Höltgen, K. R., *Francis Quarles 1592–1644: MediatiVer Dichter, Emblematiker, Royalist* (Niemeyer, Tübingen, 1978)

Hopper, V., *Mediaeval Number Symbolism* (Columbia University Studies in English and Comparative Literature No. 132, New York, 1938)

Hunt, C., *Lycidas and the Italian Critics* (Yale University Press, Newhaven, 1979)

Hunter, W. B., *Milton's Comus, Family Piece* (Troy, New York, Whitston Publishing, 1983)

Kermode, F., and J. Hollander (eds), *The Literature of Renaissance England* (Oxford University Press, Oxford, 1973)

Kermode, F., *English Pastoral Poetry from the Beginning to Marvell* (Harrap, London, 1952)

Levin, H., *The Myth of the Golden Age in the Renaissance* (Faber and Faber, London, 1969)

Lewalski, B. K., *Protestant Poetics and the Seventeenth Century Religious Lyric* (Princeton University Press, Princeton, 1979)

Lindley, D. (ed.), *The Court Masque* (Manchester University Press, Manchester, 1984)

Loughrey, B., (ed.), *The Pastoral Mode* (Macmillan. London, 1984)

McGuire, M. C., *Milton's Puritan Masque* (University of Georgia Press, Athens, Georgia, 1983)

Milner, A., *John Milton and the English Revolution: A Study in the Sociology of Literature* (Macmillan, London, 1981)

Moseley, C. W. R. D., *A Century of Emblems: An Introductory Anthology* (Scolar Press, Aldershot, 1989)

Moseley, C. W. R. D., *Shakespeare's History Plays, 'Richard II' to 'Henry V': The Making of a King* (Penguin, Harmondsworth, 1988)

Nahm, M. C., *The Artist as Creator: An Essay of Human Freedom* (Johns Hopkins University Press, Baltimore, 1956)

Norbrook, D., *Poetry and Politics in the English Renaissance* (Routledge and Kegan Paul, London, 1984)

Padley, C., *Grammatical Theory in Western Europe, 1500–1700* (Cambridge University Press, Cambridge, 1976)

Parry, G., *The Seventeenth Century: The Intellectual and Cultural Context of English Literature* (Longman, Harlow, 1989)

Parker, W. R., *Milton: A Biography* (Oxford University Press, Oxford, 1968)

Patrides, C. A., *Premises and Motifs in Renaissance Thought and Literature* (Princeton University Press, Princeton, 1982)

Patrides, C. A., *Annotated Critical Biography of John Milton* (Harvester Press, Brighton, 1987)

Patrides, C. A., and R. B. Waddington (eds), *The Age of Milton: Backgrounds to Seventeenth-Century Literature* (Manchester University Press, Manchester, 1980)

Pearcy, L. T., *The Mediated Muse: Translations of Ovid 1560–1700* (Archon Books, Hawden, Connecticut, 1984)

Potter, L., *A Preface to Milton* (Longman, Harlow, 1986)

Praz, M., *Studies in Seventeenth-Century Imagery* (Edizioni di Storia e Letteratura, Rome, 1964)

Prince, F. T., *The Italian Element in Milton's Verse* (Clarendon Press, Oxford, 1954)

Puttenham, G., *The Arte of English Poesis* (1589), eds G. D. Willcock and A. Walker (Cambridge University Press, Cambridge 1970)

Quilligan, M., *Milton's Spenser: The Politics of Reading* (Cornell University Press, Ithaca, 1983)

Roston, M., *Milton and the Baroque* (Macmillan, London, 1980)

Røstvig, M. S., *Fair Forms* (Cambridge University Press, Cambridge, 1975)

Segal, C., *Orpheus, the Myth of the Poet* (Johns Hopkins University Press, Baltimore, 1989)

Sharpe, K., *Politics and Ideas in Early Stuart England* (Pinter, London, 1989)

Sharpe, K., and S. N. Zwicker (eds), *Politics of Discourse: The Literature and History of Seventeenth-Century England* (University of California Press, Berkeley, 1987)

Sharpe. K., *Criticism and Compliment: The Politics of Literature in the England of Charles I* (Cambridge University Press, Cambridge, 1988)

Sidney, P., *Apologie for Poetrie*, 1st edn. 1595 and many modern edns

Steadman, J. M., *Nature into Myth: Mediaeval and Renaissance Moral Symbols* (Duquesne University Press, Pittsburgh, 1979)

Tillyard, P. B., *Milton's Private Correspondence and Academic Exercises* (Cambridge University Press, Cambridge, 1932)

Vickers, B., (ed.), *Rhetoric Revalued* (Columbia University Press, New York, 1982)

Vickers, B., *In Defence of Rhetoric* (Clarendon Press, Oxford, 1987)

Wilson, A. N., *The Life of John Milton* (Oxford University Press, Oxford, 1983)

Wittreich, *Visionary Poetics: Milton's Tradition and his Legacy* (Huntington Library, San Marino, Calif., 1979)

Worden, B., *Stuart England* (Phaidon, London, 1986)

Index

FOR THE BEST IN PAPERBACKS, LOOK FOR THE 🐧

In every corner of the world, on every subject under the sun, Penguin represents quality and variety – the very best in publishing today.

For complete information about books available from Penguin – including Puffins, Penguin Classics and Arkana – and how to order them, write to us at the appropriate address below. Please note that for copyright reasons the selection of books varies from country to country.

In the United Kingdom: Please write to *Dept JC, Penguin Books Ltd, FREEPOST, West Drayton, Middlesex, UB7 0BR.*

If you have any difficulty in obtaining a title, please send your order with the correct money, plus ten per cent for postage and packaging, to *PO Box No 11, West Drayton, Middlesex*

In the United States: Please write to *Dept BA, Penguin, 299 Murray Hill Parkway, East Rutherford, New Jersey 07073*

In Canada: Please write to *Penguin Books Canada Ltd, 2801 John Street, Markham, Ontario L3R 1B4*

In Australia: Please write to the *Marketing Department, Penguin Books Australia Ltd, P.O. Box 257, Ringwood, Victoria 3134*

In New Zealand: Please write to the *Marketing Department, Penguin Books (NZ) Ltd, Private Bag, Takapuna, Auckland 9*

In India: Please write to *Penguin Overseas Ltd, 706 Eros Apartments, 56 Nehru Place, New Delhi, 110019*

In the Netherlands: Please write to *Penguin Books Netherlands B.V., Postbus 3507, NL–1001 AH, Amsterdam*

In West Germany: Please write to *Penguin Books Ltd, Friedrichstrasse 10–12, D–6000 Frankfurt/Main 1*

In Spain: Please write to *Alhambra Longman S.A., Fernandez de la Hoz 9, E–28010 Madrid*

In Italy: Please write to *Penguin Italia s.r.l., Via Como 4, I-20096 Pioltello (Milano)*

In France: Please write to *Penguin France S.A., 17 rue Lejeune, F-31000 Toulouse*

In Japan: Please write to *Longman Penguin Japan Co Ltd, Yamaguchi Building, 2–12–9 Kanda Jimbocho, Chiyoda-Ku, Tokyo 101*

FOR THE BEST IN PAPERBACKS, LOOK FOR THE 🐧

PENGUIN CLASSICS

Netochka Nezvanova   Fyodor Dostoyevsky

Dostoyevsky's first book tells the story of 'Nameless Nobody' and introduces many of the themes and issues which dominate his great masterpieces.

Selections from the Carmina Burana   A verse translation by David Parlett

The famous songs from the *Carmina Burana* (made into an oratorio by Carl Orff) tell of lecherous monks and corrupt clerics, drinkers and gamblers, and the fleeting pleasures of youth.

Fear and Trembling   Søren Kierkegaard

A profound meditation on the nature of faith and submission to God's will which examines with startling originality the story of Abraham and Isaac.

Selected Prose   Charles Lamb

Lamb's famous essays (under the strange pseudonym of Elia) on anything and everything have long been celebrated for their apparently innocent charm; this major new edition allows readers to discover the darker and more interesting aspects of Lamb.

The Picture of Dorian Gray   Oscar Wilde

Wilde's superb and macabre novella, one of his supreme works, is reprinted here with a masterly Introduction and valuable notes by Peter Ackroyd.

A Treatise of Human Nature   David Hume

A universally acknowledged masterpiece by 'the greatest of all British Philosophers' – A. J. Ayer

FOR THE BEST IN PAPERBACKS, LOOK FOR THE 🐧

PENGUIN CLASSICS

The House of Ulloa Emilia Pardo Bazán

The finest achievement of one of European literature's most dynamic and controversial figures – ardent feminist, traveller, intellectual – and one of the great 19th century Spanish novels, *The House of Ulloa* traces the decline of the old aristocracy at the time of the Glorious Revolution of 1868, while exposing the moral vacuum of the new democracy.

The Republic Plato

The best-known of Plato's dialogues, *The Republic* is also one of the supreme masterpieces of Western philosophy whose influence cannot be overestimated.

The Life of Johnson James Boswell

Perhaps the finest 'life' ever written, Boswell's *Johnson* captures for all time one of the most colourful and talented figures in English literary history.

The Metamorphoses Ovid

A golden treasury of myths and legends which has proved a major influence on Western literature.

A Nietzsche Reader Friedrich Nietzsche

A superb selection from all the major works of one of the greatest thinkers and writers in world literature, translated into clear, modern English.

Madame Bovary Gustave Flaubert

With *Madame Bovary* Flaubert established the realistic novel in France; while his central character of Emma Bovary, the bored wife of a provincial doctor, remains one of the great creations of modern literature.

FOR THE BEST IN PAPERBACKS, LOOK FOR THE

PENGUIN CLASSICS

Matthew Arnold	**Selected Prose**
Jane Austen	**Emma**
	Lady Susan, The Watsons, Sanditon
	Mansfield Park
	Northanger Abbey
	Persuasion
	Pride and Prejudice
	Sense and Sensibility
Anne Brontë	**Agnes Grey**
	The Tenant of Wildfell Hall
Charlotte Brontë	**Jane Eyre**
	Shirley
	Villette
Emily Brontë	**Wuthering Heights**
Samuel Butler	**Erewhon**
	The Way of All Flesh
Thomas Carlyle	**Selected Writings**
Wilkie Collins	**The Moonstone**
	The Woman in White
Charles Darwin	**The Origin of Species**
	The Voyage of the Beagle
Benjamin Disraeli	**Sybil**
George Eliot	**Adam Bede**
	Daniel Deronda
	Felix Holt
	Middlemarch
	The Mill on the Floss
	Romola
	Scenes of Clerical Life
	Silas Marner
Elizabeth Gaskell	**Cranford** and **Cousin Phillis**
	The Life of Charlotte Brontë
	Mary Barton
	North and South
	Wives and Daughters

FOR THE BEST IN PAPERBACKS, LOOK FOR THE 🐧

PENGUIN CLASSICS

William Hazlitt	**Selected Writings**
Thomas Hobbes	**Leviathan**
Samuel Johnson/	**A Journey to the Western Islands of**
James Boswell	**Scotland and The Journal of a Tour to the Hebrides**
Charles Lamb	**Selected Prose**
Samuel Richardson	**Clarissa**
	Pamela
Richard Brinsley Sheridan	**The School for Scandal and Other Plays**
Christopher Smart	**Selected Poems**
Adam Smith	**The Wealth of Nations**
Tobias Smollett	**The Expedition of Humphry Clinker**
	The Life and Adventures of Sir Launcelot Greaves
Laurence Sterne	**The Life and Opinions of Tristram Shandy, Gentleman**
	A Sentimental Journey Through France and Italy
Jonathan Swift	**Gulliver's Travels**
Sir John Vanbrugh	**Four Comedies**

FOR THE BEST IN PAPERBACKS, LOOK FOR THE 🐧

PENGUIN BOOKS OF POETRY

American Verse
British Poetry Since 1945
Caribbean Verse in English
A Choice of Comic and Curious Verse
Contemporary American Poetry
Contemporary British Poetry
English Christian Verse
English Poetry 1918–60
English Romantic Verse
English Verse
First World War Poetry
Greek Verse
Irish Verse
Light Verse
Love Poetry
The Metaphysical Poets
Modern African Poetry
New Poetry
Poetry of the Thirties
Post-War Russian Poetry
Scottish Verse
Southern African Verse
Spanish Civil War Verse
Spanish Verse
Women Poets